PREDATOR CALLING

with Gerry Blair

The definitive book dealing with distress screaming to bring predators and other wild things close to the eye, the gun, or the camera.

Published by

 **krause
publications**

700 E. State Street • Iola, WI 54990-0001
Telephone: 715/445-2214

Please call or write for our free catalog of outdoor publications. Our toll-free number
to place an order or obtain a free catalog is 800-258-0929 or please use our regular
business telephone 715-445-2214 for editorial comment
and further information.

Library of Congress Catalog Number: 95-77319
ISBN: 0-87341-359-8
Printed in the United States of America

Dedication

Book dedications are difficult. There is the temptation to thank every human, every dog, and every gopher who has helped a bit during a long life within the hunting fast lane. Heck, in the dedication written for *Turkey Hunting With Gerry Blair* (Krause Publications), I threatened to list each of the 100,000 readers of *Turkey & Turkey Hunting* magazine. I didn't do that. To be fair I will not list the thousands who read my stuff in *Trapper & Predator Caller*. You know who you are. Thanks for the support. Thanks for the friendship.

In the dedication to *Fur Trapping* (Winchester Press), I spoke of pioneers such as Jim Bridger, Kit Carson, Old Bill Williams, and others.

The dedication I wrote for *Predator Caller's Companion* (Winchester Press), made mention of more modern pioneers; men like Murry Burnham, George Oakey, Chuck Spearman, Johnny Stewart, and too many more to mention. All contributed to the advancement of the sport. All friends.

Even though the temptation is great to do so again, to add names like Larry O. Gates, Gordo Krahn and Deb Knauer, I will not.

I dedicate this book instead to a lady who committed her love to a hunter. I dedicate this book to Ann Elizabeth Blair, my wife and best friend for 42 years. My Annie Girl succumbed to a cruel and relentless illness on June 24, 1994. She lives within my heart.

I also dedicate this book to our sons, Michael Taun and Gerry Jr. Each of those fine young men offered love and support through all of that nearly endless illness. Even though I consider myself strong, I know I would not have made it without them.

Table of Contents

Foreword

Screaming to wild ears is a most exciting sport. Screamers will surely find a thrill within, an excitement not always found during other hunts. Most hunts have the hunter making a sneak through the target's territory, hoping for an opportunistic encounter. The hunter moves and the animal hides. Screaming the good scream causes the opposite to happen. The hunter hides and uses blood-soaked screams to ask the animal to lunch. Even a super-smart critter, like a coyote, fox, a big or little cat, or even a bear, might come at the gallop.

Predators are the critters that respond most often. Meat eaters all, opportunists all, each recognizes the distress scream for what it is—groceries. Appetite and nature encourage the response.

Each of the predators has a style of response. The bobcat and the cougar most often come at the sneak. Those big and small cats respond as they normally hunt: at a careful and cautious advance that permits the close approach, and then, the charge.

Foxes, both red and gray, often come at the gallop but are just as likely to come at the sneak. Being the little guy on the block has caused these smallest of wild dogs to temper enthusiasm. That fox, before joining the meal, must discover a critical truth—will he have lunch or will he be lunch? Death from the sky—owls, hawks, and eagles—come on silent wings, sometimes lighting close to the scream to reconnoiter.

The coyote, in all of the West and some of the East, is the critter most often called. The yodel dog's relatively large size, population density, and opportunistic appetite cause him to be a screamer's best friend. Coyote with virgin ears can come like Concords, in bunches. And that hungry gang can advance at the gallop. Experienced screamers, particularly those who hunt the brush, often leave the rifle within the truck to carry one of the smoothbores I call the Big Bangers.

Prey animals also respond, including such uncalled (and unexpected) animals like the antelope, mule deer, white-tailed deer, and elk. Even the ugly javelina may come—nearly every animal with ears.

Those prey animals come, I think, because of protective instinct. They may fear a meat eater is attempting to do cousin Molly. They come to defend. Maybe. Some come, the way I see it, because they are bored. The screams tell them someone is losing a hell of a fight. Some might come running to watch Ol' Molly take it in the shorts.

Predator and prey can be naive. None I know are stupid. Each will trust a scream a time or two. Those that escape become hard-sells. A finely crafted screaming, delivered with precise circumstance, can cause even these Ph.D. critters to come one more time—most likely at the sneak. Somewhere in this book you will discover the technique needed to bring predator and prey, to bring virgin and jaded veteran. I wish you good reading and good hunting.

Chapter 1

Biological Justification for Calling

I shrugged my big body into the stingy shade of a scrawny string bark juniper and pulled on the camo-colored facemask. Through the netting and through sun-squinted eyes, I looked out on the massive mesa the Apaches call Big Prairie; a crowded and over-munched community-summer-graze filled with barely alive Herefords. The terminally ill cattle, and the freshly dead, acted as a magnet to draw in gangs of hungry coyote. I was there at the invitation of the San Carlos Apaches. I was there to scream to the carrion-eaters and to the coyotes that supplemented their beef diet with tidbits from the struggling pronghorn herd that shared the graze and the browse.

Four minutes into the screaming, a flash of fur loped from straight downwind. Thirty pounds of hungry surrounded by meat, muscle, and hair. When the yodeler passed behind a juniper, I shouldered the Sako, thumbed forward the tang safety, and prepared to do business. I figured a 52-grain Sierra traveling at a muzzle velocity of more than 3,600 fps would cause the broad-headed dog to lose interest in both beef and antelope.

Mid-March is a poor time to scream for fur. The coyote had shook the sugar tree and about every qualified bitch had been impregnated. Dog and bitch, bonded for the season and maybe bonded for life, were involved in the serious business of selecting primary and secondary den sites. Neither will show a lot of interest in the scream. The warming weather, the dogging, and photosynthetic stimulation has caused the fur to singe, curl and shag. No market for that kind of pelt. Even so, I was calling the San Carlos lands during mid-March, exactly the right time to thin the coyote population so that the antelope fawns due to hit the ground within a month would have an increased chance to survive.

Coyote can be a dreadful pronghorn predator. In certain kinds of country, wide open prairie grasslands containing little cover, too many coyote can cause herd survival to be threatened. The Big Prairie was one such habitat. Anderson Mesa, starting slightly south of Flagstaff, Arizona, is another.

Dr. Don Neff, a biologist for the Arizona Game & Fish Department for many years, completed a five-year study documenting coyote/pronghorn interaction in the Anderson Mesa study area; a hand-

6

Dr. Don Neff (left) and Norm Woolsey studied coyote predation of antelope to find such predation threatened the existence of an historic antelope herd that once numbered 8,000 animals.

some topography of grassland, ponderosa pine, juniper, and high country lakes. Five hundred square miles of antelope country. Five hundred square miles of Rocky Mountain elk and mule deer country. Five hundred square miles of coyote country.

Anderson Mesa had once housed antelope herds that numbered about eight thousand. Peak numbers, as might be expected, developed during the days when the compound poison numbered 10-80 (deadly on all dogs) was widely used. The banning of that predator control tool caused coyote numbers to become significant. Good times for the coyote caused bad times for the pronghorns. The Mesa pronghorn herd was down to a few hundred when Neff started his study. Evidence suggested the coyote to be the chief culprit.

Spotting scope observation during those crepuscular periods when the coyote was most active confirmed the suspicion. Typically, teams or gangs of coyote would patrol the mesa, searching out doe antelope. One or more of the hunting team would tease the doe into a chase. The remaining coyote would search industriously until the fawn (or fawns) was located. A secret signal would cause the teasers to leave the doe to

The Neff study suggested fawn survival within the study area was at a dismal ten percent.

return and share the meal. The coyote were so efficient at fawn killing nearly no pronghorn fawn survived to recruit into the adult population. Knowing that pronghorn does normally deliver twin fawns, biologists see a potential recruitment of 200 percent. Recruitment within the Anderson Mesa herd hovered at a dismal 20 percent. Coyote control measures such as trapping, calling, and aerial gunning, each accomplished during the peak fawning period, caused coyote numbers to diminish. As might be expected, fawn survival increased.

The Neff study ("Effect of Predation by Coyotes on Antelope Fawn Survival on Anderson Mesa," Arizona Game & Fish Special Report #8, November, 1979) established the coyote as a very efficient pronghorn predator. Some biologists believe this wild dog to be an equally efficient predator of young mule deer, young whitetail (and mature deer of both species when snow cover slows the deer to make them vulnerable), and of about every kind and age group of domestic stock. Every coyote called and killed, the way I see it, offers the opportunity of increased life span to about everything that creeps or crawls the land.

The coyote is an *equal* opportunity killer. Coyote depredation on game animals and domestic stock has been well documented. Less well documented, less publicized, is the effect the other major land predators have on prey species. The second largest North American cat (the jaguar takes top honors) is an example.

Coyote predation of sheep and other livestock causes significant financial loss to herders and ranchers. (Guy Connolly, U. S. Fish and Wildlife Service.)

Wildlife managers report an increasing incidence of lion attacks on humans—some with fatal results.

Felis concolor, also called cougar, mountain lion and *gato del monte* (cat of the mountain) is mainly a deer killer. Investigate the essentially Western habitat of this big-bodied feline (up to 200 pounds-plus within a part of the range) and you might find exploding deer populations. Sometimes. At other times you might find a few wide-ranging lions patrolling a vast area nearly devoid of deer. Too many lions, particularly within Southwestern areas where deer are water dependent, can cause the deer population to get dead.

Harley Shaw, a lion biologist for the Arizona Game & Fish Department, conducted a radio telemetry study within a central Arizona ranch, Spider-Cross U, and showed that the mountain lion became a very efficient livestock predator when deer numbers diminished. The bottom line? An adult lion will make a major kill (deer, elk or cow) about every eight days, nearly one a week. Shaw estimated a lion population of 2,000 at that time. You do not have to be a statistician to realize that lion kill a hell of a lot of deer, maybe more. Those who wish to learn more about lion/deer and lion/livestock interaction will find Shaw's "A Mountain Lion Field Guide, Special Report # 9, Arizona Game & Fish Department" to be a good read.

Too deep a predator density can also impact the health and welfare of humans. Many of the states to the west of the big river suffer through periodic flare-ups of the dreaded disease, rabies. Coyote are most often involved. Gray fox and bobcat are also, to a lesser degree. How bad does it get? And documented lion and coyote attacks on humans have increased considerably in recent years.

ITEM: A woman jogger near Cool, California, was chased, killed, partially consumed and covered. An adult mountain lion killed nearby had parts of the woman within its stomach. Locals blame an animal activist-inspired initiative banning mountain lion hunting as the cause.

ITEM: A two-year-old toddler was taken from his front yard within a California suburb by a coyote and was killed. The mother and neighbors rescued the body before it could be consumed.

ITEM: A teenage girl, waiting for the school bus in a Tucson, Arizona, neighborhood, was attacked and bitten by a rabid coyote. The painful series of anti-rabies injections saved her life.

ITEM: A rabid coyote staggered onto a South Tucson school yard and attempted an attack on several children. Custodians killed the animal.

ITEM: A mountain lion attacked an eight-year-old on vacation within the Kohls Ranch area. The father killed the animal using a .22 rifle.

There is more. Too much to cite. Suffice it to say this: In spite of what the animal-lovers say, all critters are not our friends.

And too many predators can cause problems for the predators. A fierce competition for food is the obvious result. The least skilled are undernourished and sometimes starve. Coyote and fox overpopulation can encourage sarcoptic mange, a disease that causes the hair to fall out, leaving a skin that is scabrous. In extreme cases infection and exposure can cause death. Sarcoptic mange can be transmitted to domestic dogs.

Other epizootic diseases are common to many of the predators. Most within the West carry fleas that can transmit the dreaded bubonic plague to humans. The screamings that diminish predator populations, the way I see it, minimize problems to humans, to game animals, to domestics, and to the predators themselves.

Too high a coyote density causes epizootics such as sarcoptic mange—obvious on this South Texas yodel dog.

Chapter 2

Why They Come

The animals I have met during a long lifetime of calling have responded to the screams in about every way possible. I have had eager coyote pups, out on their own for the first time, naive and desperate to get at the rabbit, come at the gallop and nearly crawl into my lap. Other coyote, jaded veterans of February, that are paranoid to the tenth power, come at the sneak—employing the stop and reconnoiter—employing the downwind circle—but still they come.

My constant calling companion Larry O. Gates and I have had mountain lions come at the sneak and bobcats come at the charge. A cat or two, sad to say, have backdoored to climb the shoulders for a short but very exciting ride. Animal response, the way I see it, is governed by that animal's nature, prior experience with distress calling, and degree of hunger.

Some come running. Predator response is determined by nature and previous experience. (Burnham Brothers)

The major reason predators respond to a scream is food-related. Many of the prey animals articulate their terror as they get the close-up look at a set of coyote tonsils, or the equally dreaded beak and talon. Flying predators like hawks, falcons, owls, and eagles, hunt and kill in a similar manner. The prey is located from aloft. The critter swoops, stoops or soars to the target, taking hold with razor-sharp talons. Those talons, much of the time, encircle the rabbit's rib cage. Death is by suffocation. The hunter holds tight and the rabbit screams, losing a bit of air. The talons tighten a bit more to further compress the lungs. Scream. Tighten. The process might take a minute or more, substantially longer if the hold is not precise. During all of that time, as air allows, the rabbit or other prey animal screams piteously. Other predators within hearing range hustle in to have a look, hoping to steal the meal. A hungry coyote, a hungry fox, or bobcat, has no conscience. Each is likely to kick a red-tailed hawk's butt bad and take away his lunch of succulent cottontail. A hawk that objects too much is likely to join the cottontail within the belly of the beast.

Birds of prey such as this golden eagle kill by suffocation—allowing time for screaming.

A part of the predator response, I am convinced, has to do with territoriality. About all predators stake out a hunting territory and vigorously defend it from poachers. A boss coyote who has a full belly, as an example, might come running if he believes a neighbor has snuck in to dip a finger in the sugar bowl.

Some critters, mostly of the grocery type, respond to the distress scream because their nature forces a protective response. Deer, antelope, and others of the ungulate persuasion will sometimes come at a charge, fearing a predator has cornered junior and is preparing to munch his tender body. As an example, Larry and I were screaming to a mesquite-choked dry wash during one winter hunt

13

Prey animals like this mule deer doe come to protect the screamee.

and hooked a hungry coyote. The critter came at the lope, following a serpentine course through the greasewood. When the coyote was decently close, Larry O. pulled the trigger on the Knight Rifle muzzleloader. The critter turned to a rug about twenty-five feet out. Larry continued to scream, hoping to interest a second customer. A few minutes later a fearful crashing of brush announced the arrival of customer number two, an outraged doe mule deer. The doe was only half mad until she saw the coyote carcass. She immediately upgraded to mad-and-a-half. Each and every hair on that outraged doe stood at attention. The ears turned back to attack mode. She suddenly reared to bring the front feet down hard near the coyote's head. Then she backed off to get a run and did it all again. Larry and I controlled our laughter as long as humanly possible and then cut it loose. The doe retreated reluctantly.

The protective nature of the doe deer can cause the distress scream to be a very effective way to hunt mule deer (the common deer around my part of the West). I have had my best luck calling to rutting bucks. Does with the bucks are most likely to respond. The buck tags along to keep track of his harem. The Child Molester Buck was one such. Read more on this degenerate in Chapter 31, "The Uncalled and the Unexpected."

The little "pig" Southwesterners call the javelina (collared peccary) is a sucker for about any well-blown distress scream. I have had herds (locally called sounders) of the little critters come at the charge, tusks clacking and mouths sending out a fearful grunting. On one memorable occasion, while taping footage for "The Masters' Secrets to Predator Calling," hoping to prove that staying still was most important when critter calling, I dressed my ample frame in a

Santa Claus suit, including red stocking cap with the cute white ball atop, and set out to call critters. A sounder of javelina came at the gallop, slid to a stop twenty feet out looking in amazement at the strangest sight they had seen, and then made a panic run for the border. I laid into the screaming again and they came back, this time to within ten feet of Ol' Santa. I am not making this up. Every bit of the action was captured on tape and is included in the video.

The strangest respondent I have had, and the most difficult to understand, is a jackrabbit coming to a jackrabbit distress scream. Common sense suggests a hare hearing the death screams of a brother hare singing his death song would run for the border. Not always true. During high hare cycles I have had as many as a half dozen of the long ears hanging around during a single screaming. Why are they there? Don't know. Maybe they're protective. Maybe they come because they know another hare is getting his harey butt kicked and they want to see it happen.

This black-tailed jackrabbit (actually a hare) came to investigate a jackrabbit distress scream.

Critters are a bit like humans in some respects. All do not own the same degree of intelligence. The young coyote of the year is a prime example. Those I have met have been so dumb their butt hurts. One such worked hard to climb atop an old time Arizona caller named Sam Dudley. Sam was hunkered down in a small depression east of Phoenix on one winter hunt when a young-of-the-year came at a charge. Sam and the critter wrestled out of the depression and out of the portable blind Sam carried. Sam flailed away with the barrel of his twelve gauge and managed to inflict a painful wound about mid-barrel. The barrel turned sort of bow shaped. Realizing it was time for the hard sell, Sam turned the ugly end of the scatter gun to the coyote and lit the fire. The gun? Sam used it for all of his life, calling it "Singing Sally" (said it sung the critters to sleep) holding Kentucky windage to compensate for the bow.

Older coyote sometimes come in high gear also, particularly early in the calling year. Even though they may have been called the previous season, the passing of time has dulled their recollection of the trickery. As an example, I was calling the slope of an antique juniper push one winter when I sighted two hard-charging bundles of fur coming from far, far away. The critters stayed neck to neck for much of the race, each imagining he or she would be the first to reach the rabbit. Seventy seconds after the sighting, the winner ran up the barrel of the full-choked twelve gauge. The auto loader took the trailer as she stood dumbfounded, wondering why hubby was kicking in the dirt.

Some animals come because they hunger. Some come because it is their nature to do so. Another might come because of curiosity or to protect another animal. No matter what the motivation, some do come, maybe at the run and maybe at the sneak. The excitement provided by that response can be damnfine, a substance that keeps the screamer working through good times and bad.

Chapter 3

Why They Do Not Come

As noted in the previous chapter, animal response can be affected by a bunch of variables. Like response, non-response can be a complicated phenomena. Only the critter knows the exact cause, and the critters I have met have refused to talk on that subject. The non-communication may have been because most of the predators were graveyard dead at the time. Even so, knowing the general nature of the critters—and knowing a bit about their lifestyle—I feel qualified to speculate on non-response.

The obvious reason an animal does not show is simple: There is not a target animal within scream range. A hunter can pick the best setup, wear the most effective camouflage and blow exquisitely painful screams until he or she gets trombone lip. If no coyote, bobcat, fox, cougar, or lion is within hearing, common sense says none will show. The no-show because of no-hear phenomena is a lot more common in the Midwest, the Mideast and the East than within the West. The reason? Predator density. Much of the West is critter crowded.

Even when the critter hears the screams, that critter may not have the decency to acknowledge. Non-response may

This Ph.D. coyote has heard the distress scream one time too many.

17

be due to a number of factors or due to a combination of factors. The non-response of a critter that hears the advertisement is most often because the critter is timid (scared scatless). That fear can come from a lack of dominance within a species (a little guy worries that a big guy might be around to kick his butt), or might come from a lack of territorial access. A coyote from a neighboring territory, for example, might hear the advertisement and might love to come for a bite of hot rabbit. Trouble is, Mean Joe Green owns the joint and turns into an animal when company shows.

Fear can also come because of cross-species dominance. A screamer who imitates the distress cry of a gray fox, as an example, is not likely to call many reds. In areas where grays and reds share a range, the gray is almost always the dominant fox. The same can be said about the gray and the coyote. Grays that do not honor the coyote at every opportunity might as well forget about Social Security and Medicare. Here in the Southwest where the kit fox is the littlest kid on the block, the smallest of the foxes stay deep within burrows during the day and come out at night with extreme trepidation. Nearly every predator, at one time or another, must ask itself the hard question. "Am I going to have dinner or am I going to be dinner?"

Non-response, when you get right down to the bottom line, might be because of something as simple as the moon phase, or because of the weather. Hell, maybe they just have a headache.

Having said all of that, it should also be stated that the main reason for a lack of interest has nothing to do with any of the above. The most common cause of lack of interest is paranoia caused by a recent and traumatic encounter with hunter screams, moans,

Even uneducated coyote can be a hard sell when weather warms.

18

groans, and whinings. The trauma of those encounters too often ends with a bang, and ends as a 52-grain chunk of copper-coated lead buzzes by at supersonic speed, maybe throwing rocks and dirt dangerously close. Common sense, under such provocation, suggests a desperate run for home and Mother.

My experience causes me to think the coyote is the kind of critter most affected by these close encounters of the .22-250 kind. The foxes, just another dog, rank a close second. Running last, barely in the race, are the cats. Bobcat and the lions I have met have shown a high tolerance for deception, some being so dumb their butt aches. The cat I call the Dumbo of Kinnikinick Canyon illustrates the point.

K. Canyon is a mean slash of gully that interrupts the somewhat level aspect of the wonderfully extensive Anderson Mesa, a vast tract of high country meadowland graced with shallow lakes and fingers of stringbark and alligator juniper. And with somewhat shallow canyons, including Kinnikinick, each decorated with the junipers and with turbinella and Gambels Oak and other low story stuff. Bear country. Lion country. Bobcat and fox country. Hell, even 'coons and cacomistles.

When an out-of-state reader visited, hoping for the opportunity to earball and eyeball the Blair screaming technique, K. Canyon came to mind almost immediately. We planned the drive so that we would be set up and screaming at precisely first light, a dandy time to scream to cats and

Cats that come almost always stay until they see the rabbit.

nearly as good to scream in fox and coyote. Stubby and I settled onto a canyon lip so that we had a decent view of the brush-choked canyon below. I was the screamer and gunner. Stubby was along to listen and to see.

False dawn surrendered to the real thing as I sent out the opening chorus of the tune I call the "Dying Rabbit Blues." Four minutes into the screaming, Stubby shouted a one word whisper across the fifteen feet that separated us. "CAT." Thinking lion, I looked until my eyeballs ached. Nothing. Stub's angle of vision permitted the sighting. Mine did not. I scrooched my butt hard left, then leaned harder left. Ahhh. A big-eared bobcat, the pretty kind with the tufted ears and hairy jowls, sat calmly a hundred yards out. I shouldered the Sako and placed the small x of the duplex six just below those hairy jowls and prepared to stroke. Even though I was off balance and my position violated every accuracy rule, I knew I could not miss. Through the magic of the magnification the bobcat looked to be as big as a VW Bug. I did stroke and I did miss. The cat continued to set and continued to be calm. I did what too many hunters do under similar situations. I bolted in a loaded round and tried a second off-balance shot. Another miss, although the cat did jerk his head as if to bite at the buzzing bee that sped close. Then the cat renewed his solemn contemplation. Somewhat rattled because of the double miss and because it was witnessed, knowing now the cat would stay until it obtained a taste of the rabbit, I took a second or so to settle my nerves, squared my body to the target, and sent a 3,650 fps chunk of lead squarely into the kitty's necessaries. Walking up, I couldn't help but notice the cat continued to look calm. Tom. Twenty two pounds. Mature and old enough to know better.

A coyote or fox that answers the call and escapes with his or her life (I am an equal opportunity killer.) is naturally disappointed. That critter is also a lot smarter. Even though that one bad experience does not cause him or her to stop being an opportunistic predator, a further advance to a screaming will be done with considerably more caution. Such a critter may come at the sneak, making frequent stops to reconnoiter the country ahead. Those that are upwind will almost surely circle downwind of the screams to let their nose verify what their nature suspects. One sniff of Redman or underarm odor and it is good-bye critter. Supply another lesson or two, and let the pupil escape, and you are almost sure to be dealing with a Ph.D. predator. Most, even though they be on death's door because of starvation, will not investigate even the real thing. The calling and recalling of a coyote is well illustrated by citing the circumstances of the Wildcat Canyon Bitch.

I was on a midwinter hunt within the pushdowns of that Arizona high country the first time I had a look at the bitch. I used the TallyHo tube to call her dog (mate) and used the Sako Forester in .22-250 to make the shot. Continuing to call, as I often do after the shot, I sighted the bitch as she wandered about within the juniper push. No chance for a shot. She howled a time or two, talking to the dog, and when he did not answer she skulked away.

I was in the same area a couple of weeks later and used the TallyHo to cause the bitch to come close, backdoor. She saw me before I saw her and made an enthusiastic run for the county line. How did I know it was the same coyote? Didn't, not for sure. Coyote in my part of the country do not wear name tags. The bitch was in the same area and was of the same color variation. I guessed from that it was her.

A week or two later, while on a hunt somewhat close, I visited the bitch one more time. I made the setup atop a pile of pushdowns and did my best to keep my head turning so as to cover every potential approach. Five minutes into the screaming I sighted the bitch making her sneak from two hundred yards out. She hung up at one hundred fifty yards. Her body language told me that was as far as she would advance. I squared, sighted, and stroked.

The author called the same bitch three times—the last having fatal results.

Calling a coyote once is somewhat frequently accomplished. Calling that same coyote twice within a semi-short time is less common. Calling that same coyote a third time, when the trauma of previous screams is fresh in the memory, is about like bowling a 300 game or golfing a hole in one. Difficult but possible under precisely perfect circumstances.

I offer a final thought on non-response. A frequent question addressed to the "Question & Answer" column I do for *Trapper & Predator Caller* magazine (Krause Publications, 700 East State Street, Iola, WI 54990-0001) has to do with critter sophistication. A common phrasing goes like this, "I call my Dad's 600-acre farm and know there are coyote there because I hear them howl. The farm has not been called, so I know the critters can't be that sophisticated. Why don't they respond?" I say this. "Even though your Dad's farm has not been called, it is unlikely the coyote spend all of their life there. Being roamers, it is likely they may have had a bad experience of the screaming kind on a farm many miles away." Generally, here in the West, if I achieve one response during five calls I consider things to be great. Zip codes having a lesser critter concentration will likely deliver even less.

Chapter 4

Tubes and Other Screamers

Predator calling has been a popular sport in the West since the early 1950s. A high predator density and vast tracts of public land caused Western hunters to take to the sport as ducks take to the water. Hunters located to the east of the big rivers were less fortunate as far as coyote numbers were considered. Many had ample populations of red and gray fox. Nearly all had more than enough raccoon. Even so, the sport of predator calling lagged. And then a funny thing happened. Big and hungry coyote from Canada started range expansion to the south. Brush wolves appeared within the East and the Midwest in increasing numbers. Yarded whitetail, unable to travel because of snow cover, offered a dandy meal. A big-footed coyote who walked deliberately could travel on top of the snow. The sharp hooves of the whitetail that attempted escape would break the crust to slow the flight. It doesn't take much of an imagination to realize the result.

Easterners, alarmed by the deer depredation, and recognizing the availability of a new kind of hunt, learned a truth long known to Western hunters. Screaming to coyote, and to other predators, can be a most exciting sport.

Many hunters new to the sport of predator calling agonize over call selection. They agonize for no good reason. I have screamed using nearly every call on the market, past and present, and have called critters with nearly all. Tube calls, in certain construction types, are remarkably similar. Battery-powered callers, in certain construction types, send out a comparable sound. I say, with little reservation, that about any mouth call and about any battery-powered caller will send out a screaming good enough to fetch a critter close.

It is also proper to say every screamer, tyro and veteran, will profit from a discussion of tube types and caller types. Later within this chapter I will deliver my opinion on the quality of scream needed to bring a predator close, using any kind of tube and any kind of circuitry.

A wood or plastic tube containing a generic metal reed is the most common of the screamers and is always the easiest to master. The interchangeable reeds stay hidden within the belly of the body. Blowing into the business end of the tube causes the stainless steel reed to vibrate. The scream is produced.

Coyote east and coyote west can impact winter stressed deer populations. (Colorado Division of Wildlife)

Varying the volume of air sent through the tube can change the sound of the scream. Cupping the hands over the end of the tube can do likewise. Change the cupping and the sound changes. A little but not much. You want the truth? One mouth sounds a lot like all other mouths when it comes to the sound produced from the metal-reeded tube. That device is basically a one-trick pony. It screams.

This lack of versatility can have a bad consequence within hard hunted areas. Critters who have heard the scream from a metal-reeded tube a time or two can develop a dreadful ennui. Because all mouths sound pretty much alike, critters within those hard hunted areas refuse to play the game.

Metal-reeded tubes have other defects. The reeds, being metal, get mighty cold when outside air temperatures chill. Hot spittle (sometimes referred to as "slobbers" in other parts of this book) hit the chilled metal. Frozen slobbers, sad to say, will almost always cause the metal-reeded tube to call in sick, and almost always at the most inopportune of times.

About every metal-reeded tube on the market uses a generic leaf-type reed, obtained from a common source. Some stainless steel reeds are pre-tuned to send out a good simulation of the jackrabbit distress scream, hoarse and coarse. Growly. A good sound for coyote, mountain lion, and bear. Other metal-reeded tubes send out a good simulation of the cottontail distress scream, a more high-toned scream and without a lot of the growl. I prefer the cottontail distress scream for some coyote and for all fox and bobcat. I have screamed using wood tubes and using hard plastic tubes. To my tin ear the resonance of the screaming is about even-Steven. Even

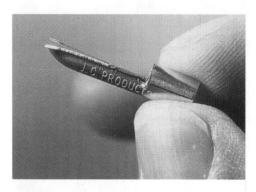

Most metal-reeded tubes hold a similar reed, obtained from a common supplier.

so, my records indicate I skin more fur when I scream using the metal reed within the wood tube. Particular favorites are the Weems Wildcall (or a custom made reproduction) or a custom made reproduction of the Trophy Model Wood Circe. I have caused each of those dandy calls (and others) to be replicated using desert ironwood or mesquite as a substitute for the original white birch of the Circe and the walnut of the Weems. The sound produced with either is damnfine.

The second kind of common call is a wood or plastic tube fitted with a thin shim of mylar plastic. The plastic reed is almost always exposed, causing some to refer to this kind of call as an exposed-reed call, or more simply, the open-reed call.

The plastic-reeded call is a bit more difficult to master than is the metal-reeded call. Strong assets cause that difficulty to be inconsequential in the big picture. I am thinking an ordinarily competent set of tonsils, with proper practice and proper instruction, will be able to master most of the assets of the plastic-reeded tube within an evening or two. Assets? The configuration of the open-reeded call causes the mylar plastic reed to be within the mouth, a place where the reed is protected from sub-zero temperature and the consequent freeze-up. The open-reed call is a dandy cold weather call.

Also, changing call position within the mouth will cause the tone of the screaming to vary, offering the asset of versatility. A good tonsil on the open-reeded tube will be able to talk fluent jackrabbit, fluent cottontail, damnfine yips and other pup distress whinings, and even the deadly howl.

Finally, no two mouths hold the mylar reed precisely the same. Consequently, no two mouths send out precisely the same scream. Educated critters are less likely to ignore a call that sounds slightly different. Varying air pressure and cupping one or two hands at the tube end can cause sound variation, just as those manipulations do within the metal-reeded tube.

All turkey hunters and some elk hunters will know a bit about the diaphragm mouth call. Few predator callers know anything at all about the diaphragm mouth call. I find that sad. Used properly, this inexpensive and versatile call can increase the size and value of the fur collection. A talented mouth can cause the call to send out decent screams, whines, yips, and sometimes howls.

The diaphragm call is made as a thin sheet of latex is stretched over a horseshoe shaped aluminum frame, tautened and secured, and then covered with duct tape of varying colors. Some diaphragm turkey calls hold as many as three layers (a few even more) of the latex. Some contain cuts and notches to cause sound variety. My experience causes me to prefer the single reed and at times the uncut and unnotched double reed for screaming. Diaphragm calls of that character deliver the truest scream and are the easiest to learn.

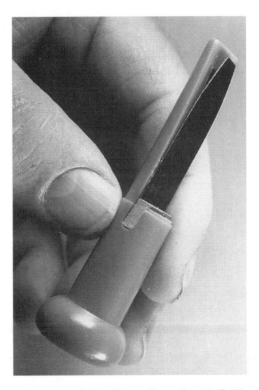

Plastic reeded calls such as this TallyHo offer versatility and freeze resistance.

Even though you may be told you must swallow a diaphragm of each color before finding proficiency, I do not believe such is true. I know of callers who have only swallowed half of the colors. Those that lived turned into decent screamers. Seriously, the diaphragm call is enclosed in the mouth so that the screamer can huff air across the reed(s). Place that sucker too far back on the roof of the mouth, hiccup, and you may have your diaphragm for lunch. The good news? Every diaphragm call I have seen contains zero calories, zero cholesterol, and zero fat.

The final category of mechanical screamers contains a group I call the close-in calls. These low volume models produce a scream or squeak predator ears can hear for a hundred yards or so. Some models have a metal reed placed within the mouth of a rubber bulb. Squeezing to expel air causes sound. Some hunters attach one of the bulbs to the fore part of the gun stock so that they might produce the squeak while holding the gun at the ready.

A second kind of close-in is the one I call the "hummer." Two flat strips of hard plastic hold a metal or rubber band reed within. Placing the call to the mouth, harmonica like, permits the articulation.

Using the natural voice is a final option for the predator hunter. Some who have the needed configuration of throat essentials, those who are willing to practice until they nearly cough themselves into a coma, can obtain a degree of screaming proficiency.

A less difficult articulation is the squeak I have come to call the "Kiss of Death." Lips suck at the hand to produce a high-pitched squeaking. More on this later.

I have not deliberately ignored the class of calls sometimes called electronic calls, but more properly called the battery-powered caller—those that play a cassette tape or play a sound chip. The very next chapter will tell all I know (maybe more) on this versatile screamer.

Diaphragm calls deliver realistic screams, moans, and whines.

Chapter 5

Tape and Chip Players

The battery-powered callers available during the early days of predator screaming were mostly miserable little buggers. One model used a bunch of D-sized batteries to power a portable record player. The distress sounds, mostly the manufacturer blowing screams, came on a 45 rpm record. The reverse side, much of the time, held dialogue that explained the basics of this exciting sport. Later generations went to tape but retained the multiple D power source. Taped distress sounds started to appear.

You are not likely to be surprised to learn that many serious callers, (I was one.) visited the electronic store to search for cassette players, amplifiers, speakers, and a power source (six volt lantern battery). The unit I assembled for a couple of hundred dollars did a fine job but was heavy and ugly as a handful of coyote vents. No matter. When the critters were close enough to see "the ugly" it was usually about BANG time. That home-built caller, in spite of defects, caused a good many coyote, cat, and fox to pack for the trip to the big gut pile in the sky.

Those who make and market the battery-powered caller have considerably improved the product since those salad days. Two styles of battery-powered callers are currently available. The first is the tried-and-true cassette player, mainly made and marketed by the Johnny Stewart Wildlife Call Company. The second kind of caller is the innovative chip player, mainly made and marketed by Burnham Brothers. Each of the construction types has all of the assets owned by all battery-powered callers. The caller types present individual strengths. It is best, I think, to offer a general evaluation of battery-powered callers and then proceed to an evaluation of each call type.

Every battery-powered caller has a strong asset. Those who hunt with one have become instantly expert in the tone and rhythm of the screaming. I emphasize that aspect and that aspect only; but there is a lot more involved. Even those who choose to be relieved of the screaming chore must be hunters—must own that elusive quality called woodsmanship. Even those who use the battery-powered caller must learn the habits and the habitats of the target animal. They must learn setup, camouflage, reading the wind, reading sign, reading animal body language, and more. Finally, when the customer shows, they must be marksman enough to make the shot.

Callers like this chip player from Burnham Brothers cause even beginners to become expert—at least at the sound.

Other assets accrue to the hunter who uses the battery-powered caller. A selection of tapes or a selection of chips lets the hunter choose the sound to be broadcast. Just as a bass fisherman might sort through the tackle box to find a lure that will work with a certain honey hole on a particular day, those who use the battery-powered caller can sort through the tape or chip collection to find a sound that will appeal to a certain kind of animal within a certain kind of country. Critters who have burnt out on the cottontail rabbit distress scream, as an example, might come running to a distressed woodpecker scream. This phenomena can be emphasized by the telling of a true story.

Robin McIntyre was a tall and lanky rookie policeman whose main claim to fame rested with his ability to ingest food. Robin, as I recall, was a four-helping man. No matter the kind of food and the kind of cooking, he would fill his plate four times and lick it clean each time. I hesitated when Robin asked to go along on a predator screaming. Hell, I didn't know if I could pack enough food for the both of us. I tried, filling the cold case with rolls of summer sausage, cheeses, home baked rolls, Ritz crackers, and such. Even a half dozen cans of the dreaded beanie weanies. Lots of coffee. A chocolate cake. Don't remember what else. Anyway, I felt good about lunch.

I felt less good when the drive to the hunting area was minutes old. Robin, smelling food, started to nibble. The groceries diminished rapidly. When I finally mentioned to him he was eating his and my lunch, he giggled. "Guess I am a lot like a coyote," he confessed. "I am an opportunistic eater." And he was. By the time we set up for the dawn stand, the grocery box held air and not much else.

The first screaming produced a pair of anxious coyotes. Both came at the race and one left at the race. The other fell to the .22-250. Considerably encouraged, I blew until I nearly got trombone lip during the next half dozen stands. Nothing. Not so much as a crow. The critters within our part of Arizona, I was convinced, had been scream-educated to the point of paranoia.

Even though it was lunchtime we did not stop. Hell, there was nothing to eat except that one early morning coyote, a critter that was beginning to smell more coyote-like with each passing minute. No thanks.

On the next stand (the last of the day, I promised myself) I broke out the battery-powered caller and entered a cottontail rabbit distress tape. Fifteen minutes of that song didn't do it. I slipped the bunny screaming out and entered in a yellowhammer flicker distress, not hoping for much. Ten minutes later I saw fur—a pair of paranoid yodelers making a sneak through the chaparral. Knowing I owed Robin something because of his eating habits, I did not mention to him we had customers coming. I used the .22-250 to "harvest" both. Robin stayed quiet during the ride home. Course, there was nothing to eat. He may have sulked because of that.

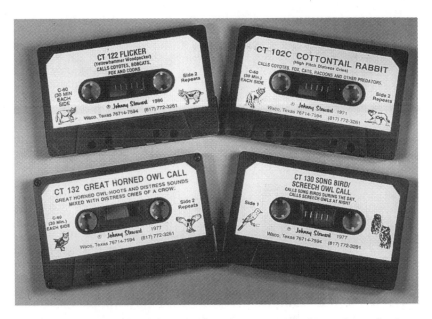

Hunters owning a selection of tapes can sort through to find an effective sound.

The battery-powered caller also shines when it comes to volume. Even though some damnfine screamers claim volume is overrated, I do not agree. Here in the West, where I may be screaming to a coyote in an adjoining zip code, a loud scream does the job. Wind can diminish the carry muscle of tube calls. I like to scream loud with the battery-powered caller during those windy days. Having the ability to cause the screaming to be isolated from the hunter can also be advantageous.

I find the battery-powered callers a good selection when calling to the camera or calling to the camcorder. Isolating the sound causes the critter to be looking over there while I am over here. The customer is less apt to discover the treachery and, consequently, hang around a bit longer, offering extended opportunity for filming or taping. Causing the caller to cooperate with a decoy can enhance the filming or taping opportunity even further. More on this in the chapter on decoys.

The Johnny Stewart MS-512 offers reliability at a bargain price.

I use an identical technique for each of the battery-powered callers. Much of the time, if there is no advantage to be gained by isolation, I keep the calling unit close. I use medium volume at the start of the call and let the screams run continuously for a couple of minutes. If there is no response I assume there is not a customer close by. I crank up the volume to full scream. I hold the unit (with speaker attached) high over my head and rotate the unit so that the directional speaker has the opportunity to look at all points of the compass. Why hold it high? Getting the speaker above the ground cover can free the sound to travel unencumbered.

After I have made the hold-high broadcast, I place the caller on the ground and ready the camera, the camcorder, or the gun for business, permitting the unit to play continuously at full volume for the duration of the setup.

The tape player made by the Johnny Stewart Wildlife Call Company is a compact unit generally consisting of the tape player, an on-off switch, a volume control and a six volt motorcycle battery (rechargeable) within the unit. A plug-in accommodates the attachment of an external speaker. The speaker comes equipped with 25 feet of cord so that the screamings may be isolated from the unit. My cassette caller is the MS-512, a model that has proved to be dependable and durable. These kinds of players reproduce the actual distress sounds of real critters, every one an expert at his or her genre of screaming.

The MS-512 comes with an adapter that permits the battery to be recharged when plugged into a household outlet. An accessory is available that permits recharging through the cigarette lighter of a vehicle, allowing the hunter to recharge while traveling from stand to stand. Such is seldom necessary. You can expect several hours of play from a fully-charged battery. There is more than enough juice to fuel a dawn to dark hunt.

Hunters who work cruelly cold country will find the battery life to be diminished due to the cold. I suggest you carry the battery-powered caller in the warm cab of the vehicle to help the batteries a bit. Also, under such Arctic conditions, a mid-hunt charging might be necessary.

Experience will show innovative ways to utilize the cassette caller. I sometimes record thirty seconds of silence at the start of the tape. Easy to do. Just put the cassette in a standard tape player/recorder, hit record, and time out thirty seconds. I then walk out

Chip players like this Burnham Brothers model offer a change of sound at the flick of a switch.

fifty or a hundred feet to the front of the setup, hit the go button, and walk leisurely back to the setup—having ample time to get hid before the music starts.

Another innovation involves the merging of two sounds onto a single tape. Gray fox fight sounds interrupted with cottontail screams or yellow hammer woodpecker screams work well. Such customizing delivers a tape that is unique. The variety of tapes available offers nearly limitless possibilities. That same variety of tapes can cause confusion when it is time to select sounds for the personal collection. Dozens of sounds are offered. At about ten bucks a tape a considerable collection can seriously dent the budget. Some hunters I know have told the kids they can eat a full meal every other day or can have grits every darn day, and use the savings to buy every sound offered. I do not consider that necessary. I suggest that new hunters, or those new to battery-powered callers, start with five basic tapes: the cottontail distress tape, the jackrabbit distress tape, the yellow hammer woodpecker distress tape, the gray fox distress tape and one of the howling locator tapes. Those who live and hunt within 'coon country might add one more tape to that basic list—the baby 'coon distress tape.

Even though the chip player eats a different kind of grocery, most that has been said about the cassette caller can be said about the chip player. The chip player does not play cassettes, not even those you may have collected for the cassette system. Players like the Compucaller pull sound from a programmed electronic chip containing four separate tracks. A switch on the face plate of the caller permits a quick change of sound. A chip programmed with the jackrabbit distress, the gray fox distress, the cottontail distress, and the bird distress, as an example, can be persuaded to change to any other sound on the chip by moving the indicator.

The screams that come from the chips are electronically produced. The cottontail distress scream is not a broadcast of a genuine cottontail screaming. It is, rather, an electronic

Hung ups and other bashfuls can be caused to move using a low volume close call.

simulation of the real thing. The chips I have heard have a short repeat time. Repeat? The electronic scream sounds for seconds and then repeats that short series of screams. And repeats, repeats, repeats.

I have had the Compucaller I own on several hunts. Even though the short repeats can sound monotonous to the hunter, the animals do not seem to mind, probably because the genuine distressed edibles can get pretty damn boring with their screaming. That makes sense to me. Those who are about to be eaten have no long time to practice the screaming. The screaming is not a prideful talent passed down from doe to bunny. One short opportunity, much of the time, and that's it. Down the gullet. Considering all of that, their lack of repertoire can be understood.

The asset of scream interchangeability was amply illustrated during a cold winter hunt in the desertlands of Arizona. A rancher who was predictably biased when it came to coyote lost his love's prize poodle to a hungry and hunting pair of yodelers. His bride, having made the trip to the West fairly recently, loved that poodle. Not physically, spiritually. Tanya, as a matter of fact, loved every animal that walked, creeped, and crawled the Western wastelands. That included the coyote. Even gophers. Her love of the coyote took a nose-dive when she witnessed the eating and killing of Poopsie (also a recent migrant from The Big Apple). Did you notice I said eat and kill, not kill and eat? Yep, Poopsie was pretty well digested while still alive. You talk about your distress screams. Anyway, such sights and sounds caused Tanya to be sick (physically) and caused her love of God's dog to considerably diminish. Tanya turned ugly. That caused Phil to get out of sorts and he dialed 911, asking for a coyote killer. The game and fish guys dropped my name. And that explains how I happened to be about the dawn desert carrying a new-in-box Compucaller, ready to do business.

The coyote, accustomed to the friendly protection offered by coyote-lover Tanya, were easy. The first came at the gallop. I let him come to sure-kill range and slapped the butt of the Mag 12 (MooseDick, the Mag-10, was in the shop for a tune-up) to my shoulder. The coyote saw the movement and made a frantic yaw to the left, a perfect move to accommodate a right-handed shooter. I placed the barrel bead on the critter's nose and lit the fire. Caught in mid-leap by the load of copper-plated BBs, the coyote did a half-gainer and hit the ground as a rug. I watched the carcass intently for a second or so to insure there would not be one of those miraculous recoveries and went back to work.

The second coyote came a lot less enthusiastically, sliding to a suspicious stop a hundred yards out to deliver the bad eye. Too far out for the full-choked twelve—too far out for a shotgun of any gauge. The yodeler faced straight to the speaker of the Compucaller, displaying the kind of body language that told me this customer would come closer if properly encouraged. I eased one hand to the Compucaller control and flicked the switch to dog distress. Low volume. The coyote keyed in on this new sound, maybe remembering the day she had Poopsie for lunch, and came at the lunge, stopping forty yards out. This time she stood at the broadside, telling me she had come as far as she intended to come. Knowing that 40 yards was about maximum for the three-inch twelve but knowing this was as good as it was likely to get, I took the shot. A few seconds later I was walking out to retrieve the double. Poopsie was avenged. Tanya (she turned out to be a decent sort, even though she later ran off with an alfalfa pellet salesman) would be happy.

A final comment on the battery-powered caller. Cassette callers like the Johnny Stewart MS-512 can be had for less than a hundred and a half. A new-in-box Compucaller will cost about twice that. Either is bargain priced, the way I see it. Such a piddling amount, prorated over a lifetime of hunting, ends up having an inconsequential cost.

Chapter 6

Howling and Howlers

There are those who are convinced that coyotes howl just for the hell of it. The yips, yodels, and howls heard through most of the West and a part of the East at dawn and dusk, to them, come from the throats of animals so full of themselves they just have to tell the world of it. Even though I do not usually comment on such anthropomorphic drivelings unless specifically invited to do so, my experience causes me to think exactly the opposite. No wild critter I have met makes any kind of noise without good reason. They do not gossip and prattle; they cannot afford to do so. Those who earn a living as hunters, and at times reluctantly accept a change of roles to become the hunted, cannot be much of a blabbermouth. To do so can cause prey animals to be alerted. To do so causes those higher on the food chain to have an improved target. Articulation, to a critter, is a basic of communication. Even though few humans understand every nuance of the coyote language, it is probable each sound carries a specific message to another coyote.

Dawn and dusk howlings are the coyote vocalizations most often heard. Those sing-alongs are mostly territorial in nature. Coyote have found a survival advantage to homesteading a particular territory and then defending that territory from poachers and other encroachers. A territorial coyote, often a territorial pair, learn about every aspect of their piece of ground. That knowledge can cause a critical advantage when it comes time to search out groceries, or to escape when the hunter comes to call. The howlings announce continued residency to the coyote in adjoining territory. Such non-aggressive territorial claims reduce confrontation between neighbors.

How do I know all of this? I read and I observe. Wildlife professionals, and those who aspire to be such, sometimes fit captured critters with a radio telemetry device that allows a discrete spying when the animal is released to the wild. One such Peeking Tom conducted a territorial study involving certain coyote within a favored coyote habitat. Nope, not Anderson Mesa but the pinion-juniper woodlands surrounding the mesa uplift. One such coyote tagged as Number 97, a handsome male trapped near the Wildcat Canyon mud tank, was released to the wild when he was a vigorous two-year-old. That dog, becoming wise in the way of survival, lived to the ripe old age of seven-years-plus. Number 97 suffered through a really bad day during the winter of his seventh year. It happened this way.

Telemetry studies suggest coyote territories vary as food availability varies.

I was in the pushdowns slightly to the east of Wildcat Tank to scream at winter coyote. Prime pelts from this high country habitat brought big dollars from the fur trade, an inducement that added incentive to my hunting activity. I was there with a Flagstaff city police supervisor to demonstrate my hunting and screaming technique. We set up to the front of a pile of pushdown stringbark and started the screaming. Minutes later Number 97 charged into view, handsome in the prime of his coyotehood. I lip-squeaked to stop the gallop, carefully sighted upon that place behind the shoulder and midway between back and chest bottom, and stroked. Number 97 died well.

Noticing the ear tag, I made an inquiry and learned a bit about 97's reputation. A wildlife biology major from Northern Arizona University had trapped and ear tagged Number 97 while he was a two-year-old (the coyote, not the biology major). Released, the coyote established dominance, took a mate, and did coyote things for the next five years, entirely within about a three square mile area surrounding Wildcat Tank.

That same study established a fact of coyote territoriality. A coyote identified as Coyote A was territorial. Coyote B occupied an adjoining territory. Both were fitted with transmitter collars. Coyote A and Coyote B honored rigid territorial boundaries for all of Coyote A's life. Finally, the radio collar attached to the neck of Coyote A sent a sad message. Coyote A had stopped moving about and was presumed to be dead. Coyote B, sending out his territorial howlings and receiving no answer from Ol' A, trotted over into A's territory to have a walk about.

Number 97 mated, lived long, and prospered—until along came Blair.

A northern Arizona study showed a female losing a mate will advertise her needs through howling.

Dawn and dusk howls, and howls at other times, can communicate circumstances other than territoriality. Such can announce degree of dominance, gender and even sexual receptivity. Through much of their range, particularly when coyote populations are crowded, only the most dominant of coyote pairs are permitted to breed. Coyote, like other wild dogs, mate pretty much for life, or at least until one of the pair dies or loses dominance. A dominant female who has lost a mate, or who has one who is too old to shake the sugar tree, may announce her needs to surrounding ears. It does not take long for Handsome Hairys to come at the gallop.

An easily identifiable coyote vocalization is the distress yip, sometimes called the pup distress. These high pitched hurtings signal trouble and ask for help. I have heard distress yippings when a dominant coyote disciplines a submissive. Politically correct body posture (the avoidance of eye contact and a slinking posture, at times laying on the back with belly and throat exposed) combined with the yippings can communicate complete submission. I have also heard the distress yips when a coyote suffers a poor hit from rifle or shotgun.

The coyote vocalizations mentioned above, the **territorial howl** (called the challenge howl or the dominance howl by some), the **female invitation** (love invite) and the **distress yip** (pup distress) are those most helpful to the coyote hunter. I have used all three to cause a coyote to come close.

The **territorial howl** can be used to attract dominant male coyote during the dogging season that begins here in the Southwest about the last of February and is likely to begin later as latitude changes. Dominant dogs have come running to the challenge during that season. I have had less luck howling in coyote outside the breeding season. I use the dominance howl then mainly as a locator call, relying on the following technique.

Even though it is illegal to shoot coyote during the dark here in Arizona (also illegal in many other Western states and within some Eastern and Midwestern states), I find it to be helpful to drive through good coyote habitat during the dark, stopping to howl about every mile, using my natural voice, a howler, or playing a howl tape through a battery-powered caller. Experience has suggested a wait of five to ten minutes after each howling as some response is delayed. Howlbacks are noted as to mileage (or mile-post) and direction. Some howl sites produce a multiple response. That information is also noted. When daylight comes I retrace the route, setting up to call to the howlbacks. A number of advantages accrue. Having heard the recent howl I am somewhat certain there is a coyote within hearing to be called. Having pinpointed location, I am able to set up using that knowledge to good advantage. I choose a hide that causes wind direction to be beneficial and that offers vision and shooting lanes located along probable approach.

The **female invitation howl,** like the dominance howl, is most effective during the dogging season. Used then, the howl is a dandy way to bring in males at a gallop.

The **pup distress** is also most effective during the time the pups are at the den and within the company of Mom & Pop, maybe April through September. The adults respond, I think, because they fear a creature is munching on Junior or Sis. They come to protect.The pup distress can be used effectively throughout the year, although response will be less vigorous than during the pupping period. The pup distress, correctly used, can be a call for all seasons. Imagination will extend the usefulness of the pup distress. A report of an actual hunting experience illustrates.

I was screaming to a pinion-juniper hillside during an early season hunt (about the first week of October, as I recall) hoping to fetch in a dumb pup or two. Dispersal happens about then, and the nearly adult-size pups of the year have the typical teenage appetite. Most lack sophistication. Even though the pelts obtained from early October coyote are not one hundred percent prime (the leather being still somewhat gray), the underfur and the guard hair are well-developed, cooperating to produce a saleable pelt.

I was three or four minutes into the stand when I sighted a flash of fur coming at the gallop, actually two flashes of fur racing to the scream. Trouble. The lead coyote was at least a hundred yards ahead of the trailer, causing it to be difficult to take both. I did as I usually do under similar circumstances. I waited until the leader passed behind a stringbark juniper and used that opportunity to shoulder the Sako, centering the small x of the duplex six at about expected reappearance. When the coyote showed in the sight, I lip-squeaked (The Kiss of Death) to cause the critter to stop. A second later the sight was centered on the critter's necessaries—back of the shoulder and about midway between back and brisket. Death came a trigger-twitch later. Moving fast I shifted to pick up the trailer, now running desperately for home and Mother. No shot. Almost by instinct I used my natural voice to send out a decent pup-distress-screaming. The runner slowed, stopped, and started the circle, hoping to taste the wind. When the coyote stopped two hundred yards out to deliver the bad eye, I braced my elbows across my drawn-up knees, sighted, and took the shot. The pup distress screaming caused my fur production to double on that stand.

I will make no effort to describe the sounds involved in the various coyote language, knowing that such description is not all that helpful. I suggest, instead, that those who are serious about howling invest in one of the howl instruction tapes. See the listing at the end of this book for recommended sources.

The right kind of vocal cords permit natural voice howls.

Chapter 7

Fur Guns/Rifles

I was after monster mulies on the North Kaibab when the song-dog sang from a ridge a quarter of a mile away. I interrupted my walk long enough to dig into the coat pocket to retrieve the nearly new Burnham Brothers Long Range Fox Call. Seconds later that sad song I call the "Dying Rabbit Blues" raped the northern Arizona high country. Not that good, as this was my first serious attempt at screaming. Even so, a couple of minutes later an out-of-breath coyote showed at the run. Amazed, I watched the advance. When the yodeler was fifty yards out he stopped to make a reconnoiter. I shouldered the ought-six deer gun and sent a custom-loaded 165 grainer through the critter's necessaries. As might be expected, the coyote was killed much more dead than need be. The corpse, sad to say, retained little dignity. That experience taught several valuable lessons. Yes, the rabbit distress scream does cause coyote to come close. Yes, about any centerfire rifle will kill a coyote graveyard dead. Yes, mule deer and elk guns like the .30-06 and all others of like genre do a messy job when it comes time to do wet work on coyote-sized critters. Kinder and gentler calibers abound.

That experience atop the "Mountain That Lays on Its Side" caused me to set out to learn all I could about the exciting sport of predator screaming. And it did even more: I set out almost immediately on the search to find the perfect fur gun.

The years of experience since the "harvesting" of that first-called coyote have convinced me of the cold hard facts. There are a lot of good fur calibers available to those who squeeze the rabbit. No one caliber, at least none I have used, can be considered to be a perfect fur gun for all facets of predator screaming. No such caliber, the way I see it, exists. A caliber that does a dandy job on long distance coyote weighing thirty pounds, maybe the .22-250, does less well when the target becomes an eight-pound fox who begs for the rabbit from twenty steps beyond the gun bore. The best a screamer can do is to choose the gun (or guns) that most often meets expectations, forgetting the perfect gun and settling for next best, the nearly perfect fur gun. A nearly perfect fur gun, no matter the caliber, must be accurate. If you can't hit 'em you can't kill 'em.

Out of the box accuracy can be decent among about all of the calibers marketed as varmint guns. I write mainly of those that have an appetite for the .224 diameter bullet. The newly resurrected Hornet,

41

The right kind of rifle can reach out to touch long distance customers—maybe do it twice.

the .222, the .222 magnum, the .223, the .22-250 and the 220 Swift. Every one of those guns, even shooting factory made ammunition, owns enough accuracy to deliver a killing blow to a coyote, a bobcat or a fox at moderate range. Trouble is, the critters I have screamed into gun range do not always cooperate and come to moderate range. An almost perfect fur gun, the way I see it, should have enough talent to consistently take critters at moderate range and have the extended talent needed to take occasional critters at immoderate range.

Considering the above, I believe it important to comment a bit more on extended-range targets. Nine out of ten of the coyotes I call will come so close I can smell the mutton on their breath. Bobcat and fox are more so. The coyote, bobcat, and fox you call will approach similarly. That tenth critter is the one you should prepare for. While on a hunt with a well-known Nebraska publisher we discovered Number 10 to be a paranoid coyote who galloped broadside at an honest 300 yards. I amazed the publisher (and myself, although I made no comment at the time) when I cleaned the earwax (and all else) from the critter's ear using a 52-grain chunk of copper-coated lead. On another hunt a Babbitt Ranch cowboy and I were calling the Redlands when a big male coyote swaggered to a ridgetop five hundred yards distant. Again, Number 10. Aiming at the moon I triggered a desperation round that found the coyotes' engine room. Luck?

The pristine pelt on this coyote showed the fur gun killed the critter but spared the fur.

Mostly. I feel it important to say the luckiest people I know are those who are best prepared. A knowledge of the gun, knowledge of the cartridge performance, and ability to judge range permitted me to place the bullet within the ballpark. Luck did the rest.

When it gets to the bottom line, screamers who hope to salvage fur from called critters do not aim at the critter, they aim at a specific part of the critter, usually the part of the rib cage immediately behind the shoulder on broadside critters and within the center of

Handloading can cause an accuracy that fills the fence with fur.

the chest on facing customers. A correctly loaded round that causes either hit is likely to penetrate the critter's necessaries and explode without exiting, providing an instant and humane death. An imprecise hit, even with one of the nearly perfect calibers, can cause fur to fly into adjoining zip codes.

Hunting with cartridges handloaded to match the appetite of a particular fur gun, and handloaded to respond to the challenges of fur hunting, is critical to fur hunting accuracy and pelt-saving performance, in my opinion. The factory loaded round is handicapped by popularity. The many who buy those mass produced cartridges hunt through the broad spectrum of hunting opportunity. The factory produced cartridge must address each of those opportunities to deliver characteristics that permit a decent performance within all.

I have heard it said that reloading is a way to save money. I do not believe such to be so. Considering initial investment, considering the cost of components, I do not believe there is a substantial savings to be found unless the reloader shoots a hell of a lot (and maybe more). The main strength to the reloaded round comes from the provided ability to tailor a round to the appetite of a specific gun and to the job ahead. And, I consider reloading to be a pleasant part of fur hunting activity. A hunter who commits to reloading is likely to shoot more. That increased shooting will almost surely cause him or her to become a better shot, an asset that can cause an increase in the fur collection.

Certain mechanical manipulations can cause an almost perfect fur gun to move a bit closer to perfect. The attachment of a quality telescope sight is an example. I freely admit a bias to the lower power magnifications. A nearly perfect choice is a variable that ranges from about 1.5 to 4.5. Isn't the gunner who throws a 52-grain chunk of copper-coated lead at a three-hundred-yard coyote handicapped by

The author prefers a trigger of about 3 pounds pull—finding such assists accuracy.

such low magnification? Not really. Here is a sad truth, learned the hard way. The critter you want to kill is not that big brute in the glass. The target, always, is that little bitty booger you see with the naked eye. The lower magnification sights, in my opinion, cause me to aim more precisely. That same lack of magnification is almost always an asset when a critter comes boot-strap close.

Careful attention to the trigger can also improve accuracy. I freely admit to being a trigger man, hating all of the eight-pound factory triggers, most likely put there by the maker to escape a degree of liability. A good trigger to me is one that crisply releases at a bit less than three pounds of pull. All of my collection of fur getters (Sorry Sarah Brady would call it an arsenal) have crisp and light-weight triggers, factory triggers adjusted by a competent gunsmith or replacement triggers installed by the same.

Knowing an evaluation of fur calibers must be made within this chapter, I reluctantly turn my attention to that. Why reluctantly? Choice of caliber is mainly subjective, the way I see it, a bit like deciding upon a blonde or a redhead. (Personally, I love both.) Those who have established caliber priority within the mind are often inflexible as they defend. Some, sad to say, have not learned to disagree without being disagreeable. Even so, my own very subjective evaluations follow.

Knowing that some will want to know, I start at the small end to write upon a round that falls far below the minimum velocity and energy needed in a fur gun. I write of the ubiquitous .22 rimfire.

The .22 Rimfire

The .22 rimfire is a dandy gun for tin cans, for tree squirrels, and for cottontails. Even shooting the .22 long rifle in hollow point, the round does not offer the range and knockdown needed to cleanly kill even small coyote, small bobcat, and fox of any size consistently. Twenty-two rimfire lovers might wonder if my opinions would change if the rifle shot the reduced lead and increased powder round some-times called "The Stinger," sometimes called "The Yellowjacket," and sometimes called something else. My opinion stays constant. Even though such manipulation results in slightly increased velocity (and almost always in a drop in accuracy), the increase is not enough to cause the round to hunt with the big dogs. Sorry.

The .22 WRFM

I hold an improved opinion of the improved .22 rimfire muscled up to become the .22 WRFM (Winchester Rim Fire Magnum). Under some circumstances, within certain range limits, I consider the .22 WRFM to be adequate for close-range fox, close range 'coon and close range cacomistle (ringtail cat). Sort of. When the hit is pre-cise. Equivocal? Sure.

Even though the gun might be shooting the 40-grain hollowpoint to a muzzle velocity of 2,000 fps, providing an impressive 364 foot pounds of energy, few critters are shot at the muzzle. That same 40-grain hol-lowpoint has substantially changed character at 100 yards. Velocity has been reduced to 1,407 fps. Energy has been reduced by about half, to 176 foot pounds. A precise hit on a fox or 'coon will usually result in a somewhat sudden death. An imprecise hit will not.

There was a time (a very short time) when I thought the .22

The 22 WRFM is gentle to fur but provides inconsistent kills on coyote.

WRFM might be a dandy gun for close coyote. I was working a pushdown during an early morning scream. Never heard of a pushdown? Such is an area of pinion-juniper woodlands ravaged by a pair of D-8 Caterpillars connected by a hundred feet of anchor chain. The dead and dying trees were bulldozed into mounds. Those mounds, after fifty years of aging, have turned into favored habitat for cottontails, rock squirrels, bushy-tailed wood rats, and a mind boggling assortment of mice and voles, all critter edibles.

I had snuggled my big body into the generous arm of a long dead juniper to make the scream. A flash of fur caused me to focus fifty yards out. I locked onto the coyote at about the time he stopped to beg for the rabbit. I took the facing shot offered, centering the crosshairs of the H&R Model 700 to the precise center of the chest. The yodel dog went down as if pole-axed. The entry hole was .224 caliber. There was no exit. No muss and no fuss. I was convinced I had come upon the ideal close-range coyote killer.

My enthusiasm was radically diminished by day's end. That day of screaming hooked three more coyote, all coming somewhat close. The first was a 65-yard opportunity at a running coyote. The autoload asset of the Model 700 permitted more than one shot. It is possible I missed, although I do not believe I did. The coyote was sure I did. He made the desperate run for home and Mother, and made it.

The other two opportunities were at about the same range. Both were at standing coyote. Each was solidly hit in the chest. Both staggered. Both made the escape. I have not used the .22 WRFM on coyote since.

The Insects

The years preceding the Big War II caused a proliferation of insects to descend upon the shooting fraternity—the .22 Hornet (1932), the .218 Bee (1938), the .219 Donaldson Wasp (1941), and the slightly earlier .219 Zipper (1937). All of the above were somewhat similar except the Hornet (early models were chambered for the .223 bullet) shot the .224 bullet. All shot decently at close range. All were moderately successful for a few years. The popularity, in my opinion, came from concept, from marketing, and because no sensible alternative was offered. All languished when improved calibers became available. You want to know why? You want the truth? None, with the possible exception of the Hornet, maintained accuracy when range was extended. When the highly-accurate .222 debuted in 1950, critter killers were damn glad to go to it. Bench rest shooters too. More on the deuce a bit farther on.

As a point of interest, Ruger restructured their Model 77/22WRM rifle during late 1993 and early 1994 to resurrect the .22 Hornet chambering. Sales have been phenomenal. Production has not kept pace with demand. If the Hornet is the best of a bad bunch, as noted above, why the popularity? I can answer only for myself. I bought my Hornet because I didn't have one. I bought the gun because I wondered how it would perform on called gray fox and the occasional raccoon. I bought it, mainly, because of nostalgia.

Screamer Martin Hendrix of Flagstaff bought his Hornet (Savage-Anshutz) for about the same reasons. A talented reloader, Martin has punched sub-minute of angle Hornet groupings (about 1/4") from the bench using Nosler Ballistic Tip bullets.

The .17 Caliber

The .17 can be a dandy gun for short-range fur and can be a fair caliber for mid-range fur. Remington legitimized this smallest of the centerfires during 1971. The .17 is a fast little booger and that speed is its main asset. A hot-loaded 20-grain or 25-grain bullet can be caused to leave the muzzle at an impressive 4,000 fps. Such will provide spectacular blowups on small critters. Such speed, as might be expected, causes the load to be flat shooting. That same speed can cause excessive pelt damage on furbearers if the hit is not precise. Reducing powder will cause a slow down and might improve accuracy. Doing so, however, causes trajectory to be less flat. Even so, those who shoot a lot of thin-bodied fox, and do so at moderate range (maybe a hundred yards or so) will find fur damage to be minimized.

The bad news? The petite pill will not buck much of a headwind and is likewise affected by staunch cross-winds. The .17 does not own the ability to take long-range fur, not as well as do most of the .224s. The small capacity of the case causes loadings to be critical. A half grain overload can increase velocity significantly and might result in an alarming pressure increase. The bottom line? The .17 is fun to shoot and does a decent job on critters out to about a couple of hundred yards.

The .222 Remington

I believe the deuce to be the most accurate of the mid-range calibers. The caliber has been a favorite of bench rest shooters since its introduction in 1950. Hunters were likewise impressed. Much of the time a factory gun fresh from the dealer's shelf would deliver minute of angle accuracy. Unlike predecessors, the deuce accuracy

The slowed .222 does dandy on fox, but loses long-range accuracy.

did not diminish as range extended.

I see the .222 as an almost perfect fur caliber for all of the East, all of the Midwest and parts of the West. Loaded close to maximum, the .222 round does a dandy job on coyote out to about 200 yards. Downloaded, the round becomes dandy for close range fox.

The .223 Remington

The .223 Remington is ballistically close to the .222 Remington Magnum, the case being a bit shorter and holding a hair less powder. I see the .223 to be about as good as the deuce and maybe a bit better in some aspects.

As many know, the .223 was developed for the military during the late fifties. Remington presented the caliber to the civilian market at about the same time. Although the round is labeled a .223, the gun shoots a .224 bullet. Commercial guns deliver good accuracy; many of the military autoloaders do not. A strong asset of the .223 is the availability of once-fired military brass. Commercial reloaders often offer reloaded .223 military at a bargain price. The case capacity of the military brass, fortunately, is about the same as the case capacity of brass intended for civil use. My .223s (including the H&K Model 630 autoloader) group both 50- and 52-grain match hollowpoints well.

The .222 Remington Magnum

The .222 Remington Magnum has a twenty percent greater case capacity than does the .222 and has about a five percent greater case capacity than does the .223. The caliber was in competition to become a military cartridge but did not succeed. A short time later (1958) the caliber appeared as a civilian offering.

The performance of the Mag-deuce is about midway between the .222 and the .22-250. The .222 Magnum delivers accuracy that is nearly equal to the legendary accuracy of the .222 and has the added advantage of increased range, out to about 275 yards.

The .222 Magnum has not enjoyed the same degree of popularity as either the .222 or the .223, and probably never will. Even though the magger is ballistically superior to the standard deuce, the eight-year head-start enjoyed by the latter causes .222 Mag sales to lag. The .223, being ballistically similar, owns the advantage of military recognition. That, and the availability of once-fired brass, causes the .223 to be most popular.

The .22-250 Remington

The .22-250 began life about 50 years ago as a wildcat. The caliber is essentially a necked down .250 Savage with a slight increase in shoulder angle. The .224 grain bullet leaves the barrel at speeds superior to the old .250-3000 Savage and delivers increased accuracy. The chambering has become the most popular varmint caliber ever developed. Considering all of that, it is surprising to note that no major gun manufacturer offered a factory chambering for this rifle until 1965, even though the .22-250 had outdistanced the popular .220 Swift years before.

I see the .22-250 as the almost perfect caliber for Western

screamers. The caliber owns impressive assets. Legitimate 300-yard plus range. Outstanding accuracy, near that provided by the .222 and the .22 Magnum. Enough muscle to take the biggest coyote and the biggest cougar.

There is not a significant difference between the .22-250 and the .220 Swift, in my opinion. Even though the Swift owns a slightly greater case capacity (about ten percent), the two chamberings are near ballistic clones when loaded to comparable pressure. Even though all advantages listed for the .22-250 will apply equally to the .220 Swift, I see the .22-250 to be the better choice. A lack of factory loadings for the Swift is the reason. Those who reload are not likely to care about factory fodder availability. For them, the Swift deserves consideration.

Larger Calibers

As noted at the start of this chapter, a caliber of any size can do a decent job of killing a called predator. I have used a the .30-06 mentioned and have also used the .25-06 (still do, at times). Screamer friends use the .243 and the .257. Such, in my opinion, can cause it to rain fox fur for a week. If such a caliber is all that is available, and if you wish to salvage the fur, download as you reload so as to avoid bullet expansion. Expect an exit hole on every shot. With luck that exit will be one that can be repaired using needle and thread.

Chapter 8

Fur Guns/Shotguns

It was a desert day to be remembered. A November night rain had traveled from Baja to water the desert. Giant saguaro, as they almost always do, took a greedy drink through their stingy root system, causing the ribbed exterior to swell with delicious enthusiasm. The long-limbed ocotillo (being a bit crazy by nature) thought the rain to be the signal of spring. Bare limbs turned new-leaf green. A few of the hard-core crazies produced flowers of a brilliant red, so pretty I could only stand to look with one eye. Ahhh, the desert after a rain.

That night rain freshened the ground and the air, causing both to look as pristine as on Creation Day. I scrunched a bit deeper into the friendly limbs of the creosote bush and sang my favorite song, "The Dying Rabbit Blues."

I heard the customers coming before sight was possible. The wet ground and the cleansed air cooperated to cause the thumping of the gallop to be drumbeat loud. A pair of storm-hungry coyote, I figured. I raised the massive maw of the ten-gauge autoloader I call "The MooseDick" and readied myself physically and mentally. Seconds later the desperate duo became an intimidating presence not more than thirty yards out. The first pattern of tightly-choked, copper-plated BBs took the leader (the easy one) full face. I was swinging to the trailer a semi-second after the boom, following as the critter made the desperate turn to begin the run for home. The second shot connected before that turn was fully complete. Those few seconds of action caused a pair of prime silver-bellies to hit the ground graveyard-dead and provided hunt excitement. The shotgun, I am convinced, deserves much of the credit for the clean kills. Knowing my limitations, knowing I am not the greatest offhand rifle shot in the world, I am betting I would not have collected two coyote on that screaming if I had carried the rifle. Hell, I might as well be totally honest. It is likely I might have missed both.

The shotgun is my gun of choice when I scream shotgun-friendly country. What kind of country is that? Tight country. Creosote-choked desert flats. Chaparral. Winter woods stripped of leaves and ground cover providing some vision opportunity, all at close range. Any kind of country where the customer has to come sure-kill close to get a look at the rabbit. How close is sure-kill close, you ask? Depends, I answer. Sure-kill range varies as the body size of the target varies, as the gauge of the gun varies, as the constriction of the bore varies, and as the nature of the gunner varies. Permit me to share opinions on each of those considerations.

Gauge is an easy explanation. The screamer who hunts coyote-size critters (30 pounds or so in the West and 40 pounds or more in the East) will do best when equipped with one of the gauges I call the big bangers. I refer to the 3.5" ten-gauge, the 3.5" twelve-gauge, and the 3" twelve-gauge. Each of those bangers have the muscle needed to reach out and touch a coyote at reasonable ranges. The bigger the bore, the way I see it, the better the banger.

The gun I call Moose-Dick can be a sensible choice for hunters who scream a lot. My gun is one of the older Ithaca Mag-10s, a big junk-yard-dog kind of a gun having the assets needed to rug out a mature dog coyote at surprising range—out to about fifty-five yards, at times a bit more. When stuffed to capacity, one of the ten gauge hulls holds two full ounces of BBs, maybe more. Even though the gas-operated autoloading action drains off a bit of recoil, the kick can be substantial. I do not mean to say the Mag-10 will kill at one end and cripple at the other. I do say that those who have the correct body size will find the recoil to be tolerable, particularly when you consider that screaming shot opportunities might be lim-

Ten-gauge autoloaders do well on coyote, fox, and bobcat.

ited to a half a handful a day. What is the correct body size for the ten gauge? I consider my own to be dandy. A six-foot frame of substantial weight. A hunting incident illustrates the good body/bad body equation.

I was on the hunt for a pair of raccoon who amused themselves by robbing the corn crib on a Texas ranch. Wildlife biologist Bill Del Monte and I traveled to the area to do a bit of night screaming. Minutes into the hunt four eyeballs showed in the beam of the Nightlite. Nope, it wasn't the rare four-eyed 'coon. It was, instead, a pair of two-eyed raccoon coming at the lope, shoulder to shoulder. Bill handled the light and illuminated the corn lovers when they paused for a reconnoiter thirty yards out. Knowing that the first shot would be easy and the second shot less easy, I gambled. I placed the barrel bead between the two heads. A trigger twitch later and both 'coon were rugged. "Holy Moly!" Bill exclaimed, "that was impressive!" And then he asked a fateful question. "Does that gun kick you?" I admitted it did not and offered Bill the opportunity to see for himself. He took dead aim at a stump and lit the fire. The recoil bruised his shoulder, backed him up and hurt his feelings. "I thought you said the gun didn't kick," he grumbled. "I said," I answered, "it didn't kick me." Even though the gun kicked each of us equally, Bill's 150-pound body was affected more than my own 250-pound body.

The assets provided by the ten-gauge autoloader are obvious—range and knockdown power. Each of those allow a clean kill at extended range. The autoloading feature permits a couple of fast followup shots if need be. Not often required when dealing with a single customer but always needed when the coyote, the fox, the bobcat, and the raccoon come like grapes, in bunches.

Ten-gauge defects can be equally obvious. Recoil has been mentioned. The cost of the gun and the cost of the shotshells can cause a hernia to all but the most muscular budgets. The ten-gauge autoloader, as most know, is currently made and marketed by the Rem-

MooseDick doubled on raccoon during a Texas hunt.

ington Arms Company, using the old Ithaca Mag-10 configuration. Purchase price will trash out a thousand dollar bill, maybe leaving enough leftover for a few boxes of fodder. The buying of that fodder, sad to say, can cause a cold wind to blow through the bank account. I figure each bang out of that big booger blows a dollar bill. Reloading, for those who are so inclined, can cut the cost in half. That's the good news. The bad news? Unless you shoot a hell of a lot (maybe more) the cost of equipment can cause savings to disappear.

Hunters who work the flyways for high traveling honkers and other waterfowl, particularly those who hope to steel the goose, will find the ten gauge to be dandy. Other all-season hunters will be less pleased. The ten gauge is not a grouse gun. It is not a quail gun, nor is it a rabbit gun. Hunters who own the small gun safe, those who must make do with one general purpose smoothbore, are advised to think twelve.

The recently revived 3.5" twelve-gauge, best typified by the Ulti-Mag pumpgun made by Mossberg, can be a sensible substitute. The 3.5" hull, as long as a ten-gauge hull but not as fat, delivers decent punch out to about fifty yards. All that was said about the ten-gauge can be said about the 3.5" twelve, reduced by about 15 percent. I see one important defect in the 3.5" twelve. Factory fodder offerings are limited. The 3.5" twelve, like the 3.5" ten, was engineered to be a steel shotgun for waterfowl. Shot shell manufacturers do not offer much for the critter caller.

Thinking positive, the cost of a gun such as the Ulti-Mag can be less than half the cost of a gun such as the Remington SP-10. And unlike the ten, the 3.5" twelve will accept the less long shotshells—the 3" twelve and the 2 3/4" twelve. Even though guns designed to handle the long twelve hulls are big and somewhat clubby, such can be crammed with reduced load shotshells and pointed at about any kind of game susceptible to a smoothbore.

Mossberg's UltiMag offers Magnum performance at a moderate price.

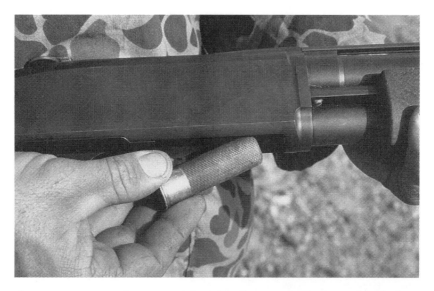

Ammo costs can decrease when big banger hulls are reloaded.

The tried-and-true twelve fitted with a chamber long enough to accept the 3" shell can be a dandy choice for screamers who intend to make one gun answer all smoothbore needs. Experience causes me to favor the autoloader, typified by the venerable Remington Model 11-87 SP. The SP stands for Special Purpose, a designation applied to guns made specifically as ambush guns, all having a non-glare metal finish (sometimes achieved through chemically altering the metal and sometimes achieved through camo painting) and all have a low luster finish to wood or plastic parts.

The three-inch twelve, in autoloader or in pumpgun, does a decent job on called critters and on flyway waterfowl. Stuffing the magazine with 2 3/4" loads of the proper shot size can cause the gun to turn attention to a mind boggling variety of feathered and furred critters.

Even though I mention only the autoloader and the pump, I am aware of other shotgun configurations, the single shot and the stack barrel and side by side doubles. Those who own that kind of gun will likely find the gun to be decent, subject to the limitations noted during the discussion of other shotgun types.

And even though I have discussed only the ten-gauge and the twelve-gauge, I am aware lesser gauges exist. I consider the six-teen-gauge, the twenty-gauge, the twenty-eight-gauge, and the .410 caliber to be unsuited for heavy-duty predators. I am not saying such cannot be used. I say, instead, that those lightweights cause the job of critter killing to be more difficult than need be.

Some mention must be made of barrel constriction, commonly called degree of choke. Tightly-choked guns cause the shot disbursement to be delayed, delivering a dense pattern at a surprising distance. Super-tight chokings have been made available to those who hide in the bushes to make a noise like a turkey's girlfriend. That kind of hunter calls the gobbler to somewhat close range (25 to 35 yards) and aims for the turkey's head—a target of about hardball size. Too large a pattern spread can cause a miss. Those tightly-choked turkey guns can do a fine job on called critters, delivering a dense pattern to the animal necessaries.

A tightly-choked gun delivering a dense pattern offers an advantage. That advantage may turn to a disadvantage. A careless shouldering or a careless aim can cause the dense pattern to be off target. Some screamers compensate. They add an extra barrel bead and sometimes fit the gun with open or glass sights. More on that within the chapter dealing with sights.

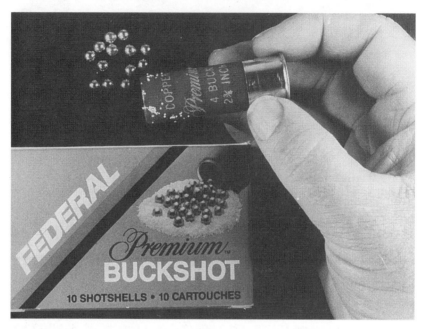

Copper-plated BB's and #4 buckshot do decently out to about a half a hundred yards.

Chapter 9

Fur Guns/Primitives

The fur takers mentioned to this point have been the kind of killers that cause the killing to be less difficult. Fast and flat centerfires like the .222, the .223 and the .22-250. Shotguns of the ten and twelve gauge subspecies. Knowing there are those who find pleasure in doing the difficult, this chapter will discuss screaming critters close to the front stuffer, the handgun, and the stick and string. I say at the start I do not intend to say a lot on the subject of screaming to the primitives, knowing that those who have answered this extra challenge will be a somewhat small percentage of the readership.

Those who enjoy the smell of black powder will find the muzzle-loader to be a decent fur getter. There is the obvious handicap caused by the one-shot capability. The reloading, even using speed loaders, offers sufficient time for the slowest of foot to make the escape before the powder is poured and patched, before the lead is ramrodded home and before the capping or priming. A second disadvantage comes from the relative inaccuracy provided by even the best of the black-smoke belchers. None I have handled offer the pinpoint accuracy provided by the deuce or by any other of the .224 genre.

The question of caliber is one that can be confusing to those not

Low velocity causes entry and exit to be discreet.

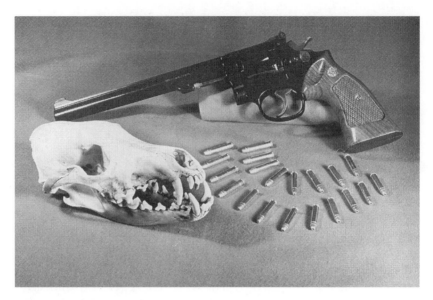

Proper technique can cause handgun hunters to take fur.

familiar with the ballistics of the muzzleloader. The slow speed of the projectile does not offer the advantage (or disadvantage) of expansion. A .36 caliber ball, a .36 caliber maxiball, a .36 caliber chunk of rock will deliver a .36 caliber entry and a .36 caliber exit. All of the above in .54 caliber will deliver an entry and an exit of .54 caliber. What is the difference? Not a hell of a lot, speaking fur-wise. I shoot a .54 caliber for all of my big game hunting and use that same .54 caliber on called critters. The entry and exit fur tears are easily repaired. The big chunk of lead delivers the big whack, causing the recipient to be graveyard dead in an instant.

Those who handgun will find paranoid predators to be a hard get. Shooting from the set can be difficult. The target, much of the time, is on the move, compounding the degree of difficulty. Here is the technique I use to handgun fur, a technique that works, some of the time.

I find it best to buddy hunt when I head out with a holstered handgun. I find it to be too tough working alone—not enough hands to do all that needs to be done. A solo hunter can do about as well if he or she trades the tube for the battery-powered caller. I find a comfortable set that places me against a tree or to the front of a bush, anything to cause my big body to blend, and set so that my body is squared to the anticipated approach. I draw up the knees and use those drawn-up knees to support the arms. Using the two-hand hold I stay ready for customers. If the critter comes running, as most do, I lip squeak, growl, or cuss to cause the critter to slide to a stop. Then I take the shot.

Taking a coyote, cat, or fox using the bow and arrow is a most difficult endeavor. A certain amount of motion is needed to make the draw and take the aim. Releasing the hold causes the arrow to fly and that causes a movement that can alarm the customer. A quick-footed coyote, sad to say, can dodge an arrow and have time left to scratch a flea. What to do? Take a tip from the archers who take stick and string to the spring turkey woods, the turkey being about equal to the coyote in degree of paranoia—use every advantage available.

As noted in the discussion on handguns, it is important to have the screamings isolated from the shooter. This can be done by having a buddy call or can be done using the battery-powered caller. It is also important to give the customer something to look at when he or she comes to do business. A coyote coming to the screams expects to SEE something. If they do not, they will not stay around for long. Consider the use of a decoy, preferably one that moves, to satisfy expectations. That decoy can deliver a second advantage: Looking at the decoy makes it less likely the critter will look at you.

The use of a brush or commercial blind, each provided with shooting ports, can be critical to success. The blind hides necessary (even unnecessary) movement from the critter. Finally, and this is important, cross the fingers. If it is in your nature to do so, pray. Taking a coyote, a fox, or a cat using bow and arrow can be REALLY difficult.

Archers need the privacy of a cloth or brush blind.

Chapter 10

Calling Equipment

I checked for snakes. Seeing no big ones I used the toe of my boot to kick away sticks and stubs and wallowed my big butt into the depression. I was beneath the cap rock of a desert rim and was halfway through a walking trapline. It was beanie-weanie time.

Minutes later I was munching happily, eating slowly to make it last. At about that time a coyote howled from across the canyon. Don't be asking me why a coyote would howl at noon-thirty on a hot desert day. Hell, maybe it smelled the beanie-weanies. Anyway, I grabbed for the Circe and blew soda crackers, beanie-weanies, and screams right on top of the howl. I nearly swallowed the tube when a gaunt desert dog popped up on the far rim of the slot canyon, maybe a hundred yards off. My only gun being a trap gun, a four inch S&W Model 63 in .22 rimfire, I did not draw and did not

The right kind of equipment can help fill the stretchers.

shoot. I stared at the yodel dog as he stared at me. The stare-down ended when the 'yote figured a half can of beanie-weanies was not worth the walk over. Watching him walk, I discovered a critter-calling truth. It is not wise to mess with a critter unless you own the equipment to deliver the extreme sanction.

The equipment carried on early fur hunts was Spartan, barely enough to get the job done. I carried a call, carried a gun and carried a knife. That was it. No camo, no face mask, no nothing. Even so I called critters. Lots of critters. (Honesty causes me to explain there were a hell of a lot of critters to be called then and not as much competition.) And then a funny thing happened. Not funny, odd. The more I called, the better I got at it, and the more equipment I carried. Not because I really needed it. Mainly because experience taught hard lessons. Calling accouterments, much of the time, causes the calling and killing of predators to be less difficult. Some such helped to put more fur on the stretcher. Others offered convenience. Some, truthfully, were neat to have. The following listing of calling accouterments helps me during my screamings. I am betting they will do the same for you.

Backup calls are dandy when customers are out front.

I never hunt without carrying more than a single screamer. I carried one until hot slobbers hit the super cold leaf of the Circe reed to cause a freeze up at a time when I had a herd of coyote coming. I hunt now equipped with a metal-reeded tube or two, a similar number of plastic-reeded calls, and maybe a diaphragm. And my mouth, to make the Kiss of Death, the growl, the moan, and all else as needed. I never leave home without it.

Most of the time I use only one call at each stand, alternating only when the one within the mouth calls in sick. I might alternate calls during the day to offer the critters a bit of variety. Carrying that collection of calls offers a further asset. Having all of those backups available brings a contentment.

I also carry a collection of guns in the truck. Never less than three. Why three? I carry my main squeeze, MooseDick, knowing that substantial circumstance of wood and steel might whine like a whipped cur if left at home. And I carry a long distance getter, usually the .22-250 Sako Forester to have the right gun for open country. I take a second centerfire, that to be decided prior to the hunt as I stand to gaze to be amazed at the contents of the gun safe. That choice, much of the time, is a dandy H&K Model 630 in .223, such being the pretty one from H&K—an accurate little sumbitch, good for putting a lot of lead into the fur, and doing it quickly.

Carrying a backup rifle on extended hunts makes sense.

Why a backup centerfire and not a backup shotgun? I have not had a shotgun call in sick during mid-hunt. Centerfires, particularly those fitted with glass sights, can be less stalwart. I offer an example.

I was far from home, far from the truck, when I attempted a half gainer from off the ice-slicked rock. Olympic judges (even the Russians) would have awarded a high score for technique. Even though naturally clumsy, I did not hit the ground head first, but came close. The Ruger went into orbit, did a couple of dandy flips, and landed so that most of the reentry impact went to the Weaver K-6, causing it to come loose from the mounts and rattle among the cold rocks in a most depressing way. Me? Hell, I was bruised and pissed off, but no broken bones. The telescope sight was another matter. I examined, cried my tears, and started the trudge back to the truck. But, no backup gun there.

I did the same thing, nearly, during one of the payback hunts mentioned earlier, another cold-weather ordeal. I was wearing wool army gloves to cause my hands to freeze less solid and made the mistake of grabbing the Sako by the barrel. Wool on cold steel did not offer much of a grip and that lovely .22-250 slid to hit butt first on the hard surface. The scope popped, the butt plate broke and a hairline crack extended from butt to rear sling stud. I was sad and glad. Sad because of the damage to one of my good friends. Glad because I had a backup available.

Unlike some who write, I do not consider myself to be the world's greatest offhand rifle shot, not even in print. I stay constantly envious of those sure shots who consistently whack far off critters (all such being a half-mile away on the windy day—all at the gallop) the first time every time.

I am not that kind of shooter and have not hunted with one who was. Dirty Harry has said a man must know his limitations, and I do. I take every advantage when it comes time to start the wet work. I set up so that I can brace arms across drawn-up knees. I borrow trees, posts, anything handy, to add stability. On one stand, having been offered a somewhat awkward angle, I leaned across Grandma Dog's broad butt. Took me 30 minutes to catch up to her after the shot. Not the coyote, Grandma Dog.

I have also used many of the bi-pod accuracy aids. Such, I am convinced, have permitted the taking of extra fur. Look for a listing of bi-pods and shooter sticks in the back section on equipment.

Those fortunate screamers who have viewed the *Beastmaster* tape know I dressed as Santa one December day to scream in a sounder of javelina, did it twice, got it all on tape. (The rumor Larry O. hummed "Jingle Bells" during the screaming is false, even though he might have if he was not busy with the camcorder.) I screamed while wearing that ridiculous costume to prove a point. The hunter who sits as still as a mountain (California excepted) will remain discrete even though not in camo. Can a screamer enjoy success while wearing street clothes? Sure. I have done it. George Oakey does not own one piece of camo, probably never will. Why wear camo then?

Savage 24-D supported on a Harris bipod is user-friendly.

65

You wear camo to become even more discreet. A lack of camo clothes might not bother some critters. Experience tells me it absolutely does bother others. Some, the ones I call the Ph.D.s, will start the desperate run for home and Mother at the least excuse. Camo clothing, including face mask and gloves, makes sense. Shotguns and rifles of the non-reflective configuration need no supplemental camouflage. Guns with a more flashy finish do. Such can be subdued using paint, using camo tape (I like the cloth kind best.) and using a camo sock. Maybe other ways I have not heard of.

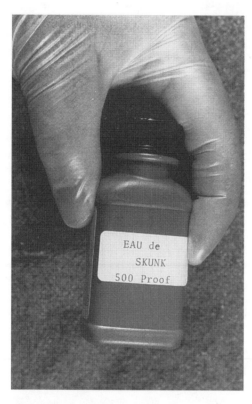

The right kind of masker can cover the smell of Oreo Cookies or Fig Newtons.

Some customers come from downwind. Others come from upwind but circle downwind to take a taste of the air, hoping to taste rabbit. Those will almost surely spook if the air tastes a lot like Gerry Blair (Oreo Cookies) or Larry Gates (Raspberry-filled Fig Newtons). Using a scent masker like pure old unadulterated skunk musk, or using an imitation like Tex Isbells CoverScent (available from Johnny Stewart Game Calls) can cause the coyote nose to stay trustful.

The critter country I hunt is of two types, the desert being one. My desert is the kind of place where everything green has stickers or spines, sometimes both. A hunter who barebutts it is likely to end up (snicker) with a rear that looks as though it has been porcupined.

I hunt high country also, a place that can be snow-covered during prime fur time. Placing a somewhat warm rear within that snow can cause a melt-down, not of the rear but of the snow. The wet rear almost always freezes—not all that uncomfortable during the freeze but damn painful during the thaw. Carrying a cloth-covered section of foam or a section of scrap carpet, something that can be placed between the butt and a hostile surface, can cause a degree of comfort.

I hate to skin on the ground, saying so within the chapter on skinning. I carry a dog choke chain on every hunt so that I might skin in the field and do so in a way that suits my nature. Those who require increased sophistication should consider the carrying of a skinning gambrel. I also carry a tail stripper and a tail splitter, each available at low cost through advertisements in *Trapper & Predator Caller* magazine.

While on the subject of skinning I feel it proper to mention a technique I call safe skinning. There was a time when I did my skinning barehanded, the way real he-men and he-women did it. I do not remain that macho. I carry surgical gloves (S-M-L at pharmacies) and pull those skin-tight rubbers on when I skin. The gloves protect the hands from blood, intestinal material, and (ugh) the ever-present poop. Thus protected, the skinner stays safe from epizootics. Cleanup, when the skinning ends, can be as easy as removing the rubbers.

The deadeye Richards mentioned earlier seldom need backup ammo, every shooting resulting in a one-shot kill (usually in the ear). Those of us who are less gifted need to carry enough ammo to make at least one reload. Carrying those reloads within the pocket can be natural. Such can be inconvenient. The sitting hunter might find it to be awkward to make the retrieve. Worse, such might do as I did on one stand. It happened this way.

I missed the running coyote four times within about as many seconds, each shot coming close

Shell holders like this arm rig offer accessibility.

enough to encourage an increase of speed. I got lucky on the fifth shot (Law of Averages) and made the connection (not in the ear). I was all happy, telling myself what a good sumbitch I was, when I sighted a second coyote headed my way. (Reckon he wanted to know what-n-heck I had killed.) I made a dive for the front pocket of a somewhat tight pair of Levis jeans, a place containing extra .22-250 rounds. The first grab brought out the key chain, three quarters, two nickels, a muddy piece of quartz collected on the way in, and several fired cases. I tossed all and went back. Two trips later I had my reload, but, too late.

What's the point? The point is, the screamer who is serious about the kill needs to carry backup ammo in a convenient location, maybe one of the clever shell holders offered by Michaels of Oregon. (See equipment listing in the back of the book.)

67

An accurate scale can cause a 20-pound fox to reduce by half.

Want more? I carry a sharpening diamond to return the edge to the skinner after each peeling. I carry a few gallon-sized ZipLocks to receive the pelt, placing it within the ice chest if weather is warm. I carry Wet Wipes (within baby supplies at pharmacies) so as to have an instrument to remove disgustables from hands. I carry an accurate field scale (Cabella's) to reduce the size of those fifty-pound bobcat and eighty-pound coyote. Your own experience will likely cause you to discover other aids. If so, drop a line (in care of Krause Publications) so that I may know. I am the kind of hunter who continually strives to improve.

Chapter 11

Decoys and Other Flimflam

The coyote came at the charge, then fifty feet out from Frankenhare the anxious critter slid to a stop. A right front foot was in the air, causing me to be amused. "That damn fool 'yote thinks he is pointer," my brain said to itself, and then that brain chuckled. At about then the coyote began a deliberate sneak, and that sneak continued until the critter was somewhat close. Suddenly, when the sneaker was ten feet out it launched to land exactly on the unconcerned decoy, that decoy being a very modest effort at taxidermy—a soft plastic form covered with the ratty hide from a black-tailed jackrabbit.

Even though the decoy did not look all that good, it apparently tasted worse. The coyote began a trot that would take the prize to a place of privacy. That trot was stopped after a step or two and the coyote spit out Ol' Frank, then slunk off into the greasewood of the Papago. Hell yes, it happened. I was there. So was Chuck Spearman. We saw it all.

A second coyote-decoy interaction took place some miles away, later in the day. Chuck and I made a stand in somewhat crowded greasewoods, a place decorated with isolated clumps of prickly pear cactus—the kind that makes the pretty yellow flowers and then the succulent red fruit. Anyway, Frankenhare was fifty feet to the front, looking mildly amused (as he always did). Chuck and I were within the scrawny arms of a creosote bush, our Canon auto-focus cameras at the ready.

The coyote came at a gallop, making what I call a run-by—a maneuver that lets the critter maintain full speed as he makes the reconnoiter. The coyote saw the decoy and his eyeballs sort of popped. The 'yote locked in on the decoy but continued the run by, a situation that can lead to excitement when in cactus country. And it did. The coyote ran full speed into a prickly pear. Chuck and I laughed out loud as the critter made the retreat. Decoys are like that, we agreed. They keep the hunt interesting because the screamers never know what in hell will happen next.

Having said all of that, it is also proper to consider a couple of other aspects to critter-calling decoys—mainly, are they all that good? Will they help to put more fur on the stretcher? I say maybe

Washing the rabbit hide caused the hair to turn curly.

Inexpensive taxidermy forms can be covered with hair to become somewhat lifelike.

and no, and then qualify. My experience with decoys causes me to think such can be dandy for those who scream to the camera or scream to the camcorder. A critter that comes to the call, the way I see it, is responding to an audio. That critter expects to see the picture when he gets close. When they do not, the light bulb lights and they get the hell gone. Such is not a great problem for gunners. A predator that comes close enough to see the rabbit is close enough to kill. You are not likely to kill that critter one bit deader if he loiters to gaze at the decoy. Such action, at times, can permit a more precise shot placement.

Even so, the main strength owned by a critter-calling decoy goes to the cameraman. Some critters that come to the call, when they see the decoy, do goofy things. A good many stick around a lot longer than they might otherwise, providing the opportunity to burn up a lot of tape or a lot of film.

I have experimented with decoys of varying personality. Frankenhare has been mentioned. Frank started his decoyhood as a hunkered hare, a critter that sat to think pure thoughts while a coyote made the sneak with murder on his mind. The original Frankenhare was not all that good. You want the truth? Many of the customers ran in and ran out and never saw Frank. Back to the laboratory.

Frankenhare II was somewhat improved. The hare hide was stretched over a running rabbit form, lending the suggestion of movement but no movement. Frankenhare III did better. Larry and I modified the running rabbit form to permit movement. We placed a steel rod through the middle of the body, extending the rods so that an inch or so protruded beyond the body. Those rod extensions were positioned within stirrups that came up out of the base. The least tug on the nose would cause Frankenhare III to nod his head agreeably. I screwed an eye hook into the nose, tied on monofilament line drawn from a Zebco reel, took the reel back to the setup, and tugged when a customer came. That little bit of movement allowed about every customer a good look. Most reacted. We became encouraged.

The concept of the moving decoy was extended. The next effort involved a battery-powered, hair-covered bit of nonsense marketed under the name "My Lovely Puppy." ("She walks and turns her head, she barks and wags her tail." I am not making this up). The little critter came with a leash (actually, a cord containing the controls) and a cute pink ribbon. $12.95 (on sale). Figuring the price was right, figuring what the hell, we bought a couple.

My Lovely Puppy was not an immediate success. The short leash caused her to sit close to the gun during the screaming. A critter looking to see her walk, bark and wag her tail was bound to see the two big guys hunkered close by.

We messed around with Lovely Puppy, hoping to make her better. We tied into the cord and inserted twenty five feet of telephone wire, small diameter stuff. Reviews were mixed. One bobcat and a few fox appreciated our puppy. Most coyote customers did not. We moved on with the search to find "the perfect decoy."

Our next effort was high tech—at least it cost considerably more. I bought a radio-controlled (about a hundred dollars or so) toy 4x4, whip antenna and all. In the field I covered most of the plastic with a tanned gray fox hide. I was ready.

Decoys must be non-threatening if they are to be most effective.

The coyote came from out of the greasewood, maybe a hundred feet or so out into the overgrazed meadow, sending the bad eye over the two or three hundred yards that separated us. Figuring it was time to give him a look at the secret weapon, I pushed a button to make the motorized fox move a bit, not a lot but enough to show life. I pushed the wrong button. The 4x4 took off at the race, fox fur flapping, antenna to the rear like some damn stinger, headed right at the coyote. The coyote turned and started a desperate depart with the 4x4 fox in hot pursuit. I have not seen a coyote (or a 4x4 fox) run so fast.

Somewhere in there we also tried out Frankenyote, another home taxidermy effort. It does not embarrass me to say we made a mistake or two. Mistake One: Being hooked on the trophy aspect, we chose the hide from the biggest coyote we had and placed that hide on the biggest taxidermy form. Mistake Two: We combined our meager talents to deliver a dominance demeanor. We realized our miscalculation the first time afield.

We set up within open greasewood at a place we had called coyote before. Frankenyote snarled from maybe fifty yards out. The coyote, either a pup or a little bitch, came at the run but slid to a stop when it saw Frank. Turning tail, the little coyote made a desperate retreat. I am almost sure I heard a pitiful yipping, but Larry says no. Anyway, trying to sort things out, we agreed that a big and dominant male coyote decoy is not great. Think about it. How would you react if you came upon John Wayne with a toothache?

Other experiments were modest. One involved using a frozen road-killed jackrabbit as a decoy; a technique that wasn't that bad early in the day but turned nasty by afternoon. We also used the tanned hide of a gray fox, laid upon a rock or draped across a limb. One configuration worked somewhat. We used monofilament line to tie the skin to the slender branch of a greasewood, leaving several inches of line between limb and fox. The least bit of wind would cause the fox to move. Several called critters, mostly coyote, showed appreciation, making an attempt to trash the fox.

Where do we stand now on the use of decoys? Sort of at the idle. Somewhere in my head there is one more decoy idea. I see Frankenhare mounted on a platform, sharing space with the remote control mechanism from a model airplane. I see that contraption out front with the Beastmasters hid in the brush, Larry manning the Camcorder and me holding the controls. A coyote appears, I push buttons to cause the rabbit to gyrate. The coyote goes crazy, charges, and runs off with all, with me and Larry in hot pursuit. Ahhh, dreams.

Chapter 12

Calling Camouflage

I sat in the sun and away from the sanctuary of greasewood and mesquite to do the screaming. Faithful companion Larry O. Gates stood behind, encumbered by the substantial weight of the Panasonic AG-460, an enhanced camcorder with an appetite for the Super VHS 1/2" tape. When the TallyHo screamer was near to my beard-covered lips I turned to ask a final question. "Larry O," I says, "I want the truth. Do I look stupid sitting here in the open, in the sun, wearing a bright red Santa Claus suit (even though it was not Christmas) while making a noise like a coyote's supper?" "Yes, Gerry, you do," Larry answered truthfully. Satisfied, I turned my broad back to the camera and started the screaming.

Blair dressed as Santa to prove a point . . . and called coyote and javelina.

Minutes later a small sounder of the pig-like critter called javelina came at the gallop and the growl. The half a handful of peccaries came ten yards close, reconnoitered and reconsidered, then trotted off while coughing out indignant whiffs. Not willing to leave well enough alone, I laid into the 'Ho one more time, sending out a delicious series of short and choppy screams. The

Fill-in flash causes this bobcat to be stark—in contrast to its commonly discreet aspect.

pigs, nearly out of sight, paused, listened, looked and threw it into reverse. Seconds later the lead boar (I assumed him to be the Boss Hog.) had his sensitive snout at my boot soles. Not willing to have him become too close a friend, I waved a hand and whiffed out a warning. That pig, and all others, made a second noisy retreat.

That encounter provided two benefits. Benefit number one was the knowledge that peccaries and other wild animals will come close to a screamer who wears a bright red Santa suit and sets in the sun, as long as that hunter sits as still as a rock and stays as quiet as a cactus. Benefit two? Superb footage for the video on predator calling we were taping.

Murry Burnham wears an extra long headnet to obscure hand movement as he screams.

I do not advocate the wearing of the Santa suit or any other conspicuous clothing during a screaming for predators. I did so in this instance to make a point, and I made that point. Having done so, it is proper to also say that the hunter who goes on the hunt for fur will be most successful if he, she, or it does so while clothed to be as inconspicuous as possible. That discrete appearance, it seems to me, will be best accomplished if the hunter wears one of the carefully crafted camo patterns available to the sport; Jim Crumley's Treebark, Toxey Hass's Mossy Oak, Bill Jordan's Realtree, and others. Each of those has been fashioned using varying contrasts of neutral and non-reflective cloths. A hunter who wears such, the hunter who sits as still as a rock and as quiet as a cactus, will be invisible to the eyes of the most paranoid of the predators.

Even so, there is more to competent camo than the wearing of pants and shirt. Complete camo calls for camo gloves, a camo headnet, camo hat, and a properly camo'ed gun.

Even the best of the vari-colored camo can be in poor taste under certain conditions. Vari-colored camo does a fine job when the hunter hunkers within the shadow of a leafed-out hardwood to toot the tube. Change the setup to a snow-covered plain and that

76

hunter will be as obvious as a college sophomore on his first date. The thing is, the thinking hunter matches his camo to the country he or she mostly hunts.

There is more to complete camo than sight camo. Nearly every predator depends on their sense of smell and sense of hearing to keep their butt safe from bigger predators. It does little good to disguise against sight and fail to disguise against sound and smell. Stay tuned while I talk (actually, write) a bit about my philosophy of complete camouflage.

According to some wildlife biologists, the coyote and many other animals do not see color, at least not in the same sense as the human eye sees color. The peccaries that came to the screaming Santa probably did not see a red Santa. It is likely they saw a black Santa. Coyote, bobcat, fox, and some other predators would have seen Santa about the same. The smart hunter, it seems to me, should not worry a lot about the color or lack of color within his or her camo. That same smart hunter should also know that animals do see contrast. An extreme example would be a midnight black cat standing atop a snow bank. That critter is obviously visible to human eyes and to animal eyes. Put a pale pussy on that same snowbank and camouflage has been accomplished.

A medium red fox standing in a mostly grey background, conversely, is likely to be nearly invisible to the predators

Bare hands on this face-masked hunter can cause customer paranoia.

that see only blacks, whites, and shades of gray. Knowing that, it makes sense to match the camo or the clothing to the CONTRAST of the hunt setting and not spend a lot of time fretting about matching to the COLOR of the hunt setting.

Honesty causes me to say that certain kinds of "street clothes" will work about as well for the predator screamer as will the most expensive of the camo patterns in some instances. A close friend and occasional hunt partner (George Oakey) does not and has not (not even one time) worn patterned camo to the screaming. Even so, George is a very successful screamer who has called and killed a ton of fur.

My own screaming costume, during the days when I was recently retired from the Arizona Highway Patrol and hunting fur to complement a meager retirement income, consisted of forest green trousers that exactly matched the shaded junipers where I did much of my screaming. Or, khaki tan trousers that precisely matched the brown of the autumn prairie. Much of the time I would wear a shirt to match. Calling snowfields caused me to break out a set of painter pants and shirt. During those times when I screamed the midnight I would opt for dead black, becoming the Mutant Ninja Screamer. All common sense stuff.

Face paint is messy, but allows visibility.

Gloves of some kind are needed to disguise the flesh tone of the hands. Those same gloves can be an asset when the temperature turns frigid. Those same gloves can create a pair of problems. Problem one has to do with the "feel" of the trigger finger. During my early days as a screamer I bought a handsome set of gloves that did a dandy job of keeping hands and fingers toasty warm and did an equally admirable job of hiding the flash of the flesh. Trouble was, the gloves completely destroyed my feel for the three-pound trigger of the Ruger .22-250. During one memorable hunt I managed to miss eight coyote in a row. To make matters worse I had a buddy along who witnessed the humiliation and felt obligated to tell all who would listen about how Blair missed a charging coyote that was 20 feet out. Those tales caused me to consider giving up screaming for good. And then, I realized my lack of markmanship started on the day I first wore the gloves. I tossed them into the truck box, called, and shot barehanded, and skinned eight of the next ten critters called. Nope, my talkative friend was not along to witness THAT part of my markmanship. Dammit.

The second handicap that comes from the wearing of gloves has to do with the volume and tone of the scream. Gloves that cover the palm of the hand used to make a sound chamber for the tube will cause the volume of the scream to diminish and will cause a change of tone. What to do? I sometimes call with the soundbox hand (the same hand fitted with the trigger finger) bare. If I feel a glove on that hand is critical, I will use a glove that has the palm part cut out. A longitudinal slit in the trigger finger cover allows that most important digit to stay snug and warm until circumstances call it to action. It is a simple matter to slip that booger out to help with the wet work. A second option, available to those who call in somewhat warm weather, is the wearing of net or mesh gloves—lightweight so that the trigger finger is not stifled, with enough flesh available to decently "box" the screams.

Camouflaging the face is not essential when calling country where the critter does not come so close you can smell the rabbit on its breath. Many of those long range opportunities let the shooter do the dirty deed before the customer has a chance to spook because of an uncamoed face. Place that same hunter in tight country, a setting where close contact is the norm, and the uncamouflaged face can cause a paranoia that will cost in lost fur. I compensate on the side of caution by wearing one of two types of face covering on every stand. Those two types are the headnet and camo makeup.

Headnets are available in a mind-boggling variety. I have used the pullover kind with no eyeholes and no mouthhole, the same with holes, the Bandido Mask, masks fitted to eyeglass frames, and masks attached to camo caps. All will work. Some work better than others. I do not favor the pullover kind, with holes or without. The kind without holes, while doing a good job of hiding the flash of my eyeglasses, causes the moisture within the breath to fog those glasses during cold weather screams. Bad. And those with no mouth opening do not offer access to the tube. Double bad. Those pullovers having appropriate holes are a bit better but will also cause fogging. And turning the head almost always causes the eye holes to squirm around to pay an unauthorized visit to the ear. The best kind of mask, at least the best for me, is one of the Bandito type, a mesh that covers the face from the eyeballs down. Pulling the camo cap low on the forehead causes most of the forehead to hide, leaving only the eyeballs uncovered. I like the kind of mask that has cloth hanging to the upper chest, leaving a lot of room so that I might move my calling hand (usually bare) up under. Doing so causes the overhang to effectively hide the flash of the flesh as the fingers flutter to provide quaver.

Camouflage makeup is a second option. Blacks, browns, and greens are applied so that flesh tones are disguised and the focus of the face is mottled. The camo creams I have used have done a decent job of hiding the face. The lack of a more substantial face cover causes the glasses to stay unfogged. There is no vision obscurement as in the case of full face covers. Disadvantages? Only one I know. The stuff is messy, rubs onto clothes, and might run when sweat-provoked. Finally, those who run around with such makeup can cause observers to be brutally frank.

I was driving a back country road during one hunt when I encountered two cowboys chousing a small herd of Herefords. I stopped the truck to relinquish right of way as is my custom. One of the 'pokes moved his grulla in for a close look. We talked for a minute or more before he made his comment. "Feller," he said, "you are the queerest looking sumbitch I have ever seen." Knowing he was right, I did not take offense.

Wearing a camouflage that neutralizes a critter's nose can be a bother but can, under certain conditions, cause an increase in the fur collection. Some critters, the real paranoids, those who have previously discovered the deception of the predator screamer, will manage to approach from dead downwind, or will approach from upwind and circle downwind to take a taste of the air. Those kind of critters, almost always, will head for home at the faint smell of Old Spice aftershave, Listerine mouthwash, or even the dreaded B.O. Even those among us who feel compelled to bathe weekly (whether they need it or not) can emit an odor that causes the paranoia to hang onto a coyote like ugly hangs to an ape.

Gun camouflage was mentioned in the chapter on shotguns. That mention mainly said there are factory-camouflaged shotguns available from Remington, Winchester, Ithaca, Mossberg, and others. All also offer shotguns and rifles (sometimes called SP for Special Purpose and sometimes called by another name) in a non-reflective finish, both stock and metal. Those who have guns, rifles or smoothbores, owning a high polish on wood and metal have options. Camo tape is inexpensive and easy to apply (not quite so easy to take off). I prefer the cloth tape over the paper tape. Such is more durable and will last longer than a part of a season. Some manufacturers offer pullover camo elastic (Gun Chaps is one) that does a decent job of hiding the shine. A more permanent camo job involves the use of spray paint on wood and metal, best done, I think, when the gun involved is a beater that can only be improved by such. Finally, a competent gunsmith can take the prettiest of guns and uglify that sucker so that it is coyote friendly.

Gun camo can cause the glare of wood and metal to become discreet.

Some mention must be made of sound camouflage. Predators hunt using all of their senses. Every one I have met has owned a highly-developed sense of hearing, some being able to hear the footsteps made by a white-footed deer mouse wearing Reeboks. That sense of sound can cause the critter to react to the distress screams while more than a mile away. That same sense of sound can cause the critter to ignore the best of those screams. What kind of sounds are most apt to spook a paranoid critter? I do not play the radio, the tape, or the CD while in calling country, particularly during times when vehicle windows are partly open. The truck bed stays free of those roll-arounds that might cause clanking.

I also make it a point to maintain absolute silence when walking to a stand. If you call with a companion, convince him or her of the value of silence before the hunt. Ask that the companion not slam the door of the truck. Say, seriously, that in the event he or she inadvertently laughs, coughs, burps, sneezes, or otherwise exercises the vocal cords you will immediately grab a stout juniper limb and begin to beat upon his or her body until he or she whines like a whipped hound. If that does not do the trick, get ugly.

The rule of silence should also be observed during the walk back to the truck. I took a neighbor to the junipers one fall day to scream at coyote. I called a pair of chargers and got lucky, putting both down with the .22-250. On the walk out my companion begin to relive the action. His

Stay silent during the walk in and walk out . . . a customer might be close.

voice spooked a big bobcat that had come back door. I had a tough shot at the 'bob running at 200 yards. Even though I almost always miss during such opportunity, the law of averages compensated in this instance and I connected. That lucky shot, the way I see it, saved my companion's life.

Chapter 13

Masking Scents

Olga spent her summer days throwing bales on her daddy's farm. A good part of the nights were spent with me. Rawboned and muscular, willing, having considerable stamina, Olgie came from sturdy stock who figured a man or woman who took a razor to the armpits was some sort of sissy. There was always the smell of honest sweat to Olga, an odor I did not find offensive then and do not find offensive now (as long as it is somewhat fresh). The thing is, Olga could never sneak up on me. I could smell her coming. Years later, when I became addicted to screaming to predators, that early life experience with Olga taught me a valuable lesson.

Every human, even those who shave the underarms somewhat regularly, have an odor. If our nose was long like a coyote nose, containing all of those super sensitive odor eaters, I am betting we could recognize Aunt Martha or Cousin Jody from a couple of hundred upwind yards. Don't believe it? I can't count the number of times I have had a paranoid coyote come to that distance and have him (or her) turn tail to make the desperate run for home. Other coyote might come to an indecent distance, being upwind, and quarter to make the circle that will allow a downwind reconnoiter. Looking for the opportunity to taste the wind. Good-bye customer. Good-bye to a substantial part of the fur check.

When I tired of those smart alecks who used their nose to save their butts, I got serious about a deodorant of the coyote kind. The stuff old-time trappers almost always called skunk piss, in actuality the amber fluid that fills the marble (taw) sized glands that decorate each side of a skunk's pooper. Using that odiferous abomination as a masker can cause some of those nose-hungry coyote, fox, and bobcat to stick around long enough to get dead.

Honesty causes me to report a divergent opinion. I know callers, some of them damn good callers, who disagree, saying the predator nose is so sophisticated it can cut through a five-gallon bucket full of skunk phew to discover the human hiding within. Maybe so. My experience has convinced me that using a masker causes me to skin extra fur every season. Coyote number 92 is a good example.

Old 92 was a husky dog who hung out in the standing and pushdown stringbarks on one of the Babbitt spreads east of my Flagstaff home; a chunk of real estate heavy hit by hunters. Screamers are so numerous during the early part of the season you almost have to take a number and wait your turn. Coyotes who do not get dead get smart. Calling there during January is about as satisfying as eating raw carrots.

Knowing better, not knowing where else to go, I went to hunt, armed with the trusty .22-250 and a film cassette filled with cotton and skunk stink. I made the first call at daylight, setting up on the edge of a stand of stringbark juniper and staring out into an area of somewhat open pushdowns. I hung the skunk on a low juniper branch (downwind of course) and slobbered out the first stanza of the "Dying Rabbit Blues."

A single skunk milking can provide enough musk to last a lifetime, maybe more.

Five minutes later I eyeballed a flash of fur from dead downwind. Here comes this big coyote at the gallop, having murder on his mind. I welcomed the brute by poking a 52-grain chunk of copper-plated lead through his necessaries. Walking out to make the retrieve I discovered an aluminum tag within one wooly ear, #97 stamped thereon. Inquiry showed Old 97 had been trapped (about 200 yards from where he died) as a two-year old by a graduate student attending Northern Arizona University. Five years before. That old dog was seven years old and had survived those seven years within a heavy hunted chunk of territory. Even so, 97 came from dead downwind and came at the trot. Senile? Maybe. I prefer to think superior calling and the judicious use of a masking scent caused his demise.

A certain kind of masking scent does a decent job of disguising all. The only effective masker is pure and unadulterated skunk musk or a chemical facsimile of the same. How does one go about obtaining THE REAL THING? Somewhat easy if you have access to a skunk and can convince your Karma to do a bit of skunk milking. Here is the way I go about it. RULE #1: Never milk a live skunk. Be sure that sucker is one hundred percent graveyard dead before making a move to the marble-size glands located on each side of the anal vent (sometimes called by more colorful names). Wear surgical gloves (available at most pharmacies) to keep the hands somewhat stink free. Place a glass or plastic container to the vent opening and

84

press gently on each side of the gland to cause the amber fluid to squirt into the bottle. Stop when the amber fluid flow stops and is replaced by a milky concentrate. Cap the bottle using a plastic or rubber closer.

If you are not into skunk milking, consider the purchase of a chemical substitute such as CoverScent marketed by the Johnny Stewart Company. This excellent product comes as a two-part liquid, each innocuous alone but turning nose-ugly when mixed.

In either event, use an empty 35 mm film cassette container (available at film processors if not otherwise) and fill that plastic container with cotton or cotton balls. Maybe cloth. About anything porous. Add a few drops of the skunk musk or of the imitator and cap, quickly. Opening the container and placing it downwind during a screaming can cause fewer of the paranoids to escape.

Less reliable alternatives are more available. I have used liquid garlic and have used pine oil, each available at many super markets. Or rub a raw onion on your shoes. None of the above will work as well as the skunk, but each is better than nothing.

Common sense suggests other cautions. Those neatniks who insist on bathing once a week (whether they need it or not) should avoid the use of smell-goods like cologne or aftershave if they intend to hunt the next day. Gas up the night before to be sure you do not, (while half asleep) slosh gas on your boots (or on anything else). Lay off the cigarettes on the drive out and during the hunt. Don't hog down a half a pot of limas. Stay clean. Once clean, there is stuff available to make your body smell like about anything you can fantasize. Maybe a sow bear in heat. I am not making this up. CAUTION: Not recommended during the bear rut.

Take the time to remove all reflective adornments before heading to the stand. I leave rings and bolo ties at home, knowing that each can cause a light flash that might alarm the most paranoid of the customers. Same deal on reflective watch bands, belt buckles and eyeglass frames.

Chapter 14

Calling the Weather

The wet clouds hugged the sere slopes of the Date Creek Mountains to create an aspect of unusual beauty. Water rich cumulonimbus, the kind cowboys call waterdogs, flowed to fill the shallow canyons. There was the smell of rain. Larry and I left the 4x4 in the sand bottom of an inconspicuous dry wash and loaded the day packs. A barely bright cloud to the east announced daylight was imminent. Minutes later we were hiking the boulder jumble that marked the boundary between desert and mountain. As we hiked, knowing we had a ways to go, I turned my thoughts to the screaming ahead, and thought of the effect the changing weather would have on predator response.

I had screamed to weather fronts before. And on about every one of those hunts predator response had been good. There is something about the aspect of an arriving or departing storm that causes the critter appetite alarm to sound. Maybe the smell of rain or the barometric pressure.

Critters feed before a front, I think, because they sense unsettled weather and sense that prey animals are likely to be less active, causing their own hunts to be less productive. Maybe the predators are smart enough to know a storm is on the way, but lack the sophisticated receptors that can define a major storm or a minor storm. Not knowing when they might eat again, maybe they go on a feeding frenzy to be safe. Hell, maybe they just don't want to get wet.

A half-hour later Larry and I set up among the granite boulders, some as big as a two-bedroom house (with den), facing down desert to discover the coyote we knew would come—sending out the first chorus of the "Dying Rabbit Blues." There is something about wetted air that causes the tone of the distress scream to be uncommonly fine. The screams are fulsome and each note is exquisitely rendered. I was working the TallyHo, working well, when the bobcat showed. Backdoor.

I did not see the cat coming—nor did Larry. One instant the bug-size (VW) boulder was bare, the next the cat was atop, creating a handsome cooperation that approximated the finest of taxidermy. A prickling of the neck hair caused me to look back. I lip-squeaked to Larry. The camcorder light lit and the 10x lens swiveled smoothly to take in the tufted-eared boulder. When I was certain Larry was on target I went to work with the call, doing my best to cause the cat to come closer. Catlike, the bob' stayed still, hoping to discover if he was going to get supper or be supper. I scrooched to square to the target and made the shot. That number one stand provided hunting excitement and delivered a prime tom cat. And as a bonus, several minutes of dandy footage for the "Masters' Secrets to Predator Calling." We were three miles from the truck by noon-thirty and had made a half-dozen stands. That effort had added a pair of handsome gray fox to the bag. The two had come to a single screaming, each bounding across the boulder jumble in a most picturesque manner. I took one at thirty-five yards and took the other as he attempted escape at about one hundred yards. Larry worked the camcorder and captured the first kill on tape.

Bobcat can use the back door to come uncomfortably close.

Two miles more, one hour before dead dark, we paused again. The afternoon screamings had added a pair of coyote to the collection. A bad camcorder angle made it impossible to tape either. Total take for the hike was one bobcat, two grays, and two coyote—pretty good all right. We could have called it quits right then and probably should have. We were one hour away from dark and two hours away from the truck. One half of the return would be made on a stormy night that showed no moon. We were in cactus country and knew it would be slow (and perhaps painful) going. We would have done precisely that if Larry had not found a fresh lion track on the soft sand of a dry wash.

Walking all of the way to the truck in the dark instead of only half way, we figured, was not that bad. We set up in the boulders to scream one more time. Larry did the screaming as I relaxed to enjoy the music, appreciating the quaver put into the TallyHo screams. Ten minutes later I perceived a slight change in tonal intensity. I looked diligently but saw nothing. I settled back for more screams.

Thirty minutes later Larry was still screaming. That screaming was interrupted when Larry's .22-250 reported. Larry was on his feet almost instantly. "Did you see him?" he shouted. I nodded a no. "Lion," he said as he headed for the ridgetop at the lope. I followed. We did not see the lion when we gained the ridgetop but did see a boulder jumble that could hide a lion. Investigation showed a crevice containing a smudge of blood, about shoulder high to a cougar. Larry, being brave, lit a gopher match and crawled into the crevice. Seconds later the lion made a desperate run. Larry crawled backwards and gave chase, eventually baying the beast within a second boulder jumble. The second shot from the .22-250 was well-placed. The tom weighed 135 pounds, an impressive weight for a desert lion.

Walking out we talked on the dandy day of screaming and talked of the effects weather can have on the quality of the hunt. Our good luck on this day, we agreed, was mostly due to the imminent storm.

Calling on the day a storm leaves can be nearly as good as calling the incoming front. Predators and prey, much of the time, lay up to miss most of the bad weather. Those predators that do hunt during the storm often have to hunt for damn little reward. Clearing weather finds the predator population with empty bellies. Being anxious to eat, they can come to the screaming with enthusiasm.

Certain kinds of weather can adversely affect calling success. The worst, the way I see it, is wind. I do not refer to the mild five or ten mph breeze that can actually encourage critters to hunt but stays

Wind direction and velocity can be critical to critter calling success.

Track screaming to a fresh snow can be dandy.

moderate to avoid bad side effects. I am talking big-time wind—the kind that makes the ground shake (or at least the limbs of trees) and the ocean roll. Such adversely affects a screaming in more than one way. The noise that is a common concomitant to such wind can cause the range of the screaming to diminish. Critters upwind, those most likely to come, cannot hear the advertisement. Critters downwind can hear a bit better but have the advantage of the wind in their nose. They are not apt to come close.

Winds that shake the limbs cause a further negative. Predators and prey alike look for movement. Prey animals do so because movement is a warning that can signal the approach of danger. Predators look for movement for the same reason but also watch for movement to signal the presence of prey. When every bush, every limb, every weed, and every leaf moves, both predator and prey become really nervous. Predators that are stressed are not likely to gamble on a distress scream. Those that do, almost always, come at the paranoid. You want the truth? Windy day calling makes me nervous too. I do not call the wind if it is practical to postpone. Having said that, honesty causes me to say I sometimes call the wind, maybe during a hunt that starts out during perfect calling weather but degrades. Maybe when I have a hunt scheduled that cannot be canceled. Experience has caused me to use techniques that can cause the screaming to be somewhat effective. Compensate for the reduced range of the call several ways. Way one: Knowing I will not cover as much country with each screaming, I shorten the distance between stands. Instead of making a screaming every mile or so as I would on a windless day I make the calls every half mile—maybe each quarter of a mile. Way two: I put away the tubes to break out the battery-powered caller, feeling the amplification delivers more volume. Way three: I do my best to select sanctuaries: hills and ridges on the lee side of the wind; hollows and basins that are somewhat protected. Way four: I sometimes position the battery-powered caller downwind a couple of hundred yards from the setup, then set up somewhat high so that vision is improved. The customer will sometimes come close to the caller and not smell the gunner. Shot opportunities under such conditions can be long range.

I do not often call during a rain because it is not pleasant to do so. I sometimes do, when a mild and intermittent rain is a concomitant to a front. Doing so can be dandy, as described at the start of this chapter. I do call during a snow, particularly when that snowing is somewhat moderate and does not come with wind. Driving remote roads during a snow, or following a snow, can be dandy—sometimes damnfine. A moderate snow does not usually discourage predators. They seem encouraged to move about and hunt. Road hunting to find tracks (always fresh) permits the hunter to scream within an area that is certain to hold a target. The response can be immediate and enthusiastic.

Cold weather, really cold weather, can cause critters to go on a feeding frenzy. Nutrition requirements go up. It takes a good many calories to keep from freezing to death. The simple act of walking or running can be more difficult, causing the expenditure of increased calories. As good as it can be, extremely cold weather can have an effect on the calls. Metal-reeded calls collect spittle from the breath and will almost always freeze. The plastic-reeded call, Crit'R•Call, TallyHo, Lohman C-250, the Johnny Stewart PC-6, that sort, do better. The plastic reed stays snug within the mouth during the screaming, preventing freeze-up.

The battery-powered caller can be a sensible choice when the weather turns frigid. Hunters need to know that cold weather can cause battery power to diminish. Always hunt with a fully charged battery. Carry the unit in the cab of the vehicle between stands to cause a warm-up. Plug in the 12-volt charger to replace lost battery power as you travel.

Chapter 15

Night Calling

I shrugged my double-X shoulders a bit deeper into the thorny arms of the Wait a Minute Bush and screamed. Nope, not because I was in pain (I was) but because I was there to scream. I was night hunting for predators and that is what night hunters do. Without a warning the big horned owl swooped to caress my cap with a furled primary. I had hardly recovered when a rustling to the rear asked for attention. Was it a snake? A snake with rattles? It was early in the fall and still warm, too high a temperature to encourage hibernation. I forgot the owl and concentrated on the crawler.

At about that time a cloud moved to release the moon, permitting a look at the creeper, a bushy-tailed wood rat looking for mesquite beans. I looked to the front and nearly lost it when I discovered an interested coyote delivering the bad eye from twenty yards. Ahhh, night calling. I love it. A hunter does not know what the night is likely to offer.

Night screaming to predators is exciting. The lack of light limits visibility, causing it to be difficult to see the customers, likewise it is difficult for the customers to see you. Perception usually comes as one big bright eye reaches out to illuminate two small bright eyes. Tension builds, then suddenly the customer looms up out of the night, often coming much closer than it would during daylight. It can be dandy.

The first question begging an answer is basic. Why in heck night hunt at all? Simply answered: There are critters to be called, animals that come reluctantly or not at all to day calls. About every land predator is most easily called at night. The raccoon is the most nocturnal of all. As noted within the chapter dealing with the masked bandit, screamers who do not work the night shift seldom see raccoon. Bobcat like the night shift but can be called during daylight if circumstances are precisely correct.

I am convinced many daytime customers of the cat kind slip in and slip out, avoiding discovery. This lack of discovery owes to two circumstances. One is the cat camouflage, a discrete fur that causes the Robert Kitty to be nearly invisible. The second circumstance has to do with bobcat hunting technique. The bob' is a sneak, using every bit of structure to creep close. Night cats are more easily discovered. Even though the camouflage stays constant, as does the hunt technique, the bright light causes the cat eyes to illuminate like a pair of miniature moons. Other land predators, dogs like coy-

Southwestern raccoon don't really grow this big. This assembled photograph was made to show the raccoon's interest in the correct kind of distress sound.

ote and foxes, are more of a switch hitter. Some, the coyote and the gray fox specifically, come dependably during the day but come most often during the night. The other fox, the red, does not. Those paranoid little boogers might respond to day calls when those day screams are heard in quiet land, places removed from habitation. Farm fox, the kind most often found within the Midwest and the East, disapprove of daytime activity, turning totally nocturnal, or nearly so. The littlest fox, sometimes called the kit and sometimes called the swift, stays one hundred percent nocturnal.

Another small predator works the night shift exclusively. I write of the critter sometimes called a cacomistile but most commonly called a ring-tail cat. Even though cat-like in habit, this small predator is a 'coon cousin, sharing that family with the raccoon and with the coatimundi. The ringtail is common to parts of Mexico, to a half a handful of Southwestern states, and is uncommon within a few more.

94

Some states prohibit night hunting. Others prohibit the use of artificial lights, allowing a screaming as long as it takes place by moonlight. Some jurisdictions permit night hunting, permit lights, but limit gun caliber. Others, more enlightened, permit night hunting with minimal restriction. It is wise to check locally to learn the hunting regulations in the area you hope to hunt.

Night hunting can carry a responsibility. Darkness will hide the customer and that customer might come close before discovery. The shooting opportunity can be sudden, and just as suddenly evaporate. The gunner that shoots at a panicked predator concentrates on the target and might not see background hazards. I write of livestock and such. The high power rifle round can travel far to do damage.

Even so, the night hunt can be safe, can be productive, and can cause one hell of a lot of hunting excitement. The animals I have night-called have owned varying attitudes to the light. The coyote is the most light shy of the ones I have called. Shine the bright part of the night light into a set of coyote eyes and be ready to shoot. My experience causes me to believe the coyote will allow a few seconds for the shot, then turn to make the retreat, most often at the gallop. Other predators are less light-shy. The raccoon is an example. The 'coon I have called have stared straight into the light, not blinking, until they learn the circumstances of the screaming. Bobcat are nearly as focused. Fox? Some yes and some no. Depends on the fox and on the kind of country he claims.

Night cats have eyes that illuminate like a pair of miniature moons.

Light technique can vary. Many night hunters, maybe even most, scan with the main light intensity held high, using the periphery of light to scan for eyes. Such provides a pair of assets. The low intensity of the peripheral light is not as likely to cause a customer to hang up, or retreat. Keeping the strong part of the beam high minimizes shadows, always a problem with light-shy critters like coyote. A low and bright light, one that moves to make the scan, cause brush and all other low structure to cast a shadow, a moving shadow. That sort of movement will often cause the customer to leave, or at the least to become too nervous to come close.

Lightforce offers a light capable of illuminating adjoining zip codes.

When eyes are sighted, when those eyes are close enough for the wet work, the light man lowers the brightest part of the beam, aiming for positive target identification and providing plenty of light for the shooter.

Some hunters place a red lens over the scanning light thinking the red light to be invisible to the predator. My experience causes me to think such is not so. The main function of the red lens is a reduction in light intensity. That reduction of light intensity likely causes the critter to be a bit more comfortable.

Shooting visibility decreases as light intensity decreases. The gunner might have more difficulty making absolute target identification. Range is substantially decreased. Using the red light causes a trade-off. The critter does not see you as well. On the flip side, the gunner does not see the critter as well.

Predator lights come in varying configurations. One such, a good one, is the cap light used by folks who spend a lot of time doing it in the dark. Miners and other such. Their lights, much of the time, consist of a helmet light powered by a muscular battery pack carried on the belt. Those battery packs are rechargeable. I have used cap lights made and marketed by KW Oldham Caplight, Nite-Lite, and the Wheat Light by Koehler. All were damnfine.

Buying such a light necessitates also buying the charger. Proper care can cause both to deliver many years of service. A hand-held spotlight of varying candlepower is commonly used. I have seen some rated to 500,000 candlepower. As might be expected, that bunch of candles can generate a lot of heat, causing it to be necessary for the light handler to use caution to avoid the bad burn. All, or nearly all, are powered by a 12-volt system, the same system found within most automobile electrical systems. Some come with rechargeable motorcycle batteries. Some can be recharged by plugging into the vehicle electrical system as the hunters travel from stand to stand.

A somewhat recent entry into the predator calling market are the lights offered by Lightforce USA, developed within the Australian bush. This finely focused light throws a spot clean out to the county line. A red filter is available to diminish light intensity. Power comes from a rechargeable battery.

A subspecies of night light are the shooting lights that attach to the top of a one-inch telescope sight. Some can be easily attached to the barrel of a shotgun also. Lightforce offers one. Burnham Brothers offers several models, one being a compact little guy offering 20,000 candlepower output (SL-18), impressive considering its power comes from a pair of 9-volt batteries. A pressure switch, mounted to the forearm of the stock, provides easy accessibility. Lenses are available in clear, red, amber, orange and blue.

Burnham Game Calls, separate from Burnham Brothers, markets a dandy shooting light (SL-1) powered by four AA batteries. This lightweight model is easily detached and can be used as a flashlight.

Nite-Lite offers an excellent shooting light that comes as a part of their Nite-Lite kit. Their scope light plugs into the same belt-carried power source (6 volts) that feeds the scanning light, some models offering 13 hours of burn time.

Those who hanker for a shooting light with real muscle need to know about the NightBlaster lights offered by Optronics. These big boogers come with a six-volt or twelve-volt power supply. All models offer a stock-mounted switch and a selection of lens color.

What advantage does the gun-mounted light offer? A solo hunter is not required to operate the hand-held spotlight and shoot at the same time, difficult even for those who are coordinated. That solo can, instead, switch off the scanning light, lay it aside, and use the gun-mounted light for the wet work.

The gun-mounted light can work about as well during team hunts. The light man locates eyes. The shooter shoulders and sights, switching on the shooting light when ready. As mentioned, some states prohibit the use of lights during night hunts, saying, I suppose, "Sure, you can night hunt, Bubba. Just don't be using no light sose you can see. Hee Hee."

Some night hunters take fur even though so handicapped. A bright moon (even a half bright moon) on snow can be dandy. So can that same moon upon fallow fields. Be aware that such conditions allow you to see the critter but lets the critter see you equally well, maybe better. Set up in the shade (yep, a bright moon casts shadows), sit still, and wear sensible clothing.

Those of us who skulk the midnight, the way I see it, have a special obligation to think safety. Visibility being limited to the scan of

Handling both the scanning light and gun can handicap the solo hunter. Gun mounted lights are an improvement.

the light, we do not often need a gun that will shoot through three zip codes and throw fur for another couple. Centerfires should be sensible. I have used the .22 WRFM (for 'coon and fox), have used the .22 Hornet and have used the deuce. All did decently.

The shotgun does dandy as a night gun. Three-and-a-half-inch ten-gauge magnums like MooseDick are the biggest of the bangers available. The twelve-gauge chambered for the 3-1/2" fodder is good. So are the three-inch twelves. All such are basically short range guns that minimize the obvious danger provided by the center fires.

Bill Del Monte with the Texas Department of Parks & Wildlife, uses a technique to call double dead 'coon and other night skulkers. Me and Ol' Bill made two calls high on the mesa but found that elevated aspect to be unproductive. The third call found us within the walls of a Texas-size canyon. Bill prepared for the screaming in a way that spoke of practice, I'm talking experience. We stood within the bed of the pickup truck (legal in Texas). Bill positioned a blanket and a pair of sandbags on the cab top to serve as shooting supports and readied the battery-powered caller and the light. I stayed ready with the flash-equipped 35 mm. When all was ready Bill swung the light so as to cover a full 360 circle, doing so at a brisk pace. "Working within tight country," he whispered, "we have to swing fast. If not, a critter can run close and not be seen." The beam suddenly slammed on the brakes, then backed up. Bill slapped my shoulder, telling he had eyes, those glowing coals being a hundred yards out. Bill kept the light moving, to cover twenty yards on each side of the eyeballs, keeping the main part of the beam high, illuminating the eyeballs using the lower intensity peripheral. "I don't know what the heck it is," he whispered. "The spacing of the eyes and the height causes me to think 'coon." I nodded agreement and stayed excited. Seconds later the guess was verified. A big boar lumbered close, circled the truck a time or two, posed as I worked the auto focus Canon, then left.

My relationship with the Texas raccoon turned ugly the next night. A neighboring rancher called to complain of raccoon depredation of his corn cribs, asking that Bill and I attempt to convince the bandits to cease and desist. We said sure. We pulled the pickup into the 'Coon Canyon when it was decently dark. Bill readied and cranked up the raccoon fight tape. The dirty guys, according to the ranch foreman, were a pair of big bruisers, probably boars. I locked and loaded MooseDick and hunkered at the ready, staying low so Bill could swing the light.

The four eyeballs showed on the canyon wall almost immediately. "Looks like ringtail cat eyes to me," Bill muttered, then continued the swing. The eyeballs did not move during the next eight or ten sweeps, then suddenly disappeared. Bill sent the scanner to search and discovered the eyeballs bobbing our way. "Those are raccoon," Bill judged. "Get ready." Hell, I was born ready and was ready then, but did not bother to say so.

The boars lumbered to 30 yards and slid to make a reconnoiter. Mistake. They mistook again when they stood shoulder to shoulder. I could not resist the temptation to show off. I placed the white barrel bead squarely between the

A raccoon distress tape played at midnight thirty can call customers.

heads and lit the fire. The boars rugged out like a couple of them Olympic swimmers that do that goofy synchronized swim. "AWESOME," Bill hollered, then began furious slapping of my shoulders (hurt like hell). He calmed down a little and said it again. "That was awesome," he says. "In all of my critter calling life I have not witnessed two critters killed with a single shot." I tried to be modest but did not have a lot of luck. "Nothing to it," I lied. "Out in Arizona I might double on critters two or three times on every hunt."

The Del Monte technique of night calling is sensible and effective. His light is a modified Nite-Lite hand-held spotlight that works from the 12-volt system of the truck. A pigtail at the rear of the cab allows easy hook up. The light has a flare guard, a protective tube extending several inches out from the glass, causing the beam to be more directional, preventing side light that can show the handler.

As mentioned, Bill likes a fast swing on setups that offer limited visibility. Swing too slowly and the customer can run in and run out between swings. The light scans more slowly in more open country.

The main beam of the red lensed light is kept high, letting the low intensity peripheral beam hunt for the eyes. "When eyes are sighted," Bill cautions, "take time to absolutely identify your target." The main beam of the light lowers to illuminate the critter, and when appropriate, the shot follows. Some new to the dark side of predator calling may think conditions to be too difficult. Even those, I am convinced, will change when they come in contact with the big-eyed critters that work the night shift. The coyote, the foxes, the cats, the snakes and all others. Ahhh, night calls, how I love 'em.

Chapter 16

Tight Country Calls

Those who gun for fur are of two general types. There are those who use rifles and those who find an advantage to the shotgun. Some of those who use the rifle, it seems to me, shoot the centerfire for the same reason a coyote howls—it is their nature to do so. My friend George Oakey is one such. George has never hunted any animal or any bird with the shotgun, preferring to demonstrate his shooting skill using a Sako in .243 or .222. That precisely focused preference can be good news to those of us who see rifles and shotguns as tools specific to circumstance.

You want the truth? There are kinds of country able to chew up the best rifleman in the world and spit that purist out in chunk bait-size servings. That country is the thick hardwoods of the East, the Midwest and the South. That country is the chaparral and just

MooseDick and me with a week's worth of brush called coyote.

102

Standing within the brush improved visibility and permitted the taking of this true triple.

plain brush of the West and Southwest. That kind of country, terrain where an eager customer might come so close you can smell his needs, and do so suddenly, is shotgun country.

Screaming the country I generically call the brush offers an obvious advantage. George and others like him do not call there. Those of us who do it in the bushes do so without the worry of extreme competition, at least not the kind of competition found in other more open areas. Critters found within the brush, some of the time, will be less pressured, less stressed, and most eager to cooperate in a screaming.

Even though I have commented a time or two on tight-country calling, doing so mainly within the chapter devoted to shotgunning, I feel it worthwhile to address the technique more specifically. There are different grades of brush. Put another way, all brush is not created equal. The brush of the low desert of the Southwest, as an example, is considerably different from the chaparral common to the transition woodlands. Both are different from the juniper forests found a bit higher within the transition woodlands. The ground cover and the hardwood overstory found to the East of the big river is different from all. Each type of terrain requires a slightly modified technique. A screamer in each must utilize the THINKING technique described in the chapter titled "Tough Calls." Experience and evaluation, much of the time, can cooperate to bring a sensible scheme. Here is an example to illustrate.

Chuck and I made the scream within a cluster of desert cover. Cholla, ocotillo, Joshuas, hohos, and greasewood competed. It was the kind of country nine out of ten hunters would sneer at. The setup where a hunter would be blinded as soon as he sat. The screamer who substituted the stand-up owned a better aspect, not much better but maybe enough.

The desert dog came at the gallop, made a desperate run-by that took him five yards to Chuck's right, and lined out for home and Mother. Chuck reacted, throwing a load of four buck at the disappearing customer. Bingo. I screamed the TallyHo to keep the stand-up alive. A littermate of the recently deceased showed within seconds, taking the usual paranoid reconnoiter then turning to retreat. A load of copper-plated BBs from MooseDick halted the escape. A third yodeler popped out of the brush and the Ithaca Mag-10

Some gray fox and all cats feel most comfortable when within the brush.

burped again. Total time elapsed? Maybe thirty seconds. Fast shooting and fast fun. A cooperation often found within the brush.

The success during that stand-up came mainly because we carried the right kind of gun and because we modified technique to respond to conditions. The most obvious change was the stand. A stander had his head high enough to own an overview that isolated the stingy spacing separating the structure. The sitter would be denied that aspect. A sitter would have his head on eye level with the greasewood and the hoho's, permitting a good look at the bush immediately to the front but little else.

Chuck and I sighted ten more coyote during that two-and-a-half day hunt and skinned half. Those eight coyote were not a two-and-a-half day total that would cause me to write home to Mother about, but were decent. More impressive when it is considered we tackled country too tough for most others.

The second obvious compromise made to accommodate the tight country screaming was the choice of guns, such being shotgun country. Experience suggests one of the class I call the big bangers. My own preference is for the biggest banger, the ten gauge chambered to take the three-and-a-half-inch hull. Those willing to accept the small handicap of reduced range can do well using a twelve-gauge chambered to take the three or three-and-half-inch shell. A full discussion of such will be found within the chapter dealing specifically with shotguns.

I often modify my setup style when calling tight country. Such cover, much of the time, will dampen the strength of the call to cause the screaming to be subdued. I compensate by shortening the distance between setups, maybe each half mile and maybe half that.

The scream is likewise modified. Experience suggests a series of desperate and choppy screams work best. The critters I have called out of the brush have come at a desperate run. I encourage that pace when I put desperation in those short duration screams, putting a drop of blood on each. I may call constantly, or nearly so, when calling the brush, as a further encouragement to the critter that might come running. The TallyHo and other open reeds do fine when I place such to the corner of my mouth and breathe out the cadence.

Do not ignore the battery-powered caller when involved with the brush. Tubes require the cooperation of at least one hand if they are to work as good as can be. That means the shotgun must be held within the free hand. That posture adds seconds to the response. There will be times when those seconds allow the customer to retreat. The battery-powered caller can be caused to scream independently, leaving the hands free to keep the gun at ready.

There is a tendency in all of us, I think, to read an instruction and literally interpret each syllable. I refer specifically to instructions you may have read suggesting you place the caller or the speaker fifty feet or so out from the gun. Forget that sort of thing when calling the brush. I use the shoulder strap to suspend the battery-powered caller, keeping the speaker above the brush a bit to extend range. Controls are a hand movement away. Turning the body slightly causes the directional feature of the speaker to address new country. Best of all, hands are freed to manage the gun, and do so quickly.

Screaming in the hardwoods can cause vision obscurement, just as tight cover calling does within other zip codes. I say so knowing that the overstory and understory are in the cold weather mode, leafless, for much of the prime fur time. Choosing an elevated set (or stand-up), maybe on the slope of a hill, can slightly improve aspect. Some screamers utilize blinds constructed to assist in the hunting of the wild turkey or white-tailed deer. Those elevated structures can provide a fine visibility. Many, maybe even most, are located in somewhat open areas, a good many adjacent to trails. I do not wish to insult the intelligence when I nag a bit about the danger inherent to the climbing of a tree carrying a loaded gun. I do feel compelled, as a friend, to make mention. Enough said.

The elevated aspect offered by the tree stand can cause a reconsideration of gun choice. Some such are likely to be open enough to permit the use of the rifle. Some might demand such. Use THINKING to decide. There will be times when the customer eschews the gallop to come at the sneak. Such, much of the time, will be heard and not seen—mostly as a rustling of the leaves or limbs. Close. There will be the temptation to begin a desperate screaming to cause the critter to show. Doing so does not get the job done, at least not often. I have found that screaming loud to a close critter has been counterproductive. Experience suggests a more low key approach. Use the Kiss of Death or another kind of close-in call (discussed fully within the chapter titled "Kisses and Other Close Calls"). I call little in such situations and call low, sending out a couple of low whines (using my voice) of two or three seconds each. I wait to see if that does the trick. If not, I play the ace, using the Kiss of Death. That "K of D," much of the time, will convince the bashful there is a trophy woodrat or cottontail nearby that is desperate to be eaten.

There is an important element to the calling of thick cover. That element involves the use of common sense. That sense of a common nature will tell you there are some brushy areas too thick to be screamed. Do not waste your time on such. Concentrate on areas offering a decent return for effort. There will be times when you will be able to set up to the edge of thick cover. Abandoned logging roads within thick cover can be dandy. Set up near to stream banks when those riparian areas offer a bit of visibility. A boat can be an asset along major waterways and lakes. The bottom line? Use THINKING to evaluate potential and select technique. Do that and you are likely to enjoy the excitement that comes with tight-country calling.

The Kiss of Death can cause a barely seen bit of fur to turn into a decent target.

Chapter 17

Teamwork

The coyote was not a virgin, I saw that immediately. He was a third of a mile out when first sighted, a barely-seen dot of fur in the distance. It took the paranoid a full five minutes to cover the next three hundred yards of pushdowns. Sometimes I could see him, sometimes not. I stayed patient and kept up the screaming. Lowering the volume of the TallyHo, blowing pitiful little screams, the kind bound to bring a tear to the eye of Hard Hearted Hanna from Butte, Montana.

My mind was made up. Even though I knew my limitations, knew that a 300-yard opportunity was not the kind of shot that fit my talents, I resolved to start the wet work the next time the yodeler paused for a reconnoiter. I shifted my eyeballs to slant sidewise, hoping to see how Joe Bob was reacting to the sight of his first called coyote. J.B. was not reacting at all. His uneducated eyes had not discovered the customer. "Just as well," I muttered to my mind, "if he can't see him, he can't spook him."

I thought wrong. Ten seconds later, at about the time I had worked through two pounds of the three pound trigger on the .22-250, perception occurred. "There comes one now," Joe Bob bellowed. He added insult when he leaped erect and laid into that 300-yard coyote with his twelve gauge. J. Bob would have been more correct if he had said, "There goes one now."

I sighed, gathered the junk, and headed for the truck. On the trudge back I amused Joe B. by telling him horror stories about the worst calling partners I had suffered through. Somewhere in that dialogue I thanked J.B. for providing the coyote with a good laugh, for allowing that same coyote to make the desperate run for home carrying the fifty dollar hide I hankered for. Do coyote laugh? I'm not sure. If any do that one damn sure did, maybe at the sight of a hunter lobbing a load of four buck at an out-of-range target, or maybe because of the tears in my own eyes.

The worst calling partner I have hunted with was the one called the hummer. Vernon LaDuke (my stepdad) is dead now so there is no longer a reason to hide his identity. Duke was a fine hunting companion in many ways. He always did his share of the camp work, sometimes more than his share. He bragged on my cooking at about every meal. He did not mention, even one time, the time I missed a trotting coyote at 20 yards. Trouble was, Duke was a

Johnny and Gerald Stewart work together to obtain outstanding wildlife photographs.

compulsive hummer and would break into a tuneless hum at the least excuse. Duke hummed, I think, because he was nervous, and critter calling always made him nervous. He became particularly nervous when I had a critter nibbling at the bait. I recall one stand vividly. I had a pair of chargers coming from out of the stringbark, each hoping to be the first to get the rabbit. Duke hummed the pair clean out of the country. I regretfully ended the partnership. Whistlers, scratchers, and squirmers can be about as bad.

Screaming to predators is like other hunts in one respect. There is more fun to be found if you share the adventure and the excitement with a buddy. A pair of callers, if each is disciplined, dedicated, and use the right technique, can take more fur, more than either would take as a solo. Do not expect twice as much, however. A team of callers will fetch in about the same number of coyote likely to respond to a single caller. A hunter who knows where the coyote lifts his leg and knows why is likely to take maybe sixty or seventy percent of those called critters. Buddy-calling can cause a better percentage but it does not take a mathematical genius to figure there is not room for doubling.

One of my all time favorite screaming companions is George Oakey of Flagstaff, a man who has hunted predators for forty years, since the mid-fifties. He has a talented touch on the tube (favoring an antique wood Circe in Trophy configuration) and is equally talented on the trigger, abilities that are in short supply among some calling companions. George and I have team hunted enough to develop a technique that maximizes our fur take. Here is the way it works.

Flagstaff screamer George Oakey owns a dandy lip and is a straight shooter.

Gun selection can be critical if a team is to take enough fur to keep the stretchers full. A solo hunter, much of the time, looks at the country and makes the choice between the shotgun and the centerfire. There will be times when the solo hunter guesses wrong. That hunter might choose a shotgun and have a bobcat hang up a hundred yards out to deliver the bad eye. That hunter might choose the centerfire and have a charger come from his back to cross his boot toes and disappear. George and I take away the guesswork. He carries a Sako, either in .243 (I keep telling him it's too damn much gun for fur) or in .222. I carry MooseDick, a junkyard dog kind of ten gauge that can cause a coyote to get dead at sixty yards. When a critter comes we let that critter come as close as they want to be, and at about then I lay into them with the load of copper-plated BBs. George cleans up on the escapees. Other times he surprises the bashfuls that dance around out of shotgun range.

We set up so that each watches an approach lane, not the same one. We do not set back to back as some early screamers advise. I usually cover the prime approach lane with the shotgun, most particularly if that approach involves trees and brush, maybe both, where the critter must come close to see the rabbit. George sets up to one side so that he can cover the more long-distance approach.

If either discovers a customer, we lip squeak to put the partner on the alert. Two guns, we figure, are always better than one gun when a critter comes to call. That lip squeak (Kiss of Death), much of the time is made when the customer is a ways out and not likely to notice. The "here comes one" signal has another benefit. Multiples are sometimes sighted. If each gunner is ready each can attend to one. How do we prevent shooting at the same critter? Easy. The shotgun guy takes the close customer. The rifleman takes the other. In the case of a double that are about equidistant, the hunter to the left takes the left-hand critter, the hunter to the right takes the right-hand critter.

I lost a critter, a good one, on one hunt because three good hunters didn't take the time to communicate. It happened this way. We were set up on a side hill below a rock rim, watching a juniper-choked canyon. Within that canyon a dirt dam caused a backwater stock tank. We were screaming to the gray fox and the bobcat we hoped would hear. Each of us carried shotguns because the tight nature of the setup caused visibility (shot opportunity) to be close range.

Mike Mell was the middle man and he was doing the calling, blowing deliciously on his plastic Circe. Twenty seconds of screams followed by a minute of silence. Repeat. I caught a flicker of movement at the ending of one series, a movement on the far side of the canyon and in a thick forest of string bark junipers. I looked until my eyeballs ached and finally found a bobcat face floating among the shadows. I looked at Mike and saw he had not made discovery. I placed my own Circe tube to my mouth and began a screaming. Mike got the message and searched until he discovered the cat. He relaxed then to let me finish the screaming. And I did. The bobcat moved out of the shadows and into the sun, showing he was a dandy blue-back worth a couple of hundred dollars within the current market. The cat looked at me and Mike and then moved across an open area of about twenty feet and then out of sight into the brush-choked drainage. We did not see that cat again for five minutes. Even so, I stayed patient and continued the scream.

Finally, the cat showed on our side of the drainage and stopped to look again. I gave him the "Kiss of Death" and he started my way at the trot, maybe sixty or seventy yards out. At about that time Mike and I heard the report from Little Gary's twelve-gauge, a hundred yards to Mike's left and a couple of hundred yards from the cat. The sound of the shotgun caused the cat to freeze in mid-stride. I panicked. Messed up. I figured the cat was bound to leave at the gallop any second. I laid into that cat with a load of four buck from the 3" twelve. The cat hit the ground, bounced erect, and disappeared into the canyon. Even though Mike and I gave chase we did not see that kitty again.

Little Gary had not shot at the cat, didn't even know it was there. His shot was at a fine silver coyote that had approached from his left, and he carried the evidence. How could we have done it differently? First, knowing then what I know now, I would not have shot at that long-distance bobcat. I now know that critters do not always spook at the sound of a shot. If I had kept on calling, continued with the lip squeak, it is likely the cat would have forgiven the shot to trot on in. Secondly, it is a good idea to develop a series of signals when team hunting. George and I use a system he used when he was involved in calling contests with Del Western during the early days. We blow a single scream if we have a fox on the hook, two screams for a coyote and three for a

Signals can cause hunting buddies to see discreet customers.

cat, bobcat or lion. Had we done so Little Gary would likely have let the coyote walk, saved the action for the bobcat.

George and I use the call as a signal in another way. We'd take turns on the tube so that neither will develop the dreaded trombone lip. When the stand master (the screamer) is ready to call it quits he blows a single long blast, indicating his desire to abandon the setup. The second hunter answers with two screams indicating he has nothing in sight. Such a system avoids the embarrassment of standing while a customer is in sight. That sort of thing happened to me during 1995, while on a hunt with an Alaskan guide who had come to America (that's what they call the lower 48) to do a bit of cat screaming.

Alaska big game guide Gary Hull gave up too soon on the bobcat, but did dandy on the coyote.

The Slammer and I were set up to call to a brush-choked canyon that was sort of fan-shaped, the narrow end being close and the wide end maybe four hundred yards out. Gary was screaming his TallyHo and had done so for about fifteen minutes. Right about then I sighted movement at the top of the fan and looked to see a bob' trot across an insignificant opening, headed our way. Our setups were apart, there was no opportunity to whisper information. Gary called for a couple of more minutes and then stood to leave. I started a desperate screaming, and when he looked, motioned for him to sit. He did. I maintained the screaming for another 30 minutes, until near dark. The bob' did not show.

Double gunning at the screaming can double the fun found afield. Done right, that double gunning can increase the fur take. Two hunters can split expenses to enjoy twice the hunts for the same money. For maximum fun, however, select the calling companion carefully. No hummers. When you find a good one, treat him or her right. They may be hard to replace.

Chapter 18

Double Trouble

I have mentioned in other chapters the asset to be found while calling after a kill, or after a missed opportunity. I repeat here, do so. If the country is good enough to give up one customer it might be good enough to give up a second. Some predators, dogs like the coyote and the fox particularly, pair for much of the year. Killing one, then calling to the other can be good business.

Those multiples that come to a single setup, but come within a somewhat separated time frame, are not true doubles and not true triples, not the way I see it. Those that come to a screaming but come separately are simply two singles, each to be dealt with as such. Predators that come like grapes, in bunches, are a different matter. The screamer is confronted with double and triple excitement. Killing more than one of the gang requires THINKING.

Every screamer will have instances where he or she is challenged by multiples. Considering options before the hunt can help awfully when it comes time to consider options while in the big middle of the situation. If you customarily scream with a partner, I suggest you and the partner communicate to develop a scheme of action. Do so before the hunt. Doing so while critters are out front is seldom productive. An important question begging an answer can be basic, who shoots what? Having a pair of screamers double kill a coyote while the neighbor runs can be depressing. Generally, if the critters are equidistant, the hunter to the right shoots the critter to the right. The hunter to the left shoots the left-hand customer.

Now, a bit more on the "keep on calling after the shot advice." There will be times when the first to respond hits the ground hard, but hits the ground so that the remains are out of sight, or maybe barely in sight. Sad experience has told me to quit the screaming right then to make the retrieve. Let me supply an example.

I was screaming the greasewoods with Chuck Spearman and his friend Gary Brittan (The Great Brittan, being the president of a Nebraska paper company). Knowing three to the screaming can be awkward, Gary and I dropped Chuck (drop & drive) a mile or so down the two track, then continued on to select our own setup.

A minute or two into the screaming I sighted a customer of the coyote kind making a sneak from a hundred yards out. The critter stopped and turned broadside, a body language that told me he had come as close as likely. I shouldered the Sako, got down on the

*Using the Drop & Drive can cause Ph.D.s to come at the run.
(Burnham Brothers)*

stock, sighted, and started the squeeze. All of that caused the coyote to become nervous. When I had tautened the trigger nearly enough to cause the ten-gauge to go bang, the critter left at the leap. I swung and continued the squeeze, causing the coyote to crash during mid-leap. The Great Brittan was impressed. Hell, I was impressed. I watched to discover a miraculous recovery.

I could not see the coyote. His tail would flag each half-minute or so, telling me he was still there. I returned to calling. Suddenly realizing I had not seen the tail in a while, I unhid and advanced at a lumber. The coyote was gone. No blood trail. Nothing. We left, sad but wiser.

Common sense says you do not continue the call when a critter is downed but flopping, particularly if that flopping causes the critter to disappear from sight. Stop the screaming, cause the finish, and make the retrieve.

The Western coyote I have met have not been pack animals, except during the fall when pups and parents hunt as a family. Multiples that come are most often doubles—Ma and Pa. That does not mean gangs do not come to a single calling. I was with Chuck Spearman, calling on an Indian reservation where the coyote is considered to be a reincarnation of Granny, when we called and counted an even dozen coyote to a single screaming. All appeared as singles and doubles. The response caused us to shoot the auto focus Canons with a gleeful desperation.

After the shot, calling can be productive when the target is gray or red fox. Those little dogs are essentially miniature coyote, the way I see it, and respond coyote-like. Here's an example.

115

I was calling the Bagdad boulders during a winter and had completed three series when a pair of gray fox galloped close, then flared at about thirty-five yards. I made the easy shot on the close fox, then swung the .222 to try for the trailer. Such, being no dummy, decided I was not the kind of neighbor worth visiting and disappeared into the rock jumble. I kept calling, staying hopeful, keeping one eye on the carcass. A couple of minutes later a second fox, maybe the same one that came as a half of the pair, peeked over a bug-sized (VW) boulder. I squared, shouldered, and shot. Staying with the scream had caused me to double the pleasure and double the fur. Do not expect a second customer to appear after every shot. It is not likely to happen. Even so, after-shot calling will work enough to make the practice worthwhile.

Shooting response to doubles and triples must be precise if the screamer is to take all that is offered. I cannot count the times I have taken the easy part of a double and then messed up to let the surviving half escape. Honesty causes me to confess to worse. There have been times the excitement of the double vision has caused me to mess up big time. I did such, nearly, on the pair of coyote called from windy winter pushdowns.

The coyotes let the forty mph crosswind cause them to be off course. Does the wind blow sound? Maybe. Those coyote thought so. Each came at the gallop but were headed wrong. I scrooched a bit behind the log, licked the call slobbers from my beard, and screamed, causing the duo to correct and come straight.

It was the winter of 1978. The pelts from that pair of high country primes would bring a hundred dollar bill, a significant sum to a recently retired highway patrol captain, struggling to supplement a stingy retirement. I watched the approach and hummed a mind song, don't mess up, don't mess up.

Coyote commonly pair, remaining so until one dies or loses dominance.

116

Flying coyote, particularly those at close range, can be a tough target.

The positioning of the pair caused a complication. The front runner was fifty yards ahead of the trailer. If I used the three-inch twelve to do business with the leader, the trailer would likely veer to escape. Wanting both, needing both, I delayed the shot until the leader was nearly on me. I loomed from behind the log with the auto loader at the ready. Any decent coyote, I figured, would veer to avoid the fence out front, maybe provide a broadside opportunity. This one did not. That sumbitch leaped. Leapt over the fence, over the log, and over me. I caught a quick look at the coyote underside (it was a male) made the turn and tried the wing shot. Missed. Shot again, missed again. I returned to the front to see number two veering forty yards out. I got on target fast to send a load of four buck that way. The coyote was down, was up, and was escaping at the wobble-legged run. Out of shells, out of patience, I followed at the lumber, finally overtaking. I finished the job using the butt of the Model 1100 and strong language. Messy.

How could I have done differently? The same situation, if it occurred today, would see a differing response. I would keep as much Blair as practical behind the log, maybe have the barrel of the twelve gauge pointed toward the fur. When the lead coyote was forty yards out I would commence a fearful growling, maybe even cuss. Do all I could to cause the lead dog to stop to discover what the hell was behind that log. When he did so I would wait the seconds needed to let the trailer catch up to honor the point. I would shoot one half the double from ambush, then raise up as needed to take the second.

Some circumstances will cause one half of the double to be as safe as if within the den, sucking on momma. Screamers need to recognize such when they occur. They need to forget about the double and concentrate on the single. Doing so allows them to leave the stand carrying fur.

No two doublings are identical. The country changes and the nature of the respondents change. I can give no good advice that will be constantly useful, excepting this. THINK on the subject of doubles. Train yourself to analyze each situation. Doing so as quickly as possible, and respond accordingly. Will that work every time? It doesn't for me and likely will not for you. The best we can hope for is an improved response.

Chapter 19

Selecting the Setup

The country out front was as flat as a road-killed rabbit. Pushdown junipers to the rear. The kind of country Western coyote love. Plenty of open country to display the speed that can cause a jackrabbit to lose his wind. The piles of pushdowns are home to cotton-tailed rabbits, wood rats, white-footed deer mice, and a mind boggling assortment of critter delectables. I had sighted pile after pile of coyote poop on the walk in. Each of those piles delivered an encouraging message. I was in coyote country. A proper screaming was likely to bring one or more to the gun. Optimism was high as I set out to find a setup.

I did not set up within the pushdowns. A coyote that came within the pushdowns would be hard to see, maybe not be seen at all before he tasted the wind to make the desperate run for home. I decided, instead, to set up outside the pushdowns, out in the open. I would scream the customer through the pushdowns and into the open, the kind of country best suited to the scope-sighted .22-250. Trouble was, there was not a good place to hide my extra-large frame. I hiked the perimeter of the pushdowns until I discovered a small grouping of leafless sagebrush. I gathered other sagebrush branches and finally had enough to form a hideout, a sort of a sagebrush overcoat. Seconds later I sent out the first notes of "The Dying Rabbit Blues."

The coyote came at the gallop when I was two minutes into the song. The critter stood panting, begging for the rabbit. Knowing the angle was bad for a shot, knowing I would almost surely miss if I did not square to the fur, I shifted slightly to start a scrooch. The coyote, obviously uncomfortable around moving sagebrush, lost his taste for rabbit and started the retreat. I lunged erect, taking parts of the sagey overcoat with me, and laid into that amazed yodeler with the Ruger. I killed a rock with the first shot and insulted a pile of pushdown with the second. The coyote hoofed it out of the country, likely laughing his butt off at the big guy in the sagebrush overcoat. What the hell is the point? The point is, I did everything right on that stand except for one detail. I settled for a setup that did not offer the shooting advantage needed to collect the fur. A screamer who hopes to skin fur somewhat regularly must learn to recognize a good setup and a bad setup.

What does it take to cause a setup to be a good 'un? The setup must be in country that houses a decent population of critters. The

The setup must offer a decent population as well as visibility.

setup must offer visibility. I divide such into two categories: vision lanes and shooting lanes. I need to see the critter as he makes the approach, hopefully in plenty of time to get ready physically and emotionally. I need to have vision enough to keep the critter in sight as he makes his desperate escape. The setup should be somewhat open so that I can swing the gun and not have to force the barrel through brush and tree limbs. I carry a set of small size pruning shears in a belt holster to trim when need be. The setup should have some structure, at least enough to mute the outline of my camo-clad frame. The setup needs to be easy to get out of. A hunter needs to get unhid in a hurry sometimes, maybe to take a second shot at a missed critter, maybe to take a first shot at a critter that comes in awkward, or maybe to try for the second leg of a double that has spooked.

Finally, the setup must offer the advantage of safety. Not from the customers, as they seldom attack a 200-pound rabbit. Safety from (shudder) snakes. Those who know me well know of my intolerance of snakes of every kind, particularly those that carry a noisemaker on their tail. Why am I a snake bigot? Don't know, I have been one ever since a five foot western diamondback (coontail) laid a lip lock on the calf of my left leg.

Anyway, here in the West, those who call early in the season and late in the season need to know that snakes are out. And they need to know snakes love brush piles. I forgot all of that on one hunt and nearly paid the price. It happened this way.

The pushdown roots to the front will interfere with shot opportunity.

Working the brush piles can cause close encounters of the rattle-snake kind.

I crawled into a cramped hole in a pile of pushdown during an October hunt, settled down, and started the music. A hungry coyote showed appreciation and came at the gallop. Trouble was, at about the same time I discovered a neighbor, a four foot diamondback, the kind that finds pleasure scaring the scat out of snake-shy screamers.

The snake slithered close, tasted my smell using that black, forked tongue, then coiled to assume the classic strike configuration. My options, as I saw them then, were few. I could fight my way free of the pushdown pile and make a run for it (a temptation I barely resisted). I could ignore the snake, pretend he wasn't coiled a couple of feet from my big butt, and concentrate on the customer, a coyote carrying about $50 worth of fur (1982 prices). Or, I could one-hand the twelve-gauge to point the barrel to the left rear (awkward), pull the trigger, and hope for good results. The snake started a hostile rattling as I moved the barrel his way. The load of four buck at the range of a foot or so spread snakeburger for yards. Even though I left that stand without fur, I left a happy man.

As stated, the ideal screaming setup will offer obvious advantages. Negatives will be few. Here are circumstances often overlooked by those new to screaming.

Even though fully camouflaged, set up in the shade when possible. A caller who sets in the sun can be obvious to a customer, particularly obvious when he or she makes a move. A shaded screamer is most difficult to see. Sun flash from the glass of the scope sight is less likely.

I pay particular attention to the wind. Experience and intuition can cooperate to help me sometime predict the avenue of approach. I set up so that the main vision area is upwind. I try to set up so that I have secondary vision lanes crosswind and maybe even downwind, knowing that the masking scent is likely to fool the critter's nose.

Calling crepuscular, calling the sunrise and the sunset, can be dandy. There is a danger to such. Pre-sunrise stands can be particularly risky. The screamer, much of the time, starts the stand before the sun has topped the horizon. Those who face east will pay a price. The sun WILL appear, and when it does, will shine directly into the screamer's eyes. This can cause irritation, can reduce visibility and can seriously hamper accuracy. Want an example?

I snuggled into a pile of pushdown on a first light screaming and did everything just right, sucking a nervous coyote to about fifty yards. The top half of the sun showed at about the same time. I could see nothing through the scope except sun flare. I tried a desperation shot, the kind of shot I seldom make. I didn't make that one either. I had trouble seeing the coyote leave. The sun was in my eyes. The moral? Set up so that the sun is in the customer's eyes, not in your own.

Calling the sunset can be nearly as bad. Sunset setups start with the sun already in position. Screamers who row with both oars in the water will see the obvious handicap and adjust the setup to compensate.

Sad experience has caused me to choose a setup that permits mobility. The critter might come at an awkward angle and you may need to move to make the shot. There may be more than one critter and you may have to scrooch to take the trailer.

I make an effort to choose a setup that holds an open area that a critter must cross on his way to the rabbit. The more open the area, the better chance of putting a 52-grain chunk of copper-plated lead within his or her necessaries. Screaming at coyote, sad to say, can

Crepuscular calling, as has been noted, is likely to increase interest.

In areas where ground cover is heavy the hunter may elect to stand for better visibility.

follow the doctrine of Murphy's Law: Anything that can go wrong will go wrong. Such is illustrated by relating a sad experience involving a canny coyote and one small and insignificant juniper bush, not even big enough to be a tree, for God's sake.

I was set up within the pocked aspect of a prairie dog (black-tailed) town in northern Arizona, a place coyote like to hang around even though I doubt they have a lot of luck dogging. Anyway, the area was mostly open, the dogs having eaten about everything alive, but had one small and insignificant (S&I) string bark juniper bush thirty feet out front. I saw that S&I stringbark when I set up in front of one just like it. I knew I should move but I did not. Three minutes into the screaming a big silver came at the lope, using the S&I juniper to cover his approach, took a quick peek around, and then turned tail to use the S&I stringbark as cover. I hate it when they do that.

I do my best to choose a setup that offers the comforts of home, or as many of those comforts as possible, knowing I will need to sit as still as a rock for at least 15 minutes and maybe more. That kind of marathon sitting demands some degree of comfort. I pick a spot free of thorns, spines, and scratchy leaves. I wriggle the back-side to discover particularly obnoxious rocks and stobs, those that will cause big-time pain after about five minutes, and remove those suckers before I start the screaming. I avoid rotting logs, knowing such are often home to ants, those little black pests that can deliver a sting that will hurt until February. I pick dry ground (I sometimes kick at wet duff until I reach a dry layer) knowing that the discomfort of a frozen butt is not conducive to rifle accuracy. Finally, I almost always carry a square of camo-covered foam and use that as a cushion on the setup. No foam handy? Substitute a two-foot square of scrap carpet. Comfort, the way I see it, lets me sit still and sit longer without squirming.

While on the subject of comfort I might as well mention my favored setup position. Some new to screaming will sit with legs crossed and heels under the body, yoga-like. Such, to me, is some-what comfortable for a minute or two. The legs then go to sleep. Not long after the pain begins. I like to sit with my backside firmly planted, a back support is dandy if available, and with my legs drawn up so that the knees are available as a brace for the elbows when it comes time to shoot. I can hold this position for fifteen min-utes and not suffer. Rifle accuracy is enhanced. I have made setups (stand-ups when visibility requires), kneeling and laying on my belly. I have not made a setup where I stood on my head, not yet anyway, but might consider such if it will help me collect the crit-ter. The point is, choose the position that is right for you and right for the country around the individual setup.

The careful consideration of stand assets should permit the sighting of the customer (or customers) as they make the approach. Most are running or at least moving and will be easily seen. Some, sad to say, make a discrete approach and are first seen as a coyote-like, fox-like, or bobcat-like blob standing to deliver the bad eye. Bobcat are the worst in the world for that sort of thing. The screamer can have trouble at identification, not knowing if it is a critter or a booger. You want the truth? I once shot a coyote-like bush, in front of a witness. Since, I have found it to be good prac-tice to scan the area for boogers (critter look-alikes) and identify all such BEFORE starting the screaming.

RIGHT. Stay low and use available cover to break up your outline.

WRONG. Even though this hunter is properly camouflaged, his skylined position will spook most predators that answer his call.

I also recommend the screamer stay alert to the actions of wildlife within the vicinity of the screaming. I was screaming from a rocky rim in central Arizona on one hunt, hoping to interest a bobcat. When fifteen minutes of screams did not provoke a customer, thinking I was whipping a dead horse, I considered calling it quits. Before I could quit, a covey of Gambel's quail, roosting in the brush below, began a nervous putting. Figuring they knew what they were talking about, I put away the tube and substituted the moaner. The quail continued to be nervous and eventually flushed. Twenty minutes of moaning caused me to sight a flash of fur within the brush fifty yards below. I put the little X of the six power duplex there and saw a suspicious eye surrounded by spotted fur. I centered on the eyeball, sucked in a breath, let half of it out, and stroked. The eye disappeared. Walking down I was elated to find a one-eyed and graveyard dead bobcat, a baileyi, one of the pretty kind. I muttered a thanks to the quail, grabbed the fur, and hiked out.

On another hunt I was calling within standing junipers, armed with a 3" twelve (pre-MooseDick days). A half a handful of Herefords grazed the area as I set up. The whitefaces looked me over suspiciously when I sent out the first series of screams. It did not take them long to return to their hunt for gamma grass. Five minutes later a heifer turned her head to direct a hard stare to my rear. I scrooched slowly until I was able to see a pair of coyote that had come back door. I dumped one and peppered the rear of the second. The third shot took the survivor when he was forty yards out. I felt like kissing ol' bossy for snitching off the sneakers, and probably would have if I could have caught her.

Selecting the setup is not that difficult. Use common sense to select one that offers concealment, favorable wind, no sun in the eyes, vision lanes, shooting lanes and comfort. Can't find a setup with all of that? Neither can I. Do as I do and do the best you can.

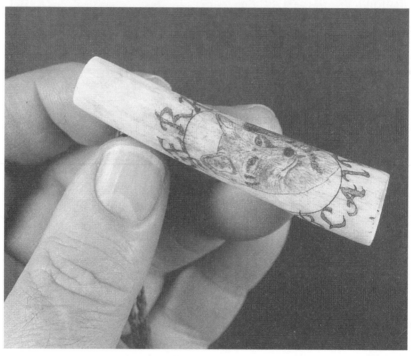

Chapter 20

Tube Technique

There is a tendency in all of us to turn something simple into something difficult. I know there is that in my own personality. Having pretty much mastered the basics of predator screaming, being able to use that boring and basic scream to fetch predators close, I find myself pushing that basic technique down the road in an effort to find improvement. Sometimes I do. And at times that improvement causes technique to improve, delivering more fur to the stretcher. Being honest, I have to say some "improvements" do not improve at all. In my collection of memories there are some that taught a sad lesson. Leaving the basics of critter calling can be a mistake. This chapter will deliver an encapsulation of the basics of the sport, tubewise.

Some of the material contained here will be repeated in other chapters. Even so, I feel it to be important to have an overview of tubes and tube technique, allowing those new to the sport to see what screaming is about, doing so in a chapter rather than in a whole book. The distress scream technique takes advantage of the opportunistic nature of predators. All, at least all I have met, use their eyes and their nose to find groceries. Every hunter knows that to be true. Less well known, however, is the regular use of another sense. I am talking ears. Every predator uses that sense of sound to locate prey that might be beyond the scan of the eye and beyond the reach of the nose.

The distress scream is heard most often, I think, because a flying predator has swooped or stooped to capture the blue plate special. That capture, a part of the time, sees the collection of a cotton-tailed rabbit, a true hare, or the hare Westerners call a jackrabbit. The capture is effected using the talons to grasp the prey outside the chest cavity. Death is accomplished by compressing that chest cavity until suffocation occurs, a process that can use up a minute or more. All of that time, commonly, the prey screams piteously. What good does that do? Don't know. Maybe the critter feels compelled to do something. Not knowing what else to do, it screams.

Anyway, other predators, those that fly the air and walk the ground, hearing the action, know something good to eat is in trouble. They come at the gallop, hoping, I suppose, to steal the meal. Predator calls are designed to permit the duplication of that distress sound. Such calls are of basic design. A wood or plastic tube containing a stainless steel reed is one. Such calls are easily mastered and do a decent job of producing the rabbit and hare distress (depending on the reed). Disadvantages? Each and all sound pretty much the same, even as they travel from mouth to mouth. Another disadvantage will be noticed during freezing weather. The moisture of the breath will collect on the thin metal reed and freeze there, causing a malfunction.

The second call type is also a tube, one that flaunts a thin shim of mylar plastic, exposed. This kind of call fits within the warmth of the mouth, does not freeze unless within a very cold mouth, and will consequently stay healthy during the coldest of weather. A second asset accrues because of call design. Moving the lips up or down on the plastic reed can cause a change of tone. Those who practice can use the plastic reeded call (sometimes called the open reed) to scream out a rabbit distress, a hare distress, a fox distress, a pup distress, and even a coyote howl. Some will bugle. The plastic reeded tube will change tone from mouth to mouth. The bad news? Not all that bad. The plastic reeded call is a bit more difficult to master, not much of a disadvantage to a caller who is serious about the screaming.

The slow death provided by hawks, eagles, and owls encourages distressful screaming, inviting all who hear to attend the feast.

A third call type is the diaphragm call favored by many turkey hunters. This device is basically a section of latex held in an aluminum frame, covered with duct tape. These calls stay within the mouth when in use and are therefore freeze-proof. Some such are marketed as predator calls. Those are, I suspect, nothing more than a single- or double-reeded turkey diaphragm re-labeled. The diaphragm call demands practice. When mastered they do a decent job of screaming and whining. A second asset involves a lack of movement and that will translate to fewer spooked critters. No hands are needed, freeing the hands to do more important tasks, maybe shooting. The volume produced, to my ears, is less than that produced by either the metal or the plastic-reeded call. A second consideration is a lack of longevity. The latex used within the diaphragm call is light sensitive and

Plastic reeded calls and diaphragms stay within the mouth to resist freezing.

will begin to deteriorate the day it is made. Spittle that collects within the latex can cause the dreaded slobber rot. I do not expect a used diaphragm call to last more than about a season. Even so, they are inexpensive and should be a part of every call collection.

The fourth call kind is the battery-powered caller that plays cassettes containing the recorded sounds of actual prey animals. Rabbits, hares, fox, birds, deer, and I don't know what all. Tapes containing howlings are also available. The tape players offer an advantage to callers who have not mastered the distress scream. The caller causes them to be immediately expert, at least as far as the screaming is concerned. Another asset comes because of the learning potential. Those new to the sport can listen to actual distress screams to learn sound and rhythm. Other assets also accrue, those to be covered within the chapter devoted to the battery-powered callers. Negatives? Not many. Mostly cost. The player and a starter tape collection will cost a couple of hundred dollars.

A second kind of battery-powered caller retrieves sound from an electronic chip. Such commonly work from a four-chip board. The operator can change to any sound on that board by flicking a selection switch. Other sounds are available through the changing of the board. Neither the chip player nor the cassette player is compatible to the other. Put another way, you cannot play chips through a cassette caller, you cannot play cassettes through the chip player.

The two most common calls, the metal-reeded tube and the plastic-reeded tube, will be discussed in depth. I cannot count the times I have been asked to describe a rabbit distress scream. Such is difficult, just as it is difficult to describe any sound without imitating that sound. Having said that, I will attempt such, saying first that

131

Kisses and other close calls can cause a bashful to come excitingly close.

some of the worst rabbit distress sounds I have heard have come from the throats of distressed rabbits. Some of the best I have heard came from the mouths of talented human screamers. Which sounds better to the customer? I am convinced the screaming from the prey animal is better. There are likely nuances, perhaps beyond the range of human hearing, that lend authenticity. An example follows.

Larry was taping footage for our "Masters' Secrets to Predator Calling" and had enlisted the efforts of a black-tailed jackrabbit to do so. The camcorder was on the tripod, set to wide angle. Larry was out front holding Jack. A squeeze of the chest caused the hare to holler. A minute or three into the holler the sound of hoof and whuff announced the arrival of a small herd of collared peccary, some running to within a few feet of Jack and Larry. The cotton-tailed rabbit distress screams I have heard have been a constant and monotonous *wah-wah-wah,* repeated for twenty to forty seconds. Mostly of moderate volume. Even though I have not talked to coyote and cats on this, I am convinced the rhythm of the screams is as important (maybe more so) as the tonal quality. The tone of the screaming is pure, no rasp is present. Some hares and all gray fox put rasp into their screamings, a hoarseness that is obtained by sending a maximum amount of air through the metal-reeded call to cause the reed to overload. That same effect can be coaxed from the plastic-reeded call when the lips are placed to bottom of the exposed part of the reed, to the stop.

Now might be as good a time as any to tell my technique of screaming, using the plastic-reeded call, the metal-reeded call, and the diaphragm, starting with the plastic-reeded call. The plastic-reeded call I use most often is the TallyHo, a call that consists of a molded plastic call body fitted with a somewhat thick plastic reed. I have used others of a similar configuration, the Crit'R•Call, Lohman's C-280, Johnny Stewart's PC-6, and too many more to mention. All are blown about the same. Blowing might be the wrong word. I do not blow into the call, even though doing so will produce a sound. The sound produced with the blow is not a sound that can be easily controlled. It is better, in my experience, to breathe air out and into the call. The breathed sound can be modified as the breath is modified, permitting a selection of sound and volume.

I begin by placing the plastic-reeded call to the corner of my mouth, finding it to be comfortable there and finding I have good control. I place my lips to the stop of the call and blow a series of moans. I cup one or both hands over the end of the tube to act as sound chambers. Opening the hand or hands as you breathe into the call causes a sound modification. Continue breathing out *wahs,* extending each *wah* to achieve a short, choppy series. If each *wah* is four beats long, insert a two beat pause between. Experiment until you find the rhythm that is comfortable, the rhythm that works for you.

A screaming jackrabbit brought a sounder of javelina so close you could smell the ugly.

Moving the lips toward the call tip can cause a change of tone. Generally, the farther toward the tip, the higher the tone. I like to position my lips to the bottom of the plastic reed when blowing jackrabbit distress. Placing the lips slightly beyond the stop can add gravel, the hoarse scream of some jackrabbit and of all gray fox. I position my lips about midway on the reed to provoke the cottontail scream. I move my mouth tipward to about the first half inch of plastic, bite down with my teeth, and breathe into the call to elicit the pup whine.

The plastic-reeded tube can also be used as a howler. Some will work better than others. All, with practice, will produce a howl that can cause a coyote to howl back, maybe even come. I place the call to the center of my mouth, extending my lips to the stop, and blow to produce the howl. As the sound begins move the lips tipward until you find the spot that produces the best pitch.

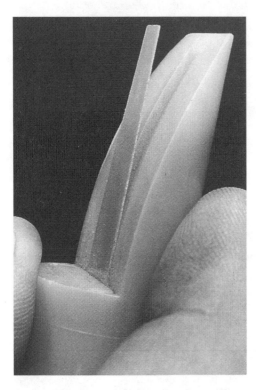

Some plastic reeded calls do well as a howler, sounding best when a funnel is used as a sound chamber.

Blowing the metal-reeded call is easy. Place your lips to the call and breathe or blow to provoke screams. Even though mouth position is not as critical as with the plastic-reeded call, habit causes me to be most comfortable when the call is to the corner of the mouth. Moderate air pressure will cause cottontail distress sounds. Maximum air pressure will cause hoarsely-coarse jackrabbit and gray fox squalls.

The calling sequence stays somewhat constant no matter what kind of call you use. I like to start the stand blowing moderate volume screams. I blow a series of screams that continue for about 20 seconds. The length of the scream series is not critical. Blow a series for ten seconds or blow a series for thirty seconds and you will likely do as well. Some callers I know blow continuously from start of stand to finish, and call critters.

I like to interrupt the screaming with periods of silence. That quiet time offers the opportunity to stay as still as a rock to scan for customers. A coyote that comes during the silent period stays a bit confused as to the call source. That can cause a hesitation that can offer an advantage when it comes time to shoot.

I continue this call/quiet alternation for the life of the stand, usually about 10 minutes for grays and reds, 15 minutes for coyote, 30 minutes for bobcat, and maybe an hour or two for cougar and bear. As is the case with most critter calling truths, that truth is not a constant. Circumstances can cause a variation of technique to be good business. That fact is best illustrated by the telling of a tale, the tale of the super paranoid coyote.

By late September the dumbest coyote in the pushdowns east of town has been skinned. The coyote that remain are the super paranoids, Ph.D.s that have seen about all of the rodeo they can stand. I told all of that to Perry Shirley when he suggested we go there for a day of screaming. "Heck," he grinned, "as good as we are, I am betting we will do dandy." And we did, sort of. It was one of those foggy mornings when the mist hung tight, limiting visibility to about a hundred yards. Perry and I called coyote on the first two stands but the customers used the fog to stay discrete. No shot opportunity. Perry discovered a sneaker on the third stand and reached out to make the touch. Other successes followed. We were starting to feel pretty good about our averages when we came up against the paranoid.

I had screamed for 15 minutes when Perry discovered the sneaker, a speck of fur five hundred yards out, standing to deliver the long-distance bad eye. I lit into the screamer and the coyote showed his appreciation. He turned tail to trot away. I sent out a hoarse screaming that caused him to look over his tail, turn, and trot a few steps closer. I continued the screaming and the coyote moved our way a couple of hundred feet, and then hung up again. I moved my lips to the tip of the plastic-reeded call and sent out a series of pup distress whines. The coyote moved closer.

I continued to mess with that coyote for a full forty minutes. Finally, as though he couldn't stand it any more, the paranoid gave up. He came straight in at a steady trot. Perry did the wet work with the .22-250 at fifty yards. A second experience illustrates further.

I was calling high plains with Chuck Spearman during a winter hunt when a long distance coyote made a lope by. Chuck did good, putting the critter down using fine and fancy shooting. We walked out to make the retrieve. Trouble was, we could not find the carcass. The long and indirect walkout, the lack of landmarks, caused us to become confused. We muddled around for 20 minutes or so looking for our fur. Suddenly, looking back to our setup, I saw a coyote make a lope by. That sucker had learned to wait a decent interval before coming to investigate a screaming. I returned on another day, called for ten minutes, stayed quiet for fifteen, and nailed that smart aleck as he made his cruise. Did we locate the carcass of the invisible coyote? Yep, walking out. The big female lay where she fell, maybe a hundred feet from the area of our search.

There is a proliferation of screamers currently available. I have used calls made by most manufacturers and have found all to be effective when properly used. The predator caller will almost surely find one or more within that offering that suits his or her needs. Having said that, it is also proper to say that some fine old-timey calls are no longer available. Two that come to mind are the wood Trophy Model Circe and the Wood Weems Wild Call. Each of those has become a valuable collector's item. Each of those, the way I see it, was as fine a metal-reeded call as any made. Some, those who hanker for one such, can measure an actual call and use a lathe and woodworking abilities to construct a replica. Hunters who have neither tools nor talent can prevail on a friend or ask a woodworker to do the job. Check the listing at book's end for information on custom call makers.

Some information is needed on call repair and it might as well appear here. First, it is bad business to fiddle with a sick call while a customer is on the hook. It is better to carry a couple of extra calls. When a screamer calls in sick, it is a simple matter to substitute one of the backups. After the dance is the proper time to do repairs.

Any mechanical device will malfunction. Predator calls are no exception. The most common malfunction to the plastic-reeded call, within my experience, is a misalignment between reed and air channel. If the reed is not precisely centered the sound turns ugly. It is simple, much of the time, to use the fingernail to reposition the reed.

A second malfunction can occur when spittle causes a scummy build up along the reverse of the plastic reed. That sort of problem can be corrected. Remove the reed and wash it in warm soapy water. Use fine steel wool to scour away the scum when need be. Dry the reed and replace it. It should work as it did when new. All plastic-reeded calls will develop slobber fatigue after a few seasons. No amount of effort will cause them to sound pristine. Replacement reeds are available and are easily installed. Refer to the information section at book's end.

Metal-reeded calls also call in sick. They did so more so during the days when the metal reeds were of a galvanized stock. Slobber rot caused an oxidation. Current metal reeds are mostly stainless steel and do better. Even so, they do wear out. I have not had luck trying to retune a metal reed. It is best, I think, to replace them. Use a tool (usually a slotted rod) to push the old reed out, working from the big hole end. Work from the little hole end to position the replacement reed.

I like to call critters using either the plastic-reeded call or the metal-reeded call, finding satisfaction when I use such a simple device, coupled with calling skill, to bring a paranoid critter to the gun or the camera. Most screamers, I am convinced, feel likewise.

Chapter 21

Kisses and Other Close Calls

Larry O. squirmed to square to the ghost, hoping to cause his eyeballs to make an identification. No luck. The hundred yards of greasewood forest combined with low light to cause the animal-like part to stay discrete. Watching, sort of, Larry laid into the TallyHo one more time, sending delicious screams across the Arizona desert. The ghost remained as still as a rock. Larry gave up and returned to business.

Larry O. Gates, a Beastmaster, was screaming to coyote that hung around high dollar housing; residences scattered through the creosote bushes, the mesquite, and all other vegetation able to live and prosper on damn little water. The coyotes, a novelty when first discovered, became bad dogs when poodle hair and kitty fur started to appear in their poop. Larry was there for revenge. The first four or five calls of the day had fetched in a half a handful of coyote. Larry had helped all to get dead, using a three-inch twelve loaded with copper-plated BB's. No coyote had shown on this call. Larry was ready to call it quits after the usual fifteen minutes. Seeing a creosote trunk that looked to be critter-like caused him to continue. Five minutes later he was ready to say quit again and almost did. First, he figured, he would use the ultimate weapon. He pressed his lips together and sucked to produce the high pitched squeal we call the Kiss of Death. The leg-like stump exploded to action, coming to view attached to a big and hungry tom bobcat. The bob was using all four of his legs to come straight at Larry, coming at the gallop. Larry had barely enough time to shoulder and shoot. The 25-pound bobcat rugged seven yards out. Trudging to the truck, Larry thought about the times he had used the Kiss of Death to cause a balky critter to come. No way to know how many. A hell of a lot, maybe more.

I have used the "K of D" other ways. I was on a dandy late fall hunt with Oakey, Thanksgiving-thirty or so, when the critters came like concords, in bunches. We were set up within the shadow of stringbarks when I sighted a shadow coming from long distance. I lip squeaked to let George know a customer was coming, maybe the first time I had done so, at least with Oakey. Oak turned his head slowly, looked my way, smiled, winked, then kissed back. And after

all of that turned to watch his assigned lane. Figuring there had been enough kissing for one stand, maybe more than enough, I returned to the screaming.

The coyote was making a gallop by sixty yards out, too far for the reach of the three-inch twelve. Not knowing what else to do I risked another kiss. A funny thing happened. Not so much funny as odd. That galloping coyote slammed on the anti-locks and skidded to a stop. Looking my way. Looking hungry. I was encouraged and kissed again. Even though George did not seem to be interested, the coyote sure was. He started a sneak on my hideout. When he was maybe thirty-five yards out I did the dirty deed. The Kiss of Death and other close-in calls can be a good friend to the screamer. There is something about the squeak and the low moan that causes the coyote, the cat, and the fox appetite alarm to sound.

Many experienced callers use some sort of close-in call to do about the same. I was working high desert down Texas way with Murry Burnham and was permitted a look at his Ace of Spades. We were set up within scrubby vegetation and Murry was blowing on a modified deer call (later marketed as the Black Beauty). Murry saw the coyote coming (we both did) from a somewhat long distance, coming slow as a paranoid should. The Ph.D. hung a couple of hundred yards out, pretty much hid in the brush and at an awkward angle for either gun. Murry's mouth started the damnedest moany groany sound I have heard and that sound caused the coyote to unhang, trotting in as if on a leash. Murry used the .222, causing the coyote to get dead. Later, after coaxing, he

The Kiss of Death can cause a bashful to turn bold.

demonstrated. He makes the sound, he said, with lips drawn over teeth, then making the suck that causes the moan.

I use mouth sounds to communicate to predators often, usually to articulate the Kiss of Death. Other good sounds for close customers are the whine and the growl. Each is easily done and each will increase the customer's interest. The growl and the whine are most often used to cause a running critter to pause, maybe used to cause a hid critter to unhide.

Those who might feel unsure about their ability to kiss, moan, growl, and whine might like to know there is a bunch of moaners and squeakers on the market, a subspecies of call marketed under the generic classification of close-in calls. Such will be of two or three general types. One is a rubber bulb of about walnut size containing a metal reed. Squeezing to force air through the reed causes a high pitched squeal, a mouse-squeak sort of a sound. I have used Velcro to fasten one of the bulbs to the forearm of the gun stock so the little sucker could be compressed while the gun was in shooting position, a handy modification during some customer situations.

Another type of close-in call is the one I call the moaner. All such consist of two slats of plastic, put together harmonica-like, with a rubber band (Burnham Brothers & Johnny Stewart) or a shim of metal (P. S. Olt) as a reed. The call is caused to moan as air is sent through. The sound produced is surprisingly Burnham-like, and is surprisingly effective. Some call companies have in the past (maybe still do) offered tube models that can be blown as a close-in call, some having devised a cunning tube that can be manipulated to sound close-in sounds as well as the generic scream.

Murry Burnham uses his mouth to moan the customers sure-kill close.

140

How far can a keen-eared critter hear the K of D, the whine, the squeal, or the moan? Depends. The carry can be affected by structure and by wind. If the setup is in somewhat open country, if there is not enough wind to mention, I consider close-in calls to be effective out to a couple of hundred yards, maybe more. Those who permit the battery-powered cassette or chip player to do the calling will want to know about close-in options. Close-in sounds are available on both the cassette player and the chip player. Those who use the cassette player can obtain tapes containing baby cottontail distress squeals and bird distress chirpings, both dandy as close-in calls. About the same is available for the chip player, that device having a handy feature. A hunter wishing to shift from long-range screams to the close-in sound need only flick a switch to make the change.

I do not use any of the close-in calls on every stand. Neither will you. The long-range scream gets the job done for me on most stands. There are times, however, when a kiss or other close-in calls cause a reluctant customer to turn eager. I urge all screamers to practice the kiss, the moan, the whine, and the growl, and urge all to include a couple of close-in calls within the collection.

Chapter 22

Tracks and Tracking

Every animal that walks the woods leaves evidence of passage. That evidence can be as obvious as a gallon or so of bear poop or can be as discreet as the partial track left by a light-footed cacomistile. The discovery and interpretation of animal tracks, animal offal, and other signs of passage can cause a good hunter to become a great hunter. How so? The most talented screamer cannot call critters if none are present to be called. And though the presence of sign does not guarantee a critter is close enough to hear the screams, the discovery of stale sign tells the hunter he or she is in critter habitat. The discovery of fresh sign delivers a more encouraging message. The animal has been here recently and may still be close. Read on to discover examples where I used tracks, poop, and a prey carcass to find fur.

The weather front from the west had caused a wet storm to deposit a sifting of snow the night before the hunt. Knowing the wetted clay base caused an uncertain surface I drove the forest two-track using more than ordinary caution, headed for dry country to do a bit of screaming to coyote. The partial track was obscure, barely seen by the roadside. Pausing to investigate I was pleased to discover the track to be two toes and a partial heel pad, almost surely made by a bobcat. A big bobcat, or at least a bobcat with one big foot. And even though the land beyond the track was juniper duff in the sun, causing a snow melt that removed the tracks, the partial track told me the Robert Kitty had been by since the snow stopped, maybe within the past four hours. Toes and heel pad suggested direction of travel. I parked, grabbed my stuff, and set off in that direction.

Even though I did not find a second track I did find a brushy canyon containing rock overhangs along the rim, a dandy place for a bobcat to lay out the last of the storm. I made the setup and started the screaming. Ten minutes later I was walking to the truck carrying the carcass of a dandy baileyi bobcat.

I used coyote crap to cause me to enjoy a day of calling action while on a hunt with Chuck Spearman, a skilled screamer and at that time publisher of *Trapper & Predator Caller* magazine. Chuck and I had spent the day calling the foothills of the KOFA mountain range for coyote. Poor luck had caused us to relocate. Even though towing the travel trailer at speed limit (perhaps a bit more) I was able to see unusual amounts of coyote scat along the roadside, all

Chuck Spearman skins a half-day collection of coyote taken from Scat Acres.

showing mesquite bean residue. I passed the area by to find a familiar camp and we called close to that camp the next day, having moderate luck. Early the next morning, well before daylight, I turned the 4x4 west, to Coyote Crap Acres.

I do not recall how many coyote Chuck and I called that day. I know it was a hell of a lot, and maybe more. It is likely we might have ignored that ten-mile stretch of country alongside the U.S. highway if not for the roadside deposits. Can you stand one more?

I was hunting a PJ ridge within the North Kaibab National Forest for mule deer. It was the late hunt, the one that has big-racked mulie bucks down on the winter range where they become somewhat vulnerable. I was out early, just as I had been for the past several days, using the binoculars to investigate side hills. Walking to a new high point I came across sign of a drag, maybe a place where a hunter had drug a deer. I took a close look and found evidence of covering. The hunter had been a mountain lion. I followed the drag trail and counted three coverings. The last hid the remains of a decent buck. I searched out a setup and started a screaming. The female lion came as a tan ghost that materialized eighty yards out. She weighed 95 pounds, big to extra big for a female lion on the Kaibab.

Even though I have written on tracks and other sign in the individual chapters on species, I consider it to be proper to write more, covering tracks and tracking from a more general aspect. Critter tracks vary in size as the age and body size of the animal varies. The track of an adult

144

bobcat, as an example, might be about two inches across. The track left by an immature bobcat might be obviously less. The point is, do not expect every track found to be exactly the same as the last.

Track identification would be less difficult if all tracks were on level ground and imprinted on dust, mud, or snow, and were fresh. And offered a series of tracks so that gait could be determined, offered the advantage found when tracks left by the front feet could be compared to tracks left by the rear feet. Common sense says such is not so. Some tracks are partials found on ground that resists imprinting. Some, as was the case with the roadside bobcat track, consist of a single partial. A single track, even a single partial, can show an overlapping of rear foot over front foot, causing further difficulty. A tracker who hopes to read all the track offers must be astute during discovery and reasonable during interpretation.

Multiple tracks offer a lot of information. A string of tracks, to the eyes of an experienced tracker, offer information on definite direction of travel, whether the animal is hunting or traveling, showing if the animal was at the walk, the trot, or the run, and even offering a determination of age (adult or sub-adult) and sometimes sex.

The widely distributed black bear, being larger than all of the U.S. land predators except the uncommon grizzly, is a fine example of a critter that leaves a lot of evidence; tracks, trashings, clawings, and the always impressive crappings. Even though the bear is mostly nocturnal, and many select exceedingly private habitat causing them to be seldom seen, the hunter who looks will find evidence of bear presence. That evidence can tell a lot to those willing to look and learn.

The track left by the hind foot of a bear is somewhat similar to the shape of the human foot. The track left by the front foot of the bear is a lot like the looks of a partially clenched human hand. A bear track, or series of tracks, can show the usual: how long ago the bear stood, walked or ran there; direction of travel; whether the bear was traveling or feeding; and even supply good evidence of bear size. How so size? Biologic inquiry has suggested an informal formula. A front foot track measuring 4-1/4" or more was likely made by a mature black bear. A hind foot track measuring 7-1/2" or more was likely made by a mature black bear.

Other bear track trivia follows: The bear is a plantigrade, just as we are. What in hell does that mean? Bear and folks like us walk on the flat of their feet, putting the weight of the body on the entire foot. The pad of the foot shows an elongated triangle fronted by oval toe-prints. The large toe on a bear, unlike the large toe on a human foot, lays to the outside of the foot. The marks left by the toes will be fronted by indentations left by the non-retractable claws. The placement of the claw marks can be an indicator to species. Some habitat has the black bear sharing the range with the grizzly bear. Even though some grizzly are larger than some black bear, all are not, causing track size alone to be an undependable identifier. The griz has much longer and more massive claws. Grizzly tracks, much of the time, have a significant gap between toe and claw.

Want more? The walking gait (or pace) of the black bear will show the hind foot imprint slightly forward of the front. The imprints left by front and rear foot will at times overlap. The inside toe might not register when the track is left in light dust or shallow mud, causing the track to show only four toes. Tracks left by a bear at the gallop are distinctive. The hind feet are brought forward of the front feet at every leap.

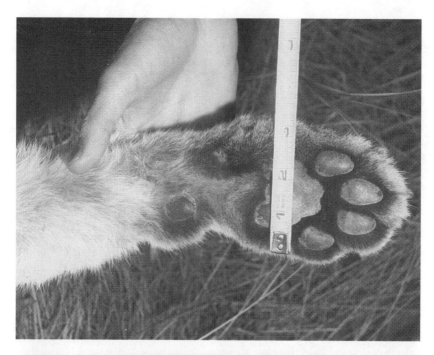

A fresh track in dust, mud, or snow can cause a lion screamer to get lucky.

Black bear are like most other land predators in their hunting and travel habits. Bear use well-established trails. The trail used might take the bear from their feeding grounds to their bedding grounds. At times there is not a difference between the two. Fresh bear tracks found within an area that shows recent feeding activity should be an encouragement. Chances are good the bear is nearby. A feeding bear leaves evidence of such. Fruit, acorns, and other masts are stripped from branches in the most messy manner. Rotting logs, those containing grubs, ants, and other edibles, are trashed. Boulders are rolled to expose edibles on the moist underside. Plops, in cattle country, will be turned for the same reason. Raccoon, skunks, crows, and ravens, and even the wild turkey are also ploppers. Finding a turned plop without supporting evidence is not enough to determine bear presence.

The generic bear has an urge to bite, claw, and rub. Trees are the main target but wooden signs receive a fair share of attention. This trashing of trees and signs is often territorial behavior. Bear scat is distinctive and can say a lot about the bear that made the deposit. The size and shape of the offal causes the deposit to be bear-specific. Contents can cause current feeding habits to be obvious. The bear that dines on meat or carrion

Bear size can be guessed by a measure of the track.

might deposit a black and odoriferous goo containing hair. A bear who has dined on insects retrieved from a rotting log might leave scat containing minor amounts of wood. A bear feeding on nuts or berries will leave scat containing nut hulls, or maybe leaves and seeds from a berry bush. Bear crap might be formed or formless. Stools may have a diameter of a couple of inches but are usually less. The formless deposit can be of impressive size. Dinner plate big. Maybe bigger.

The inquiry and evidence written about bear sign applies almost equally to the sign left by every other animal. A careful reading of the writings devoted to the sign left by specific species, to be found in the chapters describing the hunting of that species, is encouraged.

Collared Peccary (Javelina) print

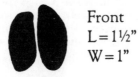

Front
L = 1½"
W = 1"

Rear
L = 1¼"
W = 1"

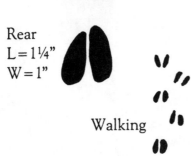

Walking

Mountain Lion print

Front
L = 3"
W = 3½"

Rear
L = 3"
W = 3"

Double Print

Front
L = 2½"
W = 2"

 Rear
L = 2"
W = 1½"

Double Print

Red Fox print

Front
L = 2¼"
W = 1½"

Rear
L = 3¼"
W = 1½"

Double Print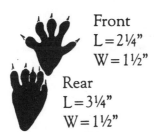

Raccoon print

Black Bear print

Front
L = 4½"
W = 3½"

Rear
L = 7"
W = 3½"

Double Print

Bobcat print

Front
L = 2"
W = 3¼"

Rear
L = 2¼"
W = 2"

Double Print

Coyote print

 Front
L = 2½"
W = 2"

 Rear
L = 2¼"
W = 1½"

Double Print

Gray Fox print

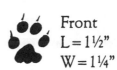 Front
L = 1½"
W = 1¼"

Rear
L = 1¼"
W = 1"

Double Print

Chapter 23

Tough Calls

A discussion of why animals come to the call appeared in an earlier chapter. A following chapter investigated the circumstances that might elicit non-response. In both chapters I mentioned the Case of the Ph.D. Critter. Ph.D.s are animals who have seen a rodeo or two and have decided dying rabbits are not for them. The earning of the doctorate comes, most often, when an animal owning a set of virgin ears comes at the gallop to find a welcome of hot lead waiting. Such, repeated a time or two, can cause the most cooperative of critters to turn to a more healthful diet. Inept callers, or unlucky ones, can beat up on a chunk of critter habitat to cause all within to become tough calls.

Even though such become paranoid to the tenth power, a screamer who uses the correct technique can scream at a paranoid individual, can scream within a heavily-called area, can compensate in other ways to find calling excitement and maybe collect a bit of fur. The technique that permits all is one I call THINKING. The tool required is basic. Those who use the THINKING technique must have a brain. Many of the critter callers I have met (maybe even most) have had such.

My honest nature causes me to say I have not used THINKING to solve tough call problems for all of my critter calling career. There was a time, at first, when I had learned the basics needed to bring a critter close somewhat regularly, when I repeated those basics on every stand and did not concern myself with those super smarts. I figured, I guess, there were plenty of dumb ones to be called. Why waste time working the Ph.D.s when two or three sophomores could be called with about the same effort?

Somewhere along the way, I am not sure just when, the critter calling turned tough. Screamers within the writing racket, guys like me, hunted hard, hunted successfully, and then wrote about both for nationally distributed publications. Interest and hunting pressure increased. The dummies disappeared early, leaving only the tough calls. When I tired of being whipped I broke out the old brain and invented THINKING.

My years of THINKING have caused me to subdivide the technique to best respond to specific problems. One such is a category I call TARGETING.

What is TARGETING? How can you use such to increase your screaming success? It works this way. Targeting is a technique that causes the screamer to carefully consider the goals of each hunt. While thinking along that path, the screamer identifies the circumstances that will most affect that goal-directed hunt, positives and negatives. An analysis of each will suggest ways to maximize results. The THINKING/TARGETING technique is best explained using an actual example.

Gary "Slammer" Hull is a big fish guide on the Kenai Peninsula during much of the summer. He also works as big a game guide, guiding hunters to caribou, moose, goat, sheep, and even griz, all such, for much of the winter. A year or so ago the Slammer wrote to offer a trade hunt. He would host me and the other Beastmaster during a big game hunt or a big fish hunt in Alaska. As payback, he asked to come to America (That is what Alaskans call the land within the lower 48) to have the Beastmasters provide a series of screamings, particularly aimed at one of the cats, maybe bob and maybe cougar. Larry and I said sure. The fall of 1994 found us on the Iliamna Barren Grounds hunting for a trophy bull.

The hunt was interesting. We were within a tent camp for eight days. It rained every day but one. On that day it snowed. The wind blew at fifty mph for every day but one. On that day the wind blew at sixty mph. Caribou, cows, calves, dink bulls, and trophy bulls were conspicuous by their absence. Hard hunting, perseverance, and luck caused each of us to take damnfine bulls. At the same time we had the opportunity to scream at a good part of Alaska.

The payback hunt started on the Iliamna Barren Grounds as Larry and I called to caribou.

The Slammer came to America three times and collected a bobcat, a couple of gray fox, many, many coyote; and was there when Larry called and killed a cougar.

The first payback hunt took place during February. Why then? THINKING/TARGETING mainly. Knowing Gary hoped for a cat we chose a time when the cats are roaming the land in an effort to shake the sugar tree. And dependent on the degree of desperation present, each was likely to make the look both night and day.

Knowing the target was of the cat kind, we hunted cat country. We drove the 4x4s to the end of the road and walked to the roughest and toughest country we could find. Not the kind of country likely to hold a lot of coyote, and that means we were in country that did not offer a lot of action. The action, when it happened, was apt to be of the kitty kind.

THINKING/TARGETING also suggested we scream out cat calls. Long moans, mostly, the kind most likely to interest a cat of the cougar kind, and also the bob'. T/T further advised to stay on the stand to give the cat customer plenty of time. Most screamings continued for a minimum of thirty minutes. Some were longer.

Gary Hull came to America three times during the paybacks. On one of those trips he was able to gun down a close-range bobcat. On another hunt he was there when Larry gunned down a cougar. The Slammer also participated in wet work involving gray fox and more coyote than I care to mention. The T/T technique made it all possible. A second example that shows T/T to good advantage follows.

The desert subdivision was high dollar housing. The folks living there were lovers. They loved every hog, every burro, and every coyote. They did, that is, before the poodles and the kitties started to disappear. Some looked suspiciously at the coyote that patrolled between the houses on a somewhat regular basis. Indoctrinated in the American concept of jurisprudence, however, many refused to make a harsh judgment as long as there remained a reasonable doubt. That reasonable doubt diminished when an examination of coyote turds showed poodle hair and kitty fur. The residents turned ugly. Some became berserk. Some (I am not making this up) collected turds, sorted them out according to the color of the evidence, and conducted a service. Right after the ceremony they called 911 and 911 called me.

Screaming to subdivision coyote can be a challenge. There is always a neophyte screamer who has messed with the coyotes' minds enough to cause paranoia. Larry and I packed up the junk and headed there with wet work on our mind. Nearly all calls took place close to the paved highway that led into and led from the luxury subdivision or close to one of the secondary roads that circled. Larry and I parked close to the road and made a walkabout to call the coyote, and we did call a few. Trouble was, the survivors turned into tough customers. Some were paranoid because of the screaming done by the tyro. Others became paranoid because of me and Larry. It did not take long for them to connect the slowing cadence of a combustion engine, the sound of a truck parking to the screaming sticks that go boom.

The Drop and Drive caused coyote to be seldom seen within the high-dollar housing lands.

What to do? We T/Ted. We thunk on it, identified problems, struggled mightily, and gave birth to the drop and drive technique. One Beastmaster slowed enough to allow the second to make the dismount and then drove on. The gunner would walk a decent distance, set up to scream away from the road, and start the music. Considerable wet work followed. Enough, at least, to provide a measure of revenge to the bereaved. Enough to cause the sighting of a coyote to be somewhat unusual.

The Beastmasters refined the DROP & DRIVE during a hunt involving Gordy Krahn, editor of *Trapper & Predator Caller* magazine. It was day three of a three-day hunt, a hunt where circumstances had caused Gordo to miss a bunch of coyote. Gordo said his scope sighted centerfire had been mishandled by the airline, causing a misalignment (now there's an alibi for you). Anyway, Larry slowed the Dodge diesel to make the drop. Gordy and I walked.

Even though the setup was in hard-hit country, close enough to the interstate to hear the rumble of the nineteen wheelers (we count the spare), we called two coyote on that setup. Not taking a chance that Gordo might embarrass himself further, I shot both, earning the new nickname of "Quickdraw." We used the DRIVE-DROP-DRIVE TECHNIQUE, modified, to hunt another bunch of uncallable land. Much of the country in northern Arizona is high plains. Flat land, some with gently rolling hills, short grass prairie. Much of that country is favored fawning areas for antelope, for deer, and for elk. The coyote know this and hit those areas hard, particularly during late spring when fawning takes place. The plains were hard to hunt. No place to hide the truck. No place to hide the hunter. A perfect place for drive and drop. One Beastmaster would dismount while the second drove away. The hunter half would find a likely looking place and lay flat on the back to stare at the sky, to scream at the pale daytime moon. The screamer would pause often to listen for the sound of galloping paws. When that happened he would raise up out of the grass to do business. Ahhh, the look on those coyote kissers.

Want another? Sure, why the hell not. We were headed for the boulder jumbles that decorate a part of central Arizona, a kind of country friendly to gangs of gray fox, clusters of cats, more than a few coyote and even the occasional cougar. That's the good news. The bad news? We were not the only screamers who knew of this critter heaven. Screamers of every shape and size, every nationality, came to the boulders for early season screamings. The dumb coyotes turned dead. Those that survived turned paranoid. A lack

The Drop and Drive works well within flat lands having no structure to hide the truck.

of action would cause many of the screamers to move on, searching for a new honey hole. After a bit of rest some of the educated critters would become somewhat trusting. A few would sneak in for a sly look at a scream, sometimes providing a shot opportunity. Knowing there was a hell of a lot of critters (maybe more) within the boulders, Larry and I whipped out the THINKING technique.

The problem, as we saw it, was one of association. The fox, the bobcat, the coyote, even the somewhat learning-challenged cougar, had come to associate the sound of the rabbit distress scream with pain and emotional trauma. What to do? This one is easy. Change the sound. We did and enjoyed moderate success. We needed to do more. We moved the THINKING technique a step further, and thus was born the infamous DOUBLE SCREAM to DOUBLE YOUR PLEASURE technique.

Knowing that all gray fox, all mountain lion and all coyote enjoy the sound of a gray fox in pain, we chose that somewhat hoarse complaint to be leg one of the double call. Larry would play the gray fox distress scream. At the same time I would sound cottontail rabbit distress screams on the TallyHo. Did it work? Hell, yes, it worked. I shot the Moose at so many fox that my shoulder hurt for a week.

Later, hoping to improve, we modified. We took the gray fox distress and a cottontailed rabbit distress and married those two sounds within one tape. That may have worked even better. Other options exist. The Gray Fox Distress and the Yellowhammer Woodpecker Distress. Baby Cottontail Distress and Gray Fox Distress. Gray Fox and Canine Puppies. Others. Such couplings offer a couple of advantages. A new sound is one. A sound that stays somewhat new is the other. Making your own combinations causes you to carry a unique sound, one not available to the generic screamer.

Bill Del Monte explains the concept of recording two or more sounds upon a single tape.

Can you stand one more? Much of the country Larry and I call is desert covered with creosote bushes, a more-than head-high shrub sometimes called greasewood. Such country can be dandy for shot-

Placing the player upon the flats and the gun upon the hill caused several Ph.D.s to turn dead.

gunners when the greasewood is spaced to permit vision and shooting lanes. Trouble is, much of the greasewood country is so thick a screamer cannot find such. Most callers drive on by to find country more friendly. Those uncalled areas turned into a coyote sanctuary, offering the kind of challenge any Beastmaster worth the name must respond to.

Some of the crowded creosote country was interrupted by knobs of rock and cactus rising above the highest creosote, enough to provide a vision down into the meager spacing between the creosote. Staying high, we figured, would allow us to look down on the coyote, maybe see enough to cause them to get dead. Calling from on high was not that successful. The coyote would come, stay within the thickest of the greasewood, and pause long enough to look up at the source of the screams. When they did not see the rabbit, saw instead four hundred pounds of hunters, they made the retreat. Back to THINKING.

A main part of the problem came about because the coyote looked high on that bare hill to reconnoiter the source of the sound. Causing the sound to stay low while we Beastmasters stayed high seemed sensible. We taped a couple of minutes of silence onto the start of a jackrabbit distress tape. How did we do that? Easy. We put tape into a recorder, rewound, then hit the record button. Didn't talk. The tape was removed after a couple of minutes.

We took the tape player to the greasewoods to hide it within a particularly thick part, one that had small openings around. We hit the GO button and made the stroll to half-way up the hill. The two minutes of silence permitted a leisurely setup. The coyotes, when they came, galloped or trotted close and then started a stalk. None even glanced to the hill. We had plenty of opportunity to shoulder, sight, and shoot. And even though the shots were somewhat long range (averaging about 200 yards), shooting .22-250s across the steady support offered by a Harris BiPod (or the knees) caused hits to be routine.

THINKING will work in about any kind of country. Even though the techniques described above might not exactly fit the situations of the kind of country you hunt, the essence of the technique of THINKING surely will.

Chapter 24

Calling Bear

We glassed the bear at about daylight, while the air was cool, before the sun heated the cactus-covered ridges to cause the air to be choked with heat waves. The critter was an insignificant black speck in the prickly pear at an estimated three-mile distance. Mike Mell cased the spotting scope with the 20X lens. "That bear will be bedding as soon as the sun shows," he mused, "and I am betting it will bed close to the feed grounds." Even though my own knowledge did not match that of my wife's cousin, a licensed big game guide, his assessment made sense. Why would the bear travel far away from the sweet and juicy fruit of the prickly pear cactus to find a bed? We gathered up our junk and returned to our open air camp. Later, after a leisurely breakfast, we loaded the day pack and the packing frames, and were on our way to the feed grounds.

I started the screaming at about 4 p.m., using a Trophy Model Circe fitted with a jackrabbit reed. I called as I almost always call to bear, blowing hard to add a hoarseness to the screams, and blowing so that the individual screams were drawn out. I did my best to cause the screaming to simulate the agony of a larger prey animal, perhaps an immature or adult deer. The bear showed thirty minutes into the call, appearing upon the back of a distant ridge, pausing to make the reconnoiter. I stayed still. When the bear started the move to descend the ridge to head for the prickly pear patch, I screamed again, reducing volume somewhat, hoping the bear would hear. He heard. The bear started to lumber our way, paused to back its butt to a boulder to enjoy a scratch, and then came again. I took the shot when the 175 pound sow was a hundred yards out. We did the dirty work and made the packout. It was near midnight when we arrived at camp.

Even though that hunt on the San Carlos Apache Indian Reservation took place many years ago, the technique of glass, stalk, and scream is as good now as it was then. Fall bear in the West often feed upon open and semi-open hillsides, permitting long distance discovery. Stalking close to such-sighted bear to make a screaming causes success to come more often.

Black bear can be found in good numbers throughout Alaska and Canada. Blacks can also be found in the mountainous areas of most of the continental United States, in the hardwood forests of the East, and in the swamps of some Southern states. North central

Mexico has a fair number. Some jurisdictions do not have a handle on total bear population. My home state of Arizona did not before a game and fish biologist used foot snares to capture and collar bear of a rough mountain range called the Mazatzals. Only adult bear were collared, for two good reasons. Placing a collar on an immature bear could cause that bear to suffocate as it matured, as the neck increased in size. Reason two had to do with territoriality. The study was aimed to determine the number of bear territories within the range. Adult bear are territorial; immature bear are not.

The study provided surprising information. The seven-year study suggested a territorial bear density within the Mazatzals (pronounced Mat-ah-zals, don't ask me why) of about one territorial bear to the square mile. The chaparral-covered canyons and ridges offer all a bear needed to prosper. Thick high brush to cover movement. A primitive area with few roads, keeping out most of the humans. Plenty of fruits and mast to keep his big belly full. And an almost complete lack of houndsmen. The high and thick chaparral causes difficulty for the hounds and for horseback houndsmen. The Mazatzal study, and other studies, caused Arizona wildlife professionals to estimate a population of 2,000-3,000 on non-Indian lands. Substantial bear populations can be found within the boundaries of the White Mountain Apache, the San Carlos Apache, and some parts of the Navajo Indian reservations. Adding such to

Some black bear are brown or red. The name refers to species, not color.

the Arizona estimate causes that total to increase. All permit bear hunting by non-Indians who have paid the proper fees.

Black bear do not live exclusively in the Arizona chaparral. Populations can be found in the mountains and in the canyons that traverse those mountains, about every part of the state, actually, excepting the deserts.

The black bear, it should be mentioned, refers to a species and not to a color. The black bear species might be black but might also be brown, cinnamon, or red. All color phases. The brown bear, sometimes used to describe the brown phase of the black bear, is correctly used to describe a sub-species of grizzly bear.

Bear mate in early summer. The mating period might last for a month. Male and female caress during that time and engage in much moaning and bawling. When the love affair ends the two go their separate ways; they do not remain even good friends. The male returns to his territory and the female to hers. The cubs are born the following winter when the sow is denned in the fitful sleep sometimes called hibernation. The one to four cubs are born small but grow rapidly on their diet of Momma's milk. They will be about a foot and a half long when they follow the sow out of the den at the starting of spring.

Head size identifies this as a BIG bear. Arizona hunter Pat Lee estimated live weight at 450 pounds.

Bear spend the summer and fall building fat so that they might survive the winter. Yearling cubs return to the den with the sow. The bear "hibernation" is a fitful sleep interrupted by periods of fitful wakefulness. The bear does not eat during this period nor does it defecate. A grass fecal plug has jammed the bowels.

Territorial bear are the biggest and baddest of the bear. And they are the smartest, the most difficult to hunt. Young bear are tolerated until they reach about two years of age. The female is tired of fooling with them then, and she is ready to breed again. Those too hardheaded to leave to find a territory of their own might be killed. The young bear so displaced, having low survival skills, are apt to wander about until they come upon a hunter.

I said in the chapter dealing with tracks and tracking that bear preferred wild and remote country. That is true. Some bear, particularly the wanderers, will do the opposite. Such become "nuisance" bear when they hang around campgrounds or close to human housing. The sentence for such behavior, much of the time, is death.

Black bear that develop a taste for beef can also be sentenced to death. A hungry bear, one coming out of hibernation with an empty belly or one headed for hibernation and hoping to do so with a reserve of fat, will find it difficult to resist the sight of a frisky and vulnerable calf. Black bear also eat carrion. Livestock that die of natural causes, even unnatural causes not bear related, often end up in a bear's belly. Such bear, much of the time, are guilty of nothing more serious than stealing a buzzard's supper. The main meal of the bear, through much of his range, is berries, fruits, and nuts. Insects. Garbage. Bear are opportunistic feeders. They take what the country has to offer.

I presented a comprehensive discussion on bear tracks and other sign within the chapter on tracks and tracking. There is no good reason to repeat that information here. It is proper, I think, to write a bit about bear, bear habits, and bear habitats.

Black bear can vary greatly in size. Many hunters have trouble estimating the trophy potential of the bear they see. Here is a simple way to recognize a fully adult bear, one with trophy potential. A bear has ears that are five inches long, true of both mature and immature bear. A bear who has ears that seem too big for the head is likely to be an immature. A bear that has ears that are widely separated by the skull, ears that seem to be insignificant in relation to head size, is likely to be a fully mature bear. A trophy.

Some idea of bear size can be determined from the track. A front foot track that measures more than 4-1/4" from heel to toe and more than 4-1/4" wide was likely left by an adult male—a boar. A hind foot track that is more than 7-1/2" long and more than 4" wide was likely made by an adult male. A really big boar bear is likely to leave a front foot track that measures more than 5-1/2" and a hind foot track that measures more than 9". Such a track is likely to have been left by a bear weighing 300 pounds or more.

As mentioned earlier in this chapter, I like a call that is on the coarse or hoarse side for a bear screaming. I prefer the sound of a series of long and drawn out screams rather than the short and choppy series I sometimes use for coyote or fox. The sound I send imitates the distress scream of a fawn deer. Might such a sound interest a bear? A wildlife professional working within bear country on the sprawling Navajo Indian Reservation says yes. Pat Ryan and Kathleen McCoy conducted a study to determine the cause of mortality among mule deer fawns. They had captured and collared a particularly vocal fawn and had left to return to the truck when they heard the fawn repeating the bleating. They returned just in time to see an adult bear leaving, with the fawn in mouth. Pat gave chase but lost the race. He returned to the truck, grabbed the antennae, and followed the beeps, eventually catching up with the fawn-loving bear. Pat used sticks, stones, and strong language to cause the bear to give up the still living fawn. No happy ending, however. Trauma, bear slobbers, maybe human handling, caused the doe to abandon the fawn. Death came a day later.

Larry finds tracks outside a Navajo aspen pole corral. Bear climbed within, killed a ewe, and left to dine alone.

The Navajo consider the bear to be one of a class of witches (called Skinwalkers) capable of changing from animal to human form. That belief provokes a fear that causes the Navajo to avoid the bear when possible. No killing, even when a bear shows he or she is a bad neighbor. Under those circumstances the Navajo wildlife people call in a non-Indian hunter to do the wet work. Larry and I hunted such a bear when the critter climbed within aspen pole corrals to select a sheep, and did so on a mighty regular basis.

The mutton-lover hung out in a rough country basin choked with Gambel's oak, and those oak were loaded with acorns. Even so, apparently, the bear tired of an all acorn diet, hankering for a bit of mutton.

Larry hunted the basin, surrounded by bear sign in the form of acorn husks and even a bit of wool. Larry used a Lohman C-280 open reed (plastic reed) call to blow out a series of desperate screams. The bear came during one such screaming and was .30-06ed. The red-brown female weighed an estimated 150 pounds. How can we be sure the bear Larry shot was the mutton lover? I could be cute and say the bear had a sheepish look about her. I will not. I say instead, there is no sure way. The bear Larry called and killed was of the same color and about the same size as the one seen raiding the corral. To the Navajo, and to Larry, that is close enough.

Prime time for bear calling is dawn and dusk. I like dawn best, sometimes starting the call before daylight, but no shooting until legal light arrives. Dusk can be nearly as good but carries a disadvantage. A slow bear, at times, will show after legal shooting light ends. The nature of the bear body causes him to be a tough kill. The hide is thick and hairy. That hide covers a layer of fat that can be inches thick. Under the fat is massive muscle and stout bone. A good bear gun should push out enough lead to get the critter's attention. The right kind of cartridge will not cause the bullet to move so fast it will explode within the hide, the fat or the muscle. Controlled expansion is best, permitting the bullet to penetrate to the necessaries.

Even under the best of circumstances screaming to a bear can be slow work. The mutton-eater Larry called in the Navajo highlands took 25 minutes to respond, even though Larry was set up close. Bear do not respond to the call dependably. Only the bear know why. I have had bear start a hard run upon hearing the first scream, running away from the screams. Others, maybe even the same bear on a different day, will run to the call. The nature of the bear, much of the time, causes it to come at the stroll. I recommend plenty of time on the bear stand, a couple of hours are not too much if encouragement is present.

A hunter might scream at a dozen setups and not call a bear. And then, unexpectedly, a big black shape (or brown, red, maybe even white) will loom up. The excitement created by that response

The glass, walk, and scream technique can be effective within open country.

causes all of the hard work to be worthwhile. Expert bear hunter Mike Mell has guided hunters to a couple of dozen bear, one a 430-pound (estimated weight) red carrying a silky coat. "Most of the bear I have called came out of brushy canyons," Mike says. That brush, much of the time, is scrub oak and manzanita, both shrubs that produce bear groceries. Mike calls most of his bear during the months of September and October, at about the beginning of the Arizona bear season. He recommends using the spotting scope to locate a feeding bear (as we did on the San Carlos hunt) and then stalking close to take the shot or make the call.

Mike Mell verifies that bear do not respond to the screaming dependably. Mike and a hunter watched a bear go into a brushy canyon during one hunt and figured he had bedded. They stalked close, to the canyon rim, and watched for nearly an hour, hoping to sight the bedded bear. No luck. Why didn't they drop off into the canyon to make an effort to flush the bear? Not a good idea, according to Mike. Too often the bear will slip away and not be seen.

After an hour of scanning Mike used the varmint call (a Trophy Model Circe) to start a screaming. Still nothing. Mike eventually threw a chunk of log down into the canyon and the bear ambled out.

Bear guide Riney Maxwell hunts rough country along the Arizona-New Mexico border. Rough country is the key to successful bear calling, according to Riney. "Rough country is where the bear stay," Riney says. "I have called dozens of bear out of that kind of country. The rougher the better." Riney screamed country that was a bit too rough during one hunt. A bear was downed within the steep bottom of a double rough canyon and Riney led his horse, following a sorry game trail, hoping to get somewhat close. The horse misstepped and fell to the bottom. The horse, a good one, was dead before he hit the bottom.

Maxwell has his best luck calling to bear early in the morning and late in the evening. He seldom calls after 10 a.m., and does not start again until about 3 p.m. Riney uses a wood Circe and prefers the jackrabbit reed, blowing loud for the first thirty second series. He pauses then to glass. Another series follows after a couple of minutes. The scream-glass cooperation continues for about thirty minutes.

"You need to give a bear plenty of time to show," Maxwell says. "The bear does not race to the call and is further slowed within rough country. Too many hunters give up too soon and walk away when a bear is on the way."

The Blue Wilderness area Maxwell hunts is some of the roughest in the state, in any state. Maxwell rides horseback to make a camp away from roads and within area too rough to interest many other hunters. On one memorable day he sighted seventeen head of bear. That is the kind of country bear hunters love. Some of that crowd of bear will almost certainly appreciate a well executed screaming. The pack out? That's another story.

Chapter 25

Calling Bobcat

There are a hell of a lot of bobcat (maybe more) in the wilds of the West. The state of Arizona, as an example, reports a harvest of about eight thousand bobs (trapping, calling, and opportunistic taking) year after year. Arizona biologists have estimated an adult population of about 40,000 bobcat. Impressive? Not really. Not when you consider that the neighboring state of California is home to an estimated 74,700 with an annual harvest of 15,000. The estimated population for the eleven Western states that are the bobcats' favored habitat totals about a quarter of a million, give or take a bobcat or two. Add the generous populations found within the Lone Star State, and in Dixie, and that total is considerably increased.

Knowing all of that, knowing of the number of bobcat around, one wonders why the bobcat and bobcat nature are so poorly understood. That lack of understanding can cause screamers to have a difficult time while hunting the bobcat.

Bobcat size is a good example. The long-legged nature of the bobcat, coupled with his furry aspect, causes hunters to be a poor judge of bobcat size. The 40- or 50-pound trophy (estimated weight) can shrink to about half that when the weight is verified on honest scales. You want the truth? I have called and killed and trapped and killed a bunch of bobcat during the last half century. Nearly all were weighed on honest scales. The largest was a tom called to the ten-gauge while on a high country hunt (Arizona) with George Oakey. That big blue back weighed 26 pounds. Conversations with other honest trappers and callers cause them say about the same.

I do not say no bobcat can be bigger. Oscar Cronk of Wiscasset, Maine, and a bluetick hound named Emerson took a 35 pounder from Maine's Allagash during 1984. A 55-pound bobcat came out of Lake County, Ohio, a few years back. Neither of those husky Roberts came close to the all-time fat cat; that honor likely goes to a 69-pound cat-and-a-half that came out of Colorado many years ago. Those fat cats, in my view, are freaks of nature, about as rare as a 600-pound human at a convention of nudists. Each is a sight not often seen but one that is remembered for one hell of a long time.

Other aspects of the bobcat nature are often as obscure. The hunter who hopes to scream a bobcat close on a regular basis cannot permit that poor perception. Knowing about bobcat habitat and

This tom cat was tracked to the lip of a brush-choked canyon and screamed to the camera.

bobcat habits can cause increased success. Bobcat can be found from southern Canada to South America and from coast to coast within the continental United States. Color can vary as geography varies. Cats of the Northwest typically show a chocolate tinting. Southwestern bobcat range from light gray to almost silver. The color of bobcat everywhere is a mixture of browns, buffs, and whites. Body fur is almost always spotted but the spots can be inconspicuous. The belly is snow-white, showing contrasting black spots. The tail is insignificant. Ears are usually tufted on fully adult bobcat.

Bobcat mostly work the night shift but will hunt night and day when so provoked by weather or hunger. Even so, screamers who do it in the dark have the best chance of fetching in a bobcat. Day callers who work the crepuscular periods of dawn and dusk will also do well. Dead noon callers will do least well.

An Arizona study caused the scat contents of 176 bobcat to be examined. The study showed the bobcat who left the scat lived mainly on the cottontail rabbit with substantial amounts of other rodents present. The rodent diet was supplemented by minor amounts of snakes, birds, lizards, fox, fish, and insects. Big bobcat eat little bobcat. Mature bobcat will take the young of antelope and deer when available and have been known to kill and consume adult deer, particularly when that adult deer is winter-stressed or is yarded. The bobcat can trot atop crusted snow and the deer cannot, causing the deer to be vulnerable.

The hunting technique of the bobcat is essentially the same as that of the mountain lion and essentially the same as the hunting technique of the feral house cat. All locate prey using excellent eyesight or a poorly developed sense of smell. The cats stalk when the prey has its head down feeding, will freeze when the head comes up, and will continue the sneak when the head goes down again. When the sneaker is close he makes a rush to take the prey, pinning small animals with razor sharp claws until the jaws can make the kill.

A hunting bobcat might cover five to eight miles during a night of hunting. The bob' will follow about the same pattern on each trip through his hunting territory, at times placing his foot at precisely the place traveled during the last trip through. The bobcat will pause at significant (to the bobcat) points within his territory to deposit scat, urine, and at times, a yellow paste from the anal glands. Territorial markings. The bobcat territory will vary as geographic conditions vary. A generous prey base coupled with huntable habitat can cause the bobcat to hunt and defend a territory as small as a few square miles. Territory size increases as available prey decreases. The territory of the male is almost always larger than that of the female. Even though a male and a female territory may overlap, the two avoid face-to-face meetings, except during late winter when it comes time to shake the sugar tree.

A bobcat mating is a mixture of aggression and submission. The mating is almost always noisy. The passionate caterwauling can be heard for a long distance. The males will leave their territories to seek out females. When one is found the tom announces his needs, using a series of growls, snarls, and moans. The female crouches to show she is interested. After an hour or so of noisy foreplay the female shows her willingness by joining the caterwauling.

A bobcat den may be in a jumble of boulders, in a cave, in a dugout, or within an abandoned mine tunnel, any place away from the weather. The litter is born about two months after the mating. There may be as many as seven kittens (the average is much less), all born blind and helpless. The female must leave the kittens to hunt and that causes them to be vulnerable, particularly to the appetite of the male bobcat. A tom that finds the den will almost surely kill and eat the kittens, causing the milk of the female to dry up and effecting her return to estrus.

Summer is a time of learning. The young travel with the female on night hunts, learning hunting and survival skills. The young will stay with the female until cold weather hits. When the food supply diminishes the female encourages the young to get the hell gone. If prey is plentiful, if the cottontail rabbit population is at a high cycle, many will survive.

As the coyote is a dog the bobcat is a cat. What the hell does that mean? Each is within a single species. Joinings between the subspecies can occur. Though uncommon, breedings between bobcat and domestic cat have produced offspring. I know of a successful mating between a bobcat and a black domestic cat. Four of the litter produced were black, resembling the domestic. The remaining three within the litter had bobtails, tufted ears, and were light gray. All of the kittens had feet obviously larger than those of a domestic cat. All had bobcat-like legs.

Fifteen years appears to be a long life for a bobcat in the wild. A bobcat in captivity lived for 32 years. The main enemy of the bobcat, aside from man, are the largest of the flying predators, other bobcat, and large land predators like the mountain lion and the coyote.

Plentiful prey during dispersal can cause the young of the year to survive.

Bobcat scat can be fox size but is usually larger. The offal is segmented (I call it the Tootsie Roll effect) so that breakage occurs at sharp right angles. When first deposited the bobcat scat is a shiny black. Exposure to air causes a crusting but the color stays black. Continued exposure causes the scat to turn gray and then to white. The scat, much of the time, consists of cottontail rabbit hair, sometimes including small fragments of undigested bone. Toilets are sometimes found, places where a bunch of bobcat scat shows repeated visits, often from more than one bobcat. Some bobcat will dig out a bowl to hold the scat. Bowl deposits may be covered or uncovered. A covered deposit indicates scat left by a territorial cat.

The bobcat track is typical of all cat tracks. Look for a somewhat round two-inch diameter track showing the characteristic heel pad, bi-lobed at the front and tri-lobed at the rear. Four toes, no claw marks. Bobcat are not a really tough call, not in the same sense a mountain lion is a tough call. As noted, there are a bunch of bobcat around, particularly within the West and the Southwest. As is the case with most predators, the bobcat must be opportunistic to prosper. A hungry bobcat (most stay so) who hears the advertisement is compelled to investigate, sometimes at the trot and sometimes at the creep. The inconspicuous nature of the bobcat, sad to say, can let him creep in and creep out without being seen. My experience causes me to think many (maybe even most) called bobcat do exactly that. The kitty eating cat of Congress illustrates.

The Congress (central Arizona) cat was an oversize tom who hung around a cluster of luxury homes scattered among the high desert, a country containing forests of creosote brush (greasewood) and with mesquite, desert ironwood, and foothills palo verde within the washes. It did not take the tom long to discover the domestic cats and small dogs who patrolled the properties, and the tom developed an appetite for all, causing the residents to become cranky. Coyote, being somewhat plentiful and always obvious because of their howlings, were the clear suspects. One resident called on Beastmaster Larry O. Gates, and asked that he do a screaming.

The first half-dozen setups caused three coyote to come. Larry used the three-inch twelve to send all to that big gutpile in the sky. During a midmorning screaming Larry looked through a greasewood to see a single critter leg, or at least something that looked somewhat like a critter leg, maybe sixty yards out. Interested, Larry continued to look and scream. The leg look-alike did not respond. Screaming continued. Minutes later, when Larry's aching eyeballs had convinced him there REALLY was a critter hiding within the greasewood, he played the ace. He compressed his lips and sucked, sending out a squeaking the Beastmasters call the Kiss of Death. The leg unhid and, attached to a big bobcat body, came at the charge. Larry did the wet work when the Robert was 20 feet out, still coming. A less observant hunter might not have discovered the leg, might not have kissed, and might have abandoned the stand to leave the tom undiscovered. An isolated incident? I don't think so. The same has happened too many times.

The bobcat that comes to the night call, the way I see it, is more likely to be discovered. The bobcat eyes illuminate like a pair of miniature moons when hit with the light, drawing attention to the obscure body. Some hunters, particularly those screaming to coyote,

The Congress cat munched poodles and allowed vocal coyote to be blamed.

do not call bobcat because they stay within open or semi-open country, good habitat for coyote but not the best habitat for bobs'. The bobcat is not fond of open country. Those I have met prefer somewhat thick cover. The brush, the kind of country a bobcat can hunt successfully, is where the groceries are found. The brush and woods, finally, offer a sanctuary when it comes time to make the desperate run away from a lion, a couple of coyote or a bigger bobcat.

A lack of hunter patience can cause the bobcat to keep his hide. Some hunters, particularly those who call to coyote or fox, abandon the stand after ten or fifteen minutes. Even though some bobcat will come during that time frame, most will not. Bobcat will travel a surprising distance to investigate a screaming but will do so at his own deliberate pace. I suggest a minimum of thirty minutes on the stand when the target is bobcat, or when the hunter suspects a bobcat might be within range of the screams. Unlike some coyote, the bobcat does not become call-shy, at least not in the same sense an experienced coyote becomes call shy. The bob' does not seem to associate the screaming and the human hiding in the brush holding the banger. A cat that is called and escapes is likely to come again, maybe even on the very next day. The Beastmaster experience with the Piggyback Cat of the Harcuvars shows this aspect of the bobcat nature.

Larry and I were on the tip-top of Pete Smith Peak in the Harcuvar Range, taping action for *The Master's Secrets to Predator Calling.* The late afternoon screaming had me hid within a clump of beargrass, singing the "Dying Rabbit Blues" through the TallyHo. Larry stood a hundred feet or so to the rear, aiming the camcorder.

Bobcat climb mainly to survive but may climb to visit a fat porcupine.

Ten minutes into the call Larry started an urgent lip squeaking. Knowing I carried the only gun, I unhid and responded at the lumber. Larry pointed downhill. Looking, I saw a bobcat leaving in a hurry. The cat, Larry said, had come to stand at his side, somewhat like a dog at heel, during the screaming, so close she could be touched.

Larry called the same area not long after, while on a muzzleloader hunt for mule deer. He made the screaming hoping to attract a rutting buck. A sense of danger caused him to look to the rear. Imagine his excitement when he saw a big bobcat, probably the same cat that had come to heel, launch from ten feet out. Perceiving a mistake while in midair, the cat sheathed her claws, hit Larry's shoulder, and bounced off. Larry turned to square to the target and did his best to have a shot opportunity with the front stuffer. Too late. The attack cat disappeared within the boulders.

Even though bobcat do not often wear nametags, Larry and I are convinced that same cat responded one more time. We were in the Harcuvar foothills with the camcorder when a bobcat showed atop a boulder a hundred yards out. Larry did the wet work with the 22-250. I taped. The cat was the same coloration and the same size as the cat called in the area on the two previous occasions, a female weighing 21 pounds.

The Canon Cat learned to love the click and hum of my autofocus and came depressingly close.

Stand selection can be crucial when the target is bobcat, maybe more so than with any other screaming excepting those addressed to cougar. The hunter must discover a habitat that is bobcat friendly. An evaluation of that habitat should cause clues that suggest where the bobcat might be at that time of day (or night). If it is dark, early morning, or late evening, the bobcat is likely to be hungry and hunting. Look for him within heavy brush that may border fields. If the call is at midday it is likely the cat will be bedded. If the day is warm the cat is most likely to be bedded on the shady side of the hill, probably half way or higher on a hillside. Cold calls will find the cat on the sunny side. Thick brush, natural caves and the gaps within a rock jumble are preferred layups.

An ideal bobcat setup will have enough cover to hide the hunter and enough to cause the cat to feel comfortable during the approach. The cover must not be so thick as to significantly diminish vision and lanes and shooting opportunity. Bobcat are not constant as they react to the call. I have called cats that stopped far out to make a reconnoiter (as did the Kitty Eating Cat), sometimes refusing to come one step closer, even when provoked by the Kiss of Death. Others come too close, and come at the gallop, as did the Piggy Back Pussy. I called a tom to thirty feet on one hunt and was busy firing the shutter of an auto-focus Canon. Something about the click of the shutter and the hum of the rewind made it happen for the bobcat. The cat went into the classic crouch and creep. I became nervous when the cat was ten feet out and invited that sumbitch to get the hell gone.

Bobcat will respond to a surprising variety of distress sounds. Cottontail screams are always popular. So are the hoarser hollers from the hare called the jackrabbit, or from any other hare. Bird distress calls work about as well. I have called bobs' using nearly all of the tube calls, plastic reed and metal reed, and using many sounds played through the battery-powered caller. I begin a bobcat screaming making low moans on a mouth call or playing a battery powered caller at about half volume. I seldom call for more than about fifteen seconds, pausing then to let the customer (if there is one about) consider. After a minute I repeat with another series. If a customer does not show within a couple of minutes or so, I crank up the volume, striving for distance, continuing such for thirty minutes or until I end the setup.

A hunter who calls a cat that remains out of sight can sometimes guess the whereabouts because of the presence of birds. A bobcat presence causes nearby birds to become paranoid. Those birds might squawk, scream, and hurl the most vile profanities. Birds will, at times, make swoops in an effort to drive the cat away. A hunter who witnesses such, even though he does not see a cat, is advised to keep calling.

Those who have trigger fingers that might become nervous under stress, as mine sometimes does, might find they miss a bobcat at embarrassingly close range. The cats I have missed seldom spook at the sound of a close miss. The hunter, much of the time, has ample time to reload and refire. A cat screamed close usually will stay close until he gets the rabbit. More information on cat calling will be found within the chapter on night calling.

Chapter 26

Calling Coyote

There was a time when the coyote was a critter of the western wastelands, actually, about all western lands. *Canis latrans* (barking dog) was not much seen before Merriwether Lewis took time out from the Lewis and Clark march to write this in his journal on May 5, 1805. "The burrowing dog of the West has large and erect ears, the head being pointed like a fox. The beast associates in bands of ten or twelve and is seldom seen singly, being unable to singly attack the deer and the antelope."

Even though he was succinct, Merriwether Lewis did a decent job of describing the critter he sometimes called the "prairie wolf." It was, as a fact, the best written description to that date. Another explorer, one who traveled to the West nearly twenty years later, closely examined a specimen of coyote collected near the present day site of Blair, Nebraska. (I am not making this up.) Thomas Say, traveling with Long's 1823 expedition to the Rocky Mountains, called the critter *Canis Latrans*. The word coyote came from the Mexicans, being a modification of the Aztec word *coyotl*.

I do not know if there were Blairs around Blair, Nebraska, during those days. If so, I am betting the Blairs and the coyote had fun together, the Blairs having more fun than the coyote. Two years past the Long Expedition, the coyote started to get on the neighbors' nerves. Folks in the Missouri legislature passed a bill encouraging counties to pay a bounty on coyote ears. The man/coyote relationship was all downhill forever after. Over the years the folks who knew the coyote best, the country folk, devised a mind-boggling assortment of desperate technique to cause old Mutton Breath to get dead. Not wishing to offend the sensibilities of those who might have a nervous stomach, I will not go into the specifics. I don't mind mentioning, however, general technique: traps, snares, strychnine, cyanide, Compound 1080, chasing with greyhounds, denning, air strikes, and so forth. Do not forget a predator screaming followed by a load of four buck in the butt. All such, it should be noted, were during the days before it became politically correct to love every wolf, every coyote, and every buck-toothed gopher on God's green earth. The coyote, to his credit, took all of this bad luck in stride, kept focused on the big picture, making more coyote, eating mutton, deer and antelope, and scratching away at fleas. The coyote, to the dismay of some, showed true grit.

The coyote has survived traps, snares, poisons, and all else, being an animal that shows true grit.

A few Westerners and a hell of a lot of Easterners, suffering from the God's Dog mentality, professed a profound love for the poorly understood coyote. The critter, they whined, had every right to eat sheep, grow a flea that can kill a human (bubonic plague), and spread rabies. The coyote problem is not now limited to the country to the west of the big river. Coyote have extended their range to include the Midwest, the Mideast, the East, and even the South, bringing western problems to all of those areas, and more. The coyote has moved to the East, taking along problems such as livestock and poultry predation, big and small game predation, rabies, and plague. Heck, in some areas, places where deep snow and extremely cold temperatures cause the whitetail deer to become winter-stressed and to yard up, the coyote pads across the crust to kill at will. Gangs of coyote have seriously impacted whitetail deer survival in those areas.

The coyote is better adapted to survive than most other land predators. Most of those are somewhat specific in diet. The lion eats the deer and the bobcat eats the rabbit. The fox eats little critters and eats vegetables and fruits. The coyote eats all of that and more, the more usually being carrion ripe enough to cause a buzzard to toss his waffles, attacking with a gusto so great it might turn a skunk trapper's stomach. Coyote have been known to hang around cattle fields to slurp up the milk-rich plops passed by the calves. And of course, the coyote will slurp up the calves also, if given a decent opportunity.

The extra large eastern coyote (brush wolf) uses size and winter cold to impact yarded deer. (Missouri Dept. of Conservation)

Had enough? OK, just so you know. I finish off the listing of coyote chow with a few inoffensives. Juniper berries, fruit from the prickly pear cactus, mesquite beans, manzanita berries. The list would be less long if I listed the things a coyote WOULD NOT eat. The coyote is a mammal owning a western weight of about thirty pounds maximum for the male and maybe five or ten pounds less for the fat female. Weight changes radically as the zip code changes. Obeying Bergstrom's Law (actually more of a constant) coyote to the north own bigger bodies and shorter legs (in relation to body size) as a heat conservation mechanism. Coyote in the Mideast and the far East own genes that permit super size. Locally called brush wolves, fully mature examples of these extra-large yodelers might weigh more than fifty pounds.

Predators as a class own uncommon intelligence. The coyote is near the top of the predator intelligence scale. Some are so smart they hunt the highway, patrolling two lane and four lane roads to collect the rabbit splats, and anything else that becomes mashed. The coyote has eyes that can discern a mouse at a hundred yards during a half moon night. His hearing is acute. The long nose is home to a bunch of sensors, causing the coyote to smell a piece of meat (alive or dead) at a quarter of a mile.

Color variation is common among coyote. Pups in a single litter might show radical color variation, but are not likely to. A coyote is commonly brown but may be roan, red, or silver. Most have a black-tipped tail. Some I have collected have had white tipped tails. Such, it seems to me, occur in pockets, verifying a gene pool origin.

Prices paid for coyote fur vary according to fashion (demand) and amount available, as is the case with all fur. An extra large Montana Pale is at the top of the line currently. These big northerns have a finely textured fur of a desirable silver gray color. The Southwestern grading is at the other end of the scale. The fur on this utility is usually blah brown, having a coarse texture to the underfur and an absence of guard hair. Size is generally small to peewee. Southwesterns are most commonly found in the Southwest (no surprise there), usually in one of the deserts. You want to hear something strange? Even in the habitat of the Southwest the pups of the year can be decent. These mostly grown teenagers have never shed. The fur is almost always finer and is almost always of a better color. Go figure.

Most coyote are night hunters, just as about all land predators are. The coyote prey is most active then and hunting effort is likely to be rewarded. Such might not be critically important to the spring and summer 'yote, a time when groceries are generously available. Such can be the difference between life and death during a tough winter when coyote walk a thin line between survival and starvation. Having said that, it is also proper to say a hungry coyote will hunt night and day. And that same hungry coyote will eat what is most available. A coyote who hangs around populated areas is likely to visit garbage dumps, garbage cans, even pet food pans containing the Purina or the table scraps. Those same coyote, when opportunity allows, will also eat the pet if that pet is the least bit smaller than Bruto the Rotweiller.

A short list of favored coyote foods appeared earlier in this chapter. Add to those ground nesting birds, large and small mammals, grasshoppers, snakes, lizards, watermelon, cantaloupe, vegetables and grass. Too much more to mention.

Coyote mate during late winter, usually during January and February. The litter is birthed about two months later (60-65 days). Litter size averages between five and ten. There are exceptions. A den found in Utah held 19 pups. A den found in Modoc County California held 14 pups.

The coyote den might be in a small natural cave, an enlarged badger hole, in a gap in a rock jumble, under an old building, or in a dugout den that extends to beneath a large boulder, maybe the roots of a tree. In the Southwest, where den sites are difficult to locate, the female coyote will dig a tunnel into the soft bank of a sand wash.

Pups of the year own finer fur (actually hair) and are of improved color.

Pup care is a function of both male and female. The pair bonds for the season and likely bonds until one dies or loses dominance. The latter is most common. The female nurses the pups, supplying a rich milk. That mother's milk is supplemented by offerings of regurgitated food, mainly meat. The meat is offered whole as the pups age. When the young are able, they travel with the adults to learn hunting and survival skills. Those who do not learn well are not likely to survive.

The coyote family remains a unit throughout the summer. They do not always hunt as one pack, separating at times into hunting groups that keep in contact through yips and howls. When the leaves turn in the fall, the unit will dissolve. Dispersal occurs. The fall dispersal can be a fine time to be a screamer. The teenage coyote, most owning limited hunting and survival skill, can be an easy target for the distress scream.

Mated coyote, as noted, remain together until one loses dominance or dies. The survivor howls to advertise for a new mate. The newlyweds defend the territory with the same vigor displayed by the oldweds. Most coyote respect territorial boundaries. Those that do not will be in for a fight. Some non-territorial coyote are allowed within to serve as a sort of a tolerated guest, most commonly young from a previous litter. These tolerated coyote will be constantly reminded of their low status. They will be nipped upon the hips by the landowners and must demonstrate their unworthiness constantly. This consists of a laying upon the back with tail between

Pups are fed a diet of milk and regurgitated meat.

the legs, legs in the air, and avoidance of eye contact and a pitiful whining. When groceries become scarce the tolerated coyote will be attacked and forced to leave. Those that resist are killed.

Territorial boundaries are verified by howl points and scent posts. The home size varies as the kind of country varies, as food supply varies. A study of collared coyote in a Northern Arizona habitat showed a typical range of 8.1 square miles. The study also suggested the coyote within the territory would move seasonally, the winter and summer range being in different parts of the territory.

Now might be a good time to comment on a point of coyote behavior. I have studied papers prepared by wildlife professionals to see where they write as though the coyote in their study area typify every coyote in the world, an error called extrapolation. One such publication stated the primary diet of the coyote was the jackrabbit; it further stated the coyote would not turn to other foods unless a serious shortage of jackrabbit existed. Such might be true in the study area (Idaho) where there exists tons of jackrabbit per square mile. Such is not true here in Arizona where we do not have enough jackrabbit to feed a small percentage of the coyote. The main prey of the coyote, in Northern Arizona, is the juniper berry during the winter, antelope and other big game fawn during the spring, and mice and voles during the summer. The coyote is like all other folks; many are individualists who modify their behavior to respond to the demands of habitat.

The coyote has a few friends, a few enemies, and a bunch of folks who ride the fence. I am in the latter group. I admire the critter for his ability to survive against serious threats. I consider the coyote to be a worthy adversary. I do not let that respect and admiration cloud good judgment when it comes time to control the coyote.

The coyote probably kills more big and small game than all other predators combined. This is mainly due to the number and nature of the critter. The Anderson Mesa Antelope Study (mentioned previously) showed a survival rate of ten to twenty percent. What in hell does that mean? It means that only about ten percent of fawns born in the study area survived. Evidence suggested the coyote to be the dirty guy. Game and fish studies in a second area showed the coyote to be a major predator of the deer fawn. Biologists have estimated that half of ground nesters like pheasant, quail, and grouse survive predation. The coyote seems to be constantly hungry. That coyote, mostly, is an opportunistic feeder, gorging, whether hungry or not, when opportunity allows. That is good news for us screamers. The coyote is likely to answer a scream even if not particularly hungry. As has been mentioned, the coyote is by nature a night feeder. Even so, the coyote will come to the call day or night, coming best at night, next best during the crepuscular periods of dawn and dusk, and least best during the day. The effect an approaching storm or a departing storm has on coyote appetite has been well covered in the chapter on weather. I see no reason to repeat all of that here, except to emphasize. Coyote often go on a feeding frenzy as a major storm approaches. Some will lay up during the worst of the storm to return to the hunt on the first clear day after the storm. Screaming at such a time can be dandy.

I am convinced the phase of the moon can influence coyote feeding habits. Tom Britt, a wildlife biologist and a regional manager for the Arizona Game & Fish Department, once participated in a night

The Anderson Mesa Study established an antelope fawn survival of about ten percent. Most were coyote-killed, as was this skinned fawn. Bloodshot ribs and neck show evidence of biting.

study of white-tailed deer populations in a Southern state. The researchers used spotlights to conduct the census. They made few sightings during the dark phases of the moon. They saw few deer, few rabbits, and few predators. Such knowledge can be helpful to those of us who hide in the brush to make a sound like a coyote's supper. A predator that does not hunt during the dark of the moon is likely to hunt the following day.

Coyote prime at the start of winter, the precise priming dependent on weather and latitude. The fur stays prime until the sun of spring causes a loss of prime and causes other obvious degradation. The first change noted is called rubbing. This is apparent on hips, showing about March. As weather warms the fur will thin and shed, causing further degradation. The hair of the back will curl (called singeing). The fur turns patchy and uneven. Any such degradation should cause the fur hunter to put away the screamers. Fur from such critters will not be salable.

Coyote come to the call in different ways. The response will be influenced by previous experience. A young coyote, one with virgin ears, will come at full gallop, anxious to own the rabbit. Multiple young will at times involve themselves in a desperate race, each hoping to be the first to claim the prize. I have had such come to five feet before deciding 200 pounds is a bit big for a rabbit. Others, older and wiser, will come at the sneak. A coyote who has hoped for rabbit but tasted hot lead loses much of his gusto for rabbit. That coyote might come but will do so the same way porcupines make love, verrry carefully.

The hunter who makes a minor mistake will likely lose this coyote. Take your shot at the first decent opportunity. Learn to read coyote body language so as to tell his thinking. A coyote that stops facing you is likely to come closer. A coyote that stops broadside is not likely to come on in. That coyote, when he moves, is likely to make a circle to taste the wind. A coyote who turns his tail to you, looks at you over his back, is a coyote about to leave.

The coyote I called from across a brushy canyon showed paranoid behavior. I watched the coyote come for a quarter of a mile. The country had been hard hit. It was obvious the customer was not coming to his first rodeo. The critter used every rock and every bush to make the sneak. It took him fifteen minutes to come to shooting range. He stopped each hundred feet or so to taste the wind, to make the reconnoiter, finally stopping two hundred yards out. The hang-up was in high grass that covered all but the coyote head. I put the crosshairs on the grass, at a place where his chest should have been, and stroked. I missed, of course, and the coyote took thirty seconds to cover the quarter of a mile approach route. That coyote, I am convinced, will not trust a dying rabbit ever again.

Mature coyote might come eagerly at season's start. Those that do not die get smart quickly.

Educated coyote will sometimes make a circle around the screaming in an effort to taste the wind, to find a taste of rabbit. If that rabbit tastes like after-shave, the coyote is gone. Masking scent will sometimes fool these nose hunters. Take your shot at a circler at the first opportunity. Nothing good is likely to be offered. Some educated coyote hang up a few hundred yards out to howl out insults. They will not come an inch even when you beg. Some writers have speculated that the howling is an effort to warn other coyote. I do not believe that to be true. The coyote I have met have not cared scat about other coyote, seeing them as competitors and not as chums. They howl, I think, to voice a frustration. They want to come but are afraid to come.

A hunter can do a number of things to respond to the frustration howler. The best course of action is to ignore the howler and continue with the call. I have called in other coyote while the howler complained. When you near the end of the setup, if you want to try for the howler, reduce the volume and the frequency of the calling. Then shut up. Sit tight and stay quiet for another ten minutes or so. Sometimes the howler will come at the sneak.

Sometimes I give the howler a taste of his own medicine, howling at him (or her), saying the same. That howling, at times, can cause the coyote to come on in. A pair of callers or a caller using a battery-powered caller can sometimes make a sneak on a howling coyote. Not often, but once in a while. If with a partner, have him or her stay at the setup to continue the call. Circle so as to approach the howler or howlers from the side. Take the shot at the first opportunity. If solo, leave the battery powered caller going, and then make the sneak, also from the side.

The squeezing of the rabbit was covered in the chapter on tubes and the chapter on battery-powered callers. I will say a bit more, however, on calls specific to the coyote. I prefer the rabbit or the jackrabbit distress scream for coyote. Those critters, through much of the coyote range, are a primary food source. Either of the two can be broadcast from the metal reeded tube or from the plastic reeded tube. I call to coyote in two general ways. One way is the short and choppy distress scream. Short duration screams with not a lot of pause between. The second screaming causes the screams to be longer, more of a moaning with a definite separation between screams, more typical of the deer family than the rabbit, but still hare-like. Which is better? Don't know. Each will work some of the time; neither will work all of the time.

I start the coyote screaming using moderate volume calls, beginning with short series, maybe only ten seconds followed by a minute or so of silence. If that effort does not provoke response I start the hard sell—full volume screams aimed at the coyote standing at the county line. I lengthen the series to twenty or thirty seconds, maybe more. Then follow with a minute or two of quiet.

A part of the screaming I do to coyote has a lot of rasp, a hoarseness reminiscent of some jackrabbit and all gray fox. Such, it seems to me, tells the coyote there is a substantial meal behind that scream, a meal worth walking the mile for. Electronic callers can be dandy for coyote. I mentioned a use or two in the chapter titled "Tough Calls." I say here that the gray fox distress tape is a good sound for coyote. So is the bird distress, the one sometimes called the Yellowhammer Woodpecker Distress and sometimes called the Flicker Distress.

It is best to ignore frustration howlers. Continuing to call might attract another coyote, maybe even the howler.

The ability to change calling sounds, to sort through the tape collection to find a sound that the critters love on that particular day, is the main asset of the battery powered caller. I generally let the tape run continuously when calling to coyote. I start the stand using moderate volume screams. After a couple of minutes of such I crank to full volume and sometimes hold the speaker high to turn it in a 360-degree circle, focusing the sound to all areas.

When tube calling, when I have a coyote in sight, I stay quiet. A critter moving your way is as good as it gets. Calling while he comes will not cause him to come faster. Calling then might cause the critter to become suspicious. At the least calling while a critter comes will provide that critter with a one hundred percent lock on your hideout. Perception is likely.

I sometimes flutter my lips as I blow the tube and flutter my hands at tube end to provoke a tremulous varying to the screaming. Such works particularly well on coyote. I almost always assess the potential of the calling stand before starting the music. I check for vision and shooting lanes. I check for obscurements. I check out ghosts, boogers that might be critter-like at some point into the call. A coyote coming to the call can be easy to see if that coyote comes from the front and comes at the run. When shotgun hunting I let the critter come to sure-kill range, shoulder, sight and shoot. The critter will be on the move but that does not matter to MooseDick. When rifle hunting I stop the coyote when he is fifty yards or so out, knowing that a too close coyote can be difficult to hit with a rifle. How do I stop that coyote? I lip squeak (Kiss of Death), growl or cuss. About any new sound will cause the coyote to pause to make a reconnoiter. The pause will not last forever. Before making the announcement, have your gun at the shoulder, ready to shoot

I have said it is proper to stay on the stand for at least 15 minutes when calling to coyote. Honesty causes me to say I do not always do so. There are times, usually in brushy country, when I abandon a stand after ten minutes, figuring any coyote in hearing has had enough time to show. Some stands, those where I receive encouragement, might have me staying considerably longer. There is no hard and fast rule on stand length, for coyote or any other critter. Evaluate each stand to decide what is right.

Calling pressure will almost always cause critter response to slow. Late in the calling season I almost always stay longer on the stand. Some screamers abandon a stand as soon as they take a shot. Hit or miss, they figure it is time to move on. Those screamers are making a big time mistake. The sound of a shot does not always cause a customer to spook. I am not talking about coyote in sight, those will almost always spook. I write of critters that may be on the way but out of sight. The bang, to them, might sound like thunder or sound like the noise produced when a jet breaks the sound barrier. I always continue the call after a kill or a miss. That effort is rewarded, much of the time, by the showing of a second customer. I illustrate.

George and I hunted a miserably cold dawn a week after Christmas. A fog bank reduced visibility to about a hundred feet. The wet air diffused the sound, making the screams delicious, coming from everywhere and nowhere. A pair of shadowy figures half-materialized in the fog. One came and the second disappeared back into the fog. The one plodded close and George Oakey placed a hundred grainer through his ribs. I continued the screaming. A minute or so later a second coyote came from hard right, at the gallop. I dumped him at thirty yards. Continuing the call had doubled our pleasure and doubled our fur.

I could tell stories of second kills until you would cry for mercy. I will not. Be convinced, however, that all critters, especially the coyote, will continue to come after a shot. A good hunter stays alert as he abandons the setup. I have sighted several coyote on the walk back to the truck. On one hunt I made it to the truck and spotted a big silver standing two hundred yards out. I exited the truck, as law requires, and caused the coyote to leave at the gallop. Even though offhand shots at two-hundred-yard galloping coyote are not my specialty, I got lucky. Staying alert added to the fur collection.

Running coyote are easily missed, most often because of insufficient lead. A coyote who is serious about speed can cover ground at about thirty miles an hour. That translates to 43 feet per second. A bullet having a muzzle velocity of 3,500 FPS will take about a fifth of a second to reach a two-hundred-yard coyote. That coyote can cover about eight feet during that time. Too much lead? Not in my book.

Where you place the bullet will affect kill and affect pelt damage. I aim for the ribs, behind the shoulder and midway between back and brisket, when shooting at broadside coyote. A properly loaded round will enter, causing a .224 (with the 22-250) diameter entry hole. The bullet that behaves will explode in the necessaries. There will not be an exit wound.

Coyote that face the gun offer a reduced target. I aim for the center of the chest, below the joining of the neck to the body. Again, the .224 entry and no exit. When aiming at a running coyote, tough shots for me, I aim at the part of the coyote easiest to hit. I would rather have a damaged pelt, I figure, than have no pelt at all.

Calling the roads can be a decent way to take coyote. I like road calling particularly well after a snow. Tracks are fresh and indicate coyote presence and movement. Parking to find a setup to call to the coyote that made the tracks always improves response. The same technique, sort of, can be used after a rain or even during dry weather when dust is present. I look for scat and fresh tracks.

Sighting a coyote while driving is always exciting. There is always the tendency to jam on the brakes and light into that sucker as he heads for Chicago. Trouble is much of the time such is illegal. And too, at least for me, seldom productive. It is better, I think, to ignore the coyote, drive out of sight, park, then make the setup and the scream. That coyote, much of the time, will come as though you had a rope around his neck.

The coyote is the main screaming target through the West and the Southwest, even in some parts of the Midwest and the East. He is a worthy opponent. Here's to him (gulp). Long may he come to my screamings.

Continuing to call after a kill can double the fur and double the fun.

191

Chapter 27

Calling Gray Fox

Every gray fox I have met has had the heart of a lion. All who earn a look into the heart of this small wild dog must admire the grit within. When I set up to scream at the gray, on a moonless midnight, in that crepuscular period the gray loves so well, or even at precisely noon thirty, I often consider the nature of the gray and thank the fox maker. Thanks for what? Thanks, Buddy, for not making that little sumbitch as big as a St. Bernard.

The gray fox nature causes him to be a dandy target for the scream. Most come to the scream with an enthusiasm that staggers the karma. Nearly all I have called have responded at the run (or at least at the trot) and have come with eyes alert, ears erect, and tail at attention. Ahhh, what a sight. The gray that Chuck and I Canoned along a desert wash is a good example.

Chuck Spearman, as anyone with scents knows, was once publisher of *Trapper & Predator Caller* magazine, a friend and a predator-calling fanatic. Chuck and I had purchased a pair of toys, identical Canon EOS-620 Auto Focus Auto Wind 35 MM cameras. And each of those smart boxes carried a dandy 300 MM telephoto lens. We headed for the winter desert, hoping to find fun. We set up within a moderately big desert dry wash, the kind that runs like a river when it rains but stays as dry as a popcorn fart the rest of the time. The banks were lined with mesquite and blue palo verde, and there was greasewood beyond that. Good country for critters.

As we usually do when calling to the camera, we set the Johnny Stewart MS-512 battery-powered cassette caller thirty feet out, hit the go button, and got a little bit excited as the tape sent out damnfine recordings of a cottontail rabbit distress scream. The gray came early into the call, maybe no more than a minute or two. The critter was about as handsome as a December fox gets. A lush winter coat and a particularly fine tail, the back fur being the typical salt and pepper with a rim of orange on the chest and belly, and then, stark white. The salt and pepper tail carried the typical black stripe. The texture of the fur was exceedingly fine, the kind buyers call the western silky.

The fox came on Chuck's side of the stand-up (we were erect to permit visibility), placing Chuck's big body between the fox and my own big body. No opportunity for photos. I relaxed to watch. Chuck rocked and rolled with his autofocus. The gray ran close to the bush hiding the caller, circled a time or two, and wheeled to whirl away, but didn't. He paused 30 feet out, looked longingly at the sound (is such possible?) and returned at the charge. That maneuver was repeated and repeated again, the repeats continuing for the fifteen minutes of the screaming. The fox watched forlornly as Chuck and I gathered the junk to leave, figuring, I guess, we were running off with his rabbit. The fox did not follow us to the truck. Knowing gray fox as I do, I would not have been surprised if it had. That aggressive behavior might have surprised someone who does not understand the gray. Some, knowing the gray to be the little guy within the woods, knowing the gray is not at the top of the food chain, knowing the gray must spend a good deal of time worrying (WORST NIGHTMARE: A close encounter of the coyote, bobcat, or cougar kind), those might presume the gray to be a bit more low key. Not true. The gray don't give a scat about all of that. A screaming, to the gray, means there is a rabbit around somewhere, and the gray is wrathy to get that rabbit.

Even though the gray is the common fox of the West and the somewhat common fox of the Midwest and the East, he is not commonly understood. A predator screamer needs extraordinary knowledge if he or she is to gain a full measure of fun from this ordinary critter.

The gray fox is common to most of the continental United States and is particularly plentiful in the Desert Southwest, a place where a generous prey base, little critters like cottontails, wood rats, 'roo rats and all such, causes the gray to live long and prosper. Gray fox are found in good numbers south of the border, down in Old Mexico. You will not find many gray (maybe none) in the high plains states, the northern Rockies, the northern parts of the Great Basin Desert, and the coastal rain forests found within Washington and Oregon.

Some gray fox range overlaps the range of the red fox. The shared habitat causes few problems. The gray follows his nature and works the brush. The red follows his nature and works the fields. As mentioned, the gray does dandy in the Southwest. The little critter thrives within the chaparral midlands and is equally at home in the high and low desert. I have screamed in grays within the ponderosa pine belt, at an elevation of eight and nine thousand feet.

I look for gray fox in rough country interrupted by many small canyons, many of them brush choked. The gray needs that kind of country to make his hunt. Unlike some members of the dog family this fox makes his living by stalking prey to get close, and then pouncing, cat-like. The presence of trees causes such habitat to be even more desirable. The gray is the only fox that is a tree climber. The gray climbs a tree often, not just when he HAS to, but when he WANTS to. Again, cat-like.

The gray also does well within boulder jumbles, within thick oak brush and manzanita, the kind the cowboys call chaparral. The gray, being nimble, can use such to stay somewhat safe. The cat-like nature of the gray has caused some to consider him to be more cat than dog. An old time trapper (aren't they all?) shared my camp one winter. During one campfire we huddled together and began philosophical discussions. "The gray fox," Stanley Pike said with a great deal of conviction, "is not a fox at all. That critter is a cat. Look at the way he hunts. Look at the retractable claws. Look at the gray's ability to climb a tree." I disagreed mildly, using logic. Stan finally compromised, saying he now considered the gray to be a cross between a dog and a cat.

Fox fur price is determined by fashion trends and by the amount of fox fur available to the trade. The fur of the gray fox, actually the hair, is not as fine or full as the fur of the red fox. Even so, the market for gray fox fur stays strong much of the time. I have sold collections of grays for a $60.00 average and I have sold collections for an $18.00 average.

The average gray will be about a yard long from nose tip to tail tip. A third of that length will be the bushy tail. Large adult fox will weigh about ten pounds, maybe more. Eastern grays, much of the time, are larger than Western grays. Gray fox fur is salt and pepper gray on the top of the back and on the tail. The under-fur is buff. The fur turns a red-brown, actually an orange, on parts of the throat, the chest, and the belly. Other parts of those areas turns to snow white. The tail is decorated with a stripe of black that extends from hips to tail tip. That tail tip is characteristically black. Even so, I have called and killed a few grays that showed a white-tipped tail.

The gray fox is mainly nocturnal, just as are other land predators. Even though that is true, the gray is easily called during daylight, particularly during the crepuscular periods following daybreak and preceding dark. The secretive nature of the gray causes him to be seldom seen, few non-hunters come across grays causing many of those to be convinced the gray is in short supply. Campers and others who may be

Gray fox climb trees mainly to stay safe—a critical talent in coyote country.

about at night have likely heard the barking and yapping of the gray and failed to recognize the source.

Gray fox are territorial. The home range is determined by the lay of the land and by prey density. The gray fox territory may extend to a few square miles in stingy country. What does the gray mainly eat? Being omnivorous (eating both meat and vegetable) the gray

195

eats what is available to eat. Prey animals include the cottontail rabbit, and at times, a jackrabbit that may be nearly as big as the gray. They also take birds, ground squirrels, mice, rats, bugs, lizards, and some snakes. Along waterways the gray will work the shore to find crawfish and frogs. Preferred fruits are juniper and manzanita berries, all other berries, and the fruits of most cacti.

Where coyote and gray fox range overlap, the coyote can be an important gray fox predator. So can the bobcat and the cougar. So are screamers like Gerry Blair, Larry O. Gates, Gordo Krahn, and all such.

The gray fox is monestrous, coming into season during January and February. Like other dogs, the pups are born a couple of months later. Litters average four or five. The pups are born fully furred and blind. The pups are attended by both male and female, the two more or less bonding for the healthy life of each.

The gray fox den might be located in an abandoned badger den, in a dugout beneath a brush pile, in one of the openings of a rock jumble, or in a natural cave. About anyplace the fox can find privacy and protection. The pups stay in the den until about five-weeks-old. Short trips to the area just outside the den begin. Those forays continue until the pups are ready to hunt. By mid-summer all are trotting along with male and female to learn the hunting skills needed to survive on their own. If it is a poor year for grocer-

The vixen becomes receptive during January and February, delivering four or five pups a couple of months later.

196

ies, the young fox will be forced to leave the territory when cold weather comes. Those that leave during those tough times, particularly those having poor survival skills, are not likely to live long. When food is plentiful the litter may stay within the territory to share with Mom and Pop.

Fox are mostly monogamous. The males stay with the females to help raise the offspring. I have called fox pairs during the fall and the winter, non-breeding times, and am convinced the two pair bond somewhat permanently.

As noted, fox hunt mainly at night. A hungry fox throws away the clock, however, and may hunt both day and night. If your state allows night calling you will find the gray responds best during the dark. You will call more fox and will find that those fox come close to the screams.

Where night hunting is not allowed screamers will have the best luck calling crepuscular, an hour or so after first light and an hour or so before last light. The fox seem to be on their feet and thinking of food during those times. Do not give up on daytime fox. They can be called then but do not often come as enthusiastically and might not make the close approach. My home state (Arizona) does not permit night hunting. I can't count the number of grays I have called during dead daylight. I know it has been one hell of a lot, maybe more.

I look for fox in brushy basins, canyons, and in mesquite-lined (yep, the gray eats mesquite beans) washes. I look for grays about any place there is an adequate prey base or an adequate supply of fruits and berries.

The gray fox must also have cover. The best food supply in the world will not sustain the gray if he does not have the kind of country needed to keep his butt safe from cousin coyote and from the other named fox lovers. The fox does not have the legs or the lungs to run a long distance and must rely on his ability to hide, maneuver, and climb.

Even so, some fox will be found in country that looks to be open. Look at that country close and you will discover fox sanctuaries, patches of brush, clusters of trees, or rocky outcrops. Gray fox love the desert. You want the truth? The desert habitat is the kind of country where gray fox (and their little cousin the Kit) do best. Cactus offers sweet fruits and offers maneuvering room to escape the less agile coyote. That same desert is home to a plenitude of tasty little rodents. Brush is almost always present. Look to the north side of hills and look within drainages. Where in hell is all of this desert and where can you get your share? Look to the southwest within the U.S. Look to parts of Southern California. Look to Nevada. Look to Arizona and look to Texas, parts of New Mexico. Look to Old Mexico. Find the desert and you will find the Western gray fox.

Eastern and Midwestern screamers are not likely to find much in the way of desert. They need to look within woodlands that border fields and look within brush-choked drainages that traverse fields. Fence lines graced by weeds and brush can be good. So can overgrown fallow fields, places where rodent density is high.

Those who scream to the east of the big rivers will find the gray to be a lot like the red and the coyote in one respect. Daytime activity

Grays sometimes take cottontail rabbits, but most often settle for smaller prey.

can cause the gray to turn nocturnal. Call the gray during the dark if you can. The grays I have met have not been fussy about the kind of song I sing. I have called grays using open reeded calls such as the TallyHo, the Crit'R•Call, the Lohman C-280 and other such. I have also called grays using metal-reeded calls like the Johnny Stewart PC-1 and the old Weems WildCall. About any metal reeded tube will do as well. Those metal reeds, as has been mentioned, are likely to freeze during really cold weather. One of the plastic reeded calls is best then.

I have also called more than a few gray fox by playing the yellow hammer woodpecker distress or the cottontail rabbit distress through a battery powered caller. I play at moderate volume and shorten the distance between setups to compensate. The gray (and any red within the area) seems to feel less threatened.

Mike Mell, a licensed guide and dandy predator caller, sucks at a piece of grass or a section of leaf to produce a sound gray fox find delightful. Mike offers a tip, "Screamers should keep on calling after they call and shoot a fox. Many times a year I call a second fox after I have called and killed the first. On one stand I called four fox and killed three of the four." Other tips follow.

Do not avoid legal hunting areas that might be close to towns, villages and houses. If you can obtain the proper permission and can hunt there safely, such areas can hold significant fox populations and are often overlooked by other hunters. When night hunting, secure permission ahead of time—midnight is a poor time to ask. Scout night calling areas during the day to learn the lay of the land, so you can select the setup that offers the most advantage. Use that day scout to identify potential shooting hazards, some such not readily apparent at night.

Gray fox can be killed with about any caliber of centerfire rifle, most shotguns and some rimfires. Options are reduced if you hope to sell or save the fur. The fox is a small-bodied critter (obviously so when you see him naked), not much bigger than a black-tailed jackrabbit. The fox frame, being fragile, will not tolerate too much trauma. My thoughts on good, bad and ugly fox guns follow.

I give the .22 rimfire an ugly rating. I have shot gray fox with the rimfire, using the .22 Long Rifle Hollow Point and using the Long Rifle Hollow Point in one of the souped up configurations, and have had inconsistent results. A few of the fox drop graveyard dead. Other fox have been inconsiderate, maybe going down, getting up, and running wobble-legged to the nearest hole. They likely die but die slowly. I am thinking we owe a quick and humane death. I do not recommend the .22 rimfire as a fox gun.

I hold an improved opinion on the .22 Winchester Rim Fire Magnum (WRFM). I have shot more than a few grays with such and have had generally good luck out to about 100 yards or so. My favorite in that caliber is the Model 700 H&R Auto-Loader. That dandy gun was marketed between 1977-1985, offered with a five shot clip but with a ten shot clip available as an option. Those who crave to have one might like to know used models are available at moderate price. Look for a publication called *Gun List*, published by Krause Publications, 700 East State Street, Iola, WI 54990.

The recently revived .22 Hornet is a good gray-fox gun, particularly within boulder jumbles.

What makes the WRFM better? Velocity. The 40 grain pill leaves the muzzle at about 2000 FPS and maintains good velocity and good punch out to about 100 yards.

The occasional bobcat that comes to the fox call can be offed handily at about that range. Customers of the coyote kind, sad to say, are too much critter for the WRFM, particularly when that coyote critter is one of the big brush wolves that hang to the east of the big rivers. I top the WRFM with a big guy scope, one of the one-inch models recommended for the centerfires. I have fitted the gun with a sling also. I sometimes carry a lot of junk to a screaming and need all of the hands I can find.

Some of the fast shooting .224 centerfires will do a decent job on fox if bullet and powder cooperate to produce a medium fast loading, pushing a non-explosive bullet. Legendary caller Murry Burnham uses a .222 loading so slow it has been passed by VW Bugs on upgrades. Murry figures that his slow loading is good out to about 100 yards. That somewhat short range is okay with Murry. Much of his fox calling takes place at night. Fox come so close you can smell the rabbit on their breath.

I like the .22 Hornet as a fox gun. Ruger modified their Model 77/22 WRFM to accept the Hornet cartridge during 1994. This clip fed bolt action is dandy for little critters like the fox, even some critters that are substantially larger.

How about shooting a Full Metal Jacketed (FMJ) bullet at fox? Maybe yes and maybe no. An FMJ loaded hot will kill the fox deader than need be. Reloaders can slow the FMJ down to achieve a decent fox load. Trouble is, slowing the bullet down takes away long range muscle.

In the right kind of country the shotgun can be dandy for fox. Stay away from somewhat open country where the fox (or any other customer) can reconnoiter from a rock a hundred yards out. Stick to tight country where the critters must come closer to get a look at the rabbit. The shotgun gets on the critter fast and throws lot of lead. The famed Morton Burnham (Murry's dad) used a shotgun almost exclusively. His choice of birdshot instead of BB's was logical for the kind of country he hunted. I prefer the BB's. Even though such might not be needed on fox, they sure come in handy when a coyote volunteers. I recommend one of the three-inch twelves and have a preference for the auto loaders. The ten-gauge, for those who have the shoulder for it, also does well.

Do not give up on shotgunning fox if your bird gun happens to be a twelve-gauge chambered for the 2-3/4" chamber. Range is reduced a bit. Shooting the so called "Standard Magnum" loads in copper plated BB's, the gun will rug out a fox out to about 30 yards. Lighter gauges do less well but can do the job if the shooter stays shot selective.

There is no such gun as the "best" fox gun. Every choice can be a trade-off. The screamer should evaluate the kind of country he or she calls most of the time, and make a guess as to which gun will do the best job there, most of the time.

Chapter 28

Lion Calling

The mountain lion is not often seen to the east of the Missouri and Mississippi rivers. Those midwestern, mideastern, and eastern states having remnant populations almost always prohibit the hunting or the killing of those few lion hardy enough to exist in habitat degraded (from the lion view) by population and ruralization. The scarcity of lion groceries, namely the white-tailed deer during the somewhat recent past, caused further difficulty. Even though enlightened game management has restored the whitetail in nearly all of the original range, the lion has not returned.

The western population of mountain lion in the eleven western states that is the main current range has stayed constant, and in some cases that population has prospered. A lion specialist for the Arizona Game & Fish Department has estimated a population of 2,000 adult lion in that state. That is a lot of lion. That many lion can and do eat a significant number of deer, elk, and livestock—including cattle that roam to graze the Arizona wild country contained in mostly public lands: National Forest lands, Bureau of Land Management (BLM) lands, and State Trust lands. The Arizona biologist has conducted studies that suggest an adult lion must make a major kill every ten days—a deer, an elk, a cow, or less frequently, a sheep or goat. It does not require much in the way of mathematical talent to discover that each of those 2,000 adult lion in the state kills a big bodied animal (usually a deer) fifty times each year.

Under certain circumstances a small population of lion, or even a single lion, can seriously impact, and sometimes extirpate, pockets of game animals. The $30,000.00 lion was one such. The $30,000.00 (1985 dollars) lion probably thought he had died and gone to heaven when the Arizona Game & Fish Department transplanted the 22 desert bighorn sheep into the Tres Alamos Range (Central Arizona) at an estimated cost of $2,000.00 per sheep. Before the transplant the big tom ranged the Tres Alamos, the Harcuvar Range, and, most likely, the Harquahala Range, looking for the scattered mule deer that hung out on the mountains, in the canyons, and on the desert floor. The deer diet was supplemented, when opportunity permitted, with javelina, a critter uncommon to all of that range. The transplant changed all of that. Dropping a herd of sheep into a water poor area caused those sheep to cluster around one of the few sources of con-

stant water, a trick tank in one of the Tres Alamos drainages. It did not take the lion long to learn about his new neighbors. Eight of the 22 sheep carried radio collars containing a mortality feature—if the sheep did not move his or her head for an hour or two, that lack of movement would cause the collar to say so.

Ewe #981 was the first collared sheep to bite the dust. An investigative team found the remains of the carcass in a dense thicket of Palo Verde, prickly pear cacti, and galleta grass. The carcass had been moved and covered at least two times, as a lion is likely to do with one. Tooth punctures in the hide that had covered the throat showed the lion was an adult.

More bad news followed. All of the collared sheep and most of the uncollared sheep went to feed the lion. The sheep transplant failed, because of one or two hungry lions. Why didn't the Game and Fish guys get rid of the lion or lions so that the sheep would have the opportunity to establish? Don't know. Probably because it was not politically correct to do so.

Congress, Arizona, hunter and trapper Larry O. Gates, a Beastmaster, had no such hesitation. While in the Tres Alamos to check traps on a fox and bobcat line, Larry sighted one of the remaining sheep, maybe the only remaining sheep, a young ram. The next day, checking traps again as Arizona law required, Larry found fresh sheep tracks that showed the sheep was on the run. Fresh mountain lion tracks were atop the sheep tracks. A skilled predator caller, Larry set up to make a series of calls in the area, blowing an open reeded model called the TallyHo.

Seconds into the second stand a small herd of desert mule deer broke and ran from a brushy wash. Twenty minutes later Larry sighted a flash of fur, maybe one of the mule deer sneaking back for a look. More calling caused the critter to come somewhat close, but always in the brush so that identification was difficult. Larry called for ten minutes more, decided that thirty minutes was enough, and prepared to move on. Before doing so, however, he made a final scan. The lion stood in the shade of a mesquite eighty yards out. The Tres Alamos tom weighed 132 pounds on certified scales, mighty big for a desert lion.

The nocturnal nature of the mountain lion, its tendency to travel long patterns, and the beast's secretive nature cause the lion to be seldom seen and poorly perceived. Lion country can be about any kind of country. The Arizona low desert is home to a subspecies humorously called the Yuma Puma. That same state has catamounts (from the Mexican Gato del Monte, or cat of the mountain) roaming in the state's highest mountain ranges, those having elevations that approach 14,000 feet.

A favored lion habitat is the transition woodlands, a country chopped by tough canyons and covered with scrub oak, Gambels Oak, Turbinella Oak, and manzanita and other brushes, the kind the cowboys call chaparral. Such country offers groceries to mule deer and whitetail, both lion edibles. The ground cover is made to order for lion hunting technique, a technique that has the lion sneaking close to the prey, and when close enough, the blinding burst of speed to make the assault.

Felis concolor is Latin for cat of the same color. That color, almost always, is a light brown, about the color of tanned leather. The adult lion will measure about five feet from nose to the rear of the

Lion depredation caused a $30,000 desert bighorn sheep transplant to fail.

hips. The slender tail will extend for another three feet. Fully grown lions weigh from eighty to about two-hundred pounds. The adult male is almost always larger than the adult female.

Lion kittens can be born at any time of the year but are most likely to be born during late spring, coinciding with the birthing of prey animals like deer and elk. The kittens are spotted for the first few months of life. The birthing, feeding, and protection of the kittens is strictly a female function. Most of the present population of mountain lion is in the western United States, all of Mexico, and parts of Canada. Other states have minor populations with some eastern and southern states reporting increased sightings. It is not known if populations are actually on the increase. The increased sightings might be because of a more sophisticated census.

Western lion seem to prefer rimrock country in the Transition Life Zone, characterized by pinion/juniper woodlands, land interrupted by steep canyons and rocky rims. The main food of the lion is the deer, most often the big bodied mule deer of the West. Many populations of such deer are migratory, staying high during the summer and then retreating to lower elevation ahead of winter snows. The lion, almost always, follows.

A biologist for the Arizona Game Department has estimated an adult lion will make a kill each eight days and that kill is most often a deer. If deer are not plentiful the kill may be an elk, a feral burro, a bighorn sheep, or livestock. Cattle depredation seems to be greatest in the states of Arizona, New Mexico and Texas, most often in areas where calves are born in lion habitat. Stock killing increases when deer densities are low.

Blind calling to mountain lion, that is, setting out to call lion habitat indiscriminately, is not likely to produce a lot of action. The wide ranging habits of the lion and the low lion density can cooperate to cause it to be unlikely a lion will be near enough to hear the screaming. Many of the lion I have called have come while I was screaming to other ears, most often coyote or bobcat. The lions that came to a screaming in the Kinnikinik Indian Ruins are typical.

It was late in the season to be calling for fur. Under ordinary circumstances I would not be perched atop the rubble of this ancient Indian village playing the "Dying Rabbit Blues" to a pair of game biologists. I was there because of coyote predation of antelope, a predation that threatened the existence of an historic antelope herd. Knowing that the antelope were due to drop their twin fawns soon, and knowing that gangs of hungry coyote would go on the hunt almost immediately, we were there to remove some of the antelope eaters from the habitat.

The ruin stand was the third screaming made that morning. The first two were duds. Not so much as a raven. Knowing the target was coyote and that fifteen minutes is plenty of time to allow a coyote to respond, I had terminated both screamings at about that time. The ruin call took place at the junction of two major drainages. Canyons. Kinnikinick and Grapevine. Each of them brush-choked and rimmed by pinion pine and juniper. PJ in forest service language. The kind of country favored by lion succulents such as mule deer and Rocky Mountain elk.

I slobbered into the screaming with enthusiasm, ready for action. The two Game and Fish guys were also ready. Ten minutes into the call I saw movement sixty yards out. Thinking it might be a tawny

Beastmaster Larry O. Gates called and killed this 132-pound tom within the sheep transplant area, but too late to help the sheep.

205

Biologists have estimated a mature lion must make a major kill each eight to ten days.

coyote I squared to the flash of fur, shouldered the 22-250 and readied myself for some wet work. Imagine my surprise when the small x of the duplex six centered on a lion head. I moved the crosshairs down to touch the lion throat and begin the squeeze that would cause the three pound trigger on the Ruger 77 to release the sear. Halfway there I paused to wonder if my wallet contained a lion tag. Knowing it was a poor time to gamble, having two Game and Fish guys sitting near, I released the pressure on the trigger, unshouldered the gun, and made a search of the wallet. No tag. All of this time the lion stayed still and stayed interested. Finally, whispering hoarsely, I asked Don and Norm if they might have a lion tag. Neither did. We let that lion walk and let another lion walk that came up to the rear of Don, maybe fifteen feet close. Damn. Calling a double on lion and not a two dollar tag among the three of us. Two days later, the rancher who leased grazing rights to the area found a cow elk and calf killed and partially eaten by a pair of lions.

Elk are a common prey of the mountain lion in areas where range overlaps. The target, much of the time, is a cow or a calf. Mature bulls are oversize and can be more than just a mouthful. The same is not true of deer. Radio transmitting collars and tracking devices have caused biologists to discount the fallacy that the lion takes only the old and the sick. Lions, studies suggest, take the deer that is most easily killed. Probably pregnant does during the spring, fawns during the summer, and mature bucks during the rut, when a swollen neck and swollen testicles cause the breeding buck to become careless. Do lion also kill the old and the sick? Sure they do. The lion is an equal opportunity killer.

As mentioned, the lion grabs his groceries using a technique that sees a cooperation between sneak and run. A hungry lion stays alert as he or she patrols the territory. When a prey animal is sighted, the lion begins a slow and stealthy stalk. If the intended is a mule deer or a white-tailed deer, as it often is, the lion will advance when the deer's head is down. When the head is up the lion will turn to stone, at times pausing in midstride. The head goes down and the lion sneaks. When the lion is close enough, and the lion almost always knows, he turns to a blurred streak of tawny lightning, making a leap that puts him atop the deer's back. Razor sharp claws dig into the shoulders. Massive jaw muscles cause the substantial canine teeth to bite through neck muscles to search for the vertebrae. Small deer go to the ground almost immediately. Large deer, small elk, and livestock almost always make a run for it, hoping to end the deadly embrace. That effort is seldom successful.

The lion will eat his fill of the fresh kill and cover the leftovers with leaves and sticks, maybe snow or dirt—whatever is available. That lion will return to the kill when his appetite alarm sounds once again. The remains will be dragged to a somewhat clean place and the lion will feed, covering the carcass when through. When the weather is cold, keeping the meat somewhat fresh, the lion may feed from a carcass for as long as two weeks. One lion, observed during an Idaho study, fed from the carcass of an elk for nineteen days.

This aspect of the lion nature can cause a benefit to the predator caller. Screamers who find an active kill, those who set up to make a series of screamings in the area, have an excellent chance at success.

Gerry Blair screamed this lion from rough country so that dogs could make the tree. The 97-pound female was tranquilized, fitted with a radio collar, and released.

Adult male lion are loners. Mature toms get together with the ladies when it comes time to shake the sugar tree, but leave abruptly when the fun and games end. The mating might continue for several days and is almost always accomplished to the tune of much moaning, groaning, snarling, growling, and caterwauling. The female selects a den site located in any natural shelter, perhaps a cave or the overhang of a rim. A pregnant female may or may not use that same sanctuary when it comes time to deliver another litter but will usually return to the same general area. The female delivers a litter only once each two or three years.That litter can come at any time of the year but is most often delivered during the summer, a time when the young of prey ungulates offer easy hunting.

The litter of cubs, averaging three, are totally dependent on the female for the first months of life and need total protection, even from the mature tom who may have sired them. Male mountain lion, when opportunity allows, will kill and eat the cubs. That loss can cause the female to return to estrus and the male has one more chance to shake the sugar tree. The cubs stay somewhat dependent for the first year of life. The Parissawampits Lady ran with a female offspring that was nearly two years old and was about as big as Momma. How do I know that? Hell, I was there. It happened this way.

The radio-collared adult female lion ran a rough piece of real estate called Parissawampits Canyon, a brush choked gash that began atop the North Kaibab Plateau and fed off into the dismal depths below the North Rim of the Grand Canyon. The batteries of the radio collar at her neck began to weaken and it was time for recapture and recollar, a function most often accomplished using a pack of precisely trained hounds. Trouble was, the Lady ran country too rough for the hounds, or at least too rough for the hunters to follow. I was asked to help, asked to make a screaming that would cause the Lady to come out of her wilderness sanctuary.

I did and she did. The game guy sitting beside me during the screaming held an antenna that monitored movement. The lady came to about two hundred yards, out of sight in the brush, and that was close enough. Harley used the radio to call in the hounds.

The chase was short but exciting. A lion was treed in less than a mile. Trouble was, the lion was not The Lady. The lion halfway up the 150-foot-tall ponderosa pine was an eighteen-month-old uncollared female, probably the nearly adult offspring of The Lady. What did we do? What could we do? We used a modified Thompson Contender to shoot a dart into that ponderosa pussy, climbed to her, attached a rope, and lowered her gently to the ground. A radio collar fitted with a two year supply of batteries was attached to HER neck. And then back into the mystery of her territory in Parissawampits Canyon.

All lion are motivated to be territorial. Adult lion who have their own territory are at the top of the pecking order. Those who patrol and defend a territory that offers the most to the lion survival are the best of the best. Territorial lion adapt to the nature of their territory. Lion in the Spider Ranch Study (chaparral of west-central Arizona) showed little variation between summer and winter range. Lion in a North Kaibab Study (at considerably higher elevation) showed a preference for summer and winter territories that were some distance apart. The cause, most likely, was due to the migratory nature of the mule deer that is the lion's main source of groceries on the Kaibab.

Lion sign is often discreet, but careful observers will be able to seek it out.

Lion territory can vary as the sex of the lion and the wealth of the territory varies. Female lion on the Spider Ranch had home areas that varied from ten to almost seventy square miles. Adult toms in the same area had home areas that averaged fifty-nine square miles. Studies in northern states have established home areas much larger.

Lion sign is most often discreet, that is, not easily discovered during a casual investigation. Those who have learned to look, however, will find ample evidence of lion wanderings. The sign most often is as oversize cat tracks in dust, mud, or snow. Tracks left by large dogs can somewhat resemble lion tracks, at least in size. A close inspection will make positive identification possible. The heel pad of the lion is like the heel pad of all cats, that is, bi-lobed at the front and tri-lobed at the rear. (See sketch.) Dog tracks show a heel pad characteristic of the dog family, triangular in shape, coming to a point at the front, and bi-lobed at the rear. The tracks left by dogs almost always show toenail marks; tracks left by lion seldom do. Finally, the lion is a most efficient traveler. Unless pursued or on the chase for groceries, the lion does not move at more than a deliberate walk. Feet are firmly placed, leaving no disturbance outside of the track itself. Drag marks left by feet and by tail are often visible in deep snow.

Lion tracks left on level ground show that the print left by the rear foot will partially or totally overlap that left by the front foot. Tracks left by members of the dog family, by comparison, are most often left when the dog is at a trot. Dirt and gravel around the imprint is often disturbed. Dogs also have a tendency to move with the body at a slight angle to the line of travel, causing an offset in the front and hind feet so that overlap is avoided.

Lion scratches are sometimes found, showing where the lion urinated or defecated to mark territory. Look along rocky rims, in major drainages, in saddles and along trails. Such are most apt to be found when the territory of adult males overlap. The scratch will be seen as a series of long furrows. Scat may or may not be present. Dung heaps are an aspect of lion territoriality. Such may be made by both male and female. Some, left near a kill site, might act as an aid to rediscovery of the carcass, or might be left there to establish ownership of the remains. Others, most likely, are territorial markings, pure and simple. Mounds are constructed markings most likely made by females, particularly by females who have litters close by. Look for a dome of pine needles or other debris about five feet in diameter, somewhat resembling a covered kill but containing no animal remains.

A kill site, when fresh, is positive evidence a lion is nearby. Members of the cat family and the grizzly bear are the only U.S. predators who commonly cover a kill. A kill not covered might also be a lion kill as they do not always cover. Drag marks will show the number of visits.

As noted, blind calling for lion can be a tough way to take a lion. Most lion killed by screamers are taken opportunistically as the lion comes to a scream directed at a coyote or a bobcat. Even so, experience has convinced me a dedicated hunter can use certain circumstances to increase his or her chance of calling in the second largest of the North American cats, the jaguar being the largest.

I have said random calling does not often cause a lion to come. I say also that certain techniques of screaming will increase the like-

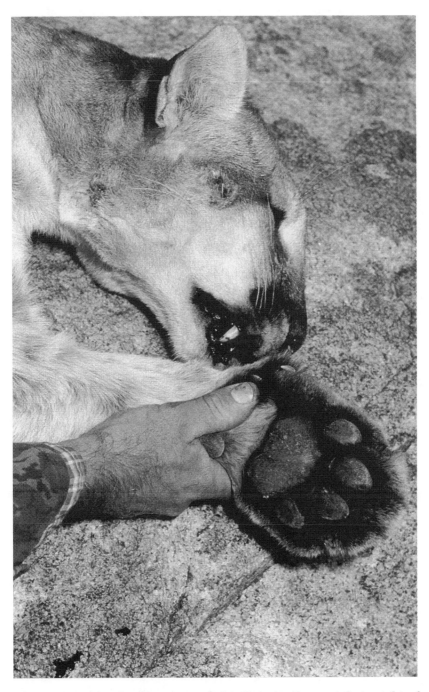

This mature tom had been in a fight. Note tooth wounds to right of ear and on neck. Upper lip shows a four inch tear.

lihood of calling a lion. Calling over or near a fresh and still active kill is the technique that offers the best opportunity to succeed. How does a hunter discover the presence of such? Develop contacts with those who spend a lot of their time in the wild country. Field folks employed by the U.S. Forest Service. The same in the State Game Managers. Become friendly with ranchers, a group almost always eager to cooperate in the killing of a stock-killing lion. Any and all others who know a lion kill when they see one.

Calling in an area that shows fresh lion sign can also be dandy. Fresh tracks, fresh scat, or a fresh scratch shows a lion was close by in the recent past. Driving forest roads on the morning after a night snow can be effective. Lion tracks found then are absolutely fresh, made since the snow stopped. Following those tracks to pause and scream at selected sites can produce. Larry and I have used each and all of those listed techniques to call and kill lion—random calling in lion habitat, having a lion come while calling to other species, calling a kill, calling a fresh track, and calling the snow. Each will work some of the time. None will work all of the time.

Track screaming after a snow can be productive. Experienced hunters follow the tracks, stopping to scream each half mile or so.

I call to lion about as I do to other animals, modifying technique to suit the lion nature. I prefer to use an open reeded call (Crit'R•Call, TallyHo, or Lohman C-280) and blow that call so as to produce a scream that is more deep-toned and having some rasp to it. A lion, the way I see it, is more likely to walk a mile to find a deer dinner than to walk a mile to gobble down a cottontail rabbit. I blow loud and strive for a rhythm that approximates the rhythm sounded by a deer fawn in distress. I scream for 30 seconds or so and rest my lip for a minute, then blow another 30-second series, repeating for the length of the stand. How long do I scream to a lion? Depends upon the circumstances. If I am screaming over a kill or over fresh sign I scream until the lion shows, almost. Larry and I screamed a boulder jumble for more than an hour after finding a smoking hot track in the sand of a desert dry wash. The 135-pound tom showed near the end of legal light. I have, more than once, continued the screaming for more than two hours. On the average, given moderate encouragement, I deliver no less than one-half hour of screams.

Every lion I have killed, every lion Larry has killed, fell to a .224" diameter bullet sent from the bore of a 22-250 at about 3700 fps muzzle velocity. Any caliber larger will do as well. Calibers lower become iffy. Even though a proper hit on a lion will cause that lion to get dead, every hit is not precise. I would worry about wounding when using calibers to the low end of the centerfire range. There are a lot of lion in the West, more than most realize. The hunter who spends a lot of time at the screaming, those who deliver the right technique, will eventually call lion. Doing so can be the highlight of any predator calling career.

Chapter 29

Calling Raccoon

I have heard it said "God must have loved the common man because he made so many of them." The same must be true of raccoons. You want the truth? In some parts of the country, maybe even most parts, there are a hell of a lot of raccoon (maybe more) skulking the midnight. That midnight skulk delivers mischief much of the time. That aspect of the raccoon personality can be a benefit to those of us who hide among the hardwoods, or the corn, to make a noise like a raccoon's supper. Landowners, even those cold-eyed ones who turn ugly when the question of access is asked, become emotional and chummy when they learn you are there to call and kill 'coon. The circumstances surrounding the wet work involving the Ms. Sadie situation illustrates the point.

Ms. Sadie was the kind of critter who loved every gopher and every sewer rat in this wide world. Didn't love 'em physically, of course, but loved them because they were "wild things," as she loved the rabbits, the chickens, the ducks, and the geese that roamed her property.

Sadie's collection of cluckers and quackers caused a lot of interest among the wildlife that roamed the adjoining national forest. The coyote, the bobcat, the gray fox, and the raccoon saw Sadie's loved ones as groceries. The mysterious disappearance of a part of the goose flock caused concern. On a moonless midnight Sadie was jolted awake. One of the remaining geese was honking piteously. Sadie grabbed a light and went to the rescue. Too late. She arrived in time to see the final phase of a messy struggle between the goose and a big boar 'coon. Sadie did not have the decency to wait until daylight to call me.

Having my sleep disturbed, particularly by a bunny hugger, causes a change of personality. My eyes narrow to bloodshot slits. Frown wrinkles cover my forehead. I am not a nice person. I had no cage traps big enough to hold a big boar 'coon, I lied to Sadie. The only help I could offer involved the ultimate sanction, wet work. It was that or kiss the rest of her geese (and probably the chickens and the rabbits) *adios*. Sadie gulped a couple of times and did just as any animal lover would do when confronted by a situation where something that belonged to her was threatened by something that did not belong to her. She did not come right out and say "kill every one of those miserable scumbags," but she nodded a go ahead. And I did.

The same thing, sort of, happened on a Texas ranch. The property was a vast holding devoted to cattle and to the controlled (and expensive) "harvest" of wildlife. Locked gates. Fences so high you needed an oxygen mask to climb over. Signs saying "Trespassers will be shot. Survivors will be shot again." That sort of thing.

Anyway, a colony of raccoon set up to work the corn feeders positioned to attract white-tailed deer and wild turkey so that the rich sports from Dallas/Fort Worth could shoot from the comfort of nearby blinds. The ranch foreman called a friend and he called me. Several nights later, after a series of proclamations from the awesome maw of the ten-gauge autoloader I call MooseDick, the corn supply was saved.

How does one go about screaming in a raccoon? Not as easy as it might seem but not impossible. The raccoon nature causes them to mostly resist the standard distress screams. I am not saying they will not come to a rabbit distress because they sometimes will. But not dependably. The best sound I have found for 'coon is a sound that incorporates a 'coon kit distress holler. The effectiveness of that kit screaming seems to be enhanced when the piteous kit calls interact with the mean snarls of an enraged boar raccoon. I heard that cooperation the first time during a Texas hunt with wildlife professional Bill DelMonte of Nolan and vicinity.

Bill DelMonte makes his living doing biology work for the Texas Department of Wildlife & Recreation. His off-time, during one period, was spent recording a series of wildlife distress

RACCOON FIGHT
Actual Live Recorded — Calls Varmints
℗ 1983, BILL E. DEL MONTE

Live Call
Ph. (915) 798-3152

Bill DelMonte's raccoon fight tape is one of the most effective at bringing out 'coon.

sounds, such sounds being marketed under the old Live Call label and later sold to the Johnny Stewart Company to be marketed under their label. The harmony achieved in his Raccoon Fight tape was and is the most effective 'coon calling sound I have heard.

Our first night among the 'coon caused us to drive night roads, senderos in Texas talk, to play the raccoon fight tape from the bed of the truck, legal in Texas law. We called 'coon close many times during a two-hour period, all coming close to the truck, all circling the truck, looking for a way up. Those who hope to use the Raccoon Fight Tape to call 'coon must have a device to cause the magnetic meanderings on the tape to turn to screams. I use and recommend the Johnny Stewart MS™512, a compact cassette player powered by a 12-volt motorcycle battery (rechargeable). Nope, I do not own stock in the Johnny Stewart Company. I consider the MS-512 to be

The raccoon skulks the midnight, most often with mischief on his mind.

a reliable and sturdy player, available at moderate cost. Check advertisements in the already mentioned *Trapper & Predator Caller* to discover rock bottom pricing.

Successful 'coon calling, it seems to me, results when the hunter fully understands raccoon needs and raccoon nature. Read on to learn all I know (maybe more) on the raccoon. The raccoon is a heavy-bodied critter that might weigh forty pounds or more. An adult animal measures about three feet from nose to tip of tail. Body fur is coarse and will range from dark to a light and grizzled gray. The raccoon has a distinctive black face mask, a characteristic that has caused him to be called a woods bandit. The ten-inch tail is ringed with alternating bands of dirty white and black, provoking a second nickname, Old Ringtail.

The raccoon is prolific and has increased his range. The omnivorous 'coon moves into old and newly developed agricultural areas to make a home close to his groceries. Predator control projects in much of the intermountain West has caused the raccoon to prosper. A place is made for the raccoon when larger land predators are thinned.

The raccoon is adaptable. He is often found within the city limits of even the largest city. Some metropolitan landfills host a respectable raccoon population. Other raccoons, in metro and rural areas, are somewhat constant visitors to backyards—on the search for food.

Raccoon are intermittent hibernators, choosing hollow trees, caves, and spaces within boulder jumbles.

The raccoon is not a fussy eater. Garbage dump coons might spend a lifetime eating the delicacies found in the dump. Waterway 'coons make their living catching and eating crawfish, minnows, frogs, and even snakes. Even though the food has just been retrieved from the water, the raccoon will sometimes wash it thoroughly before eating. That same raccoon will lose most of his fastidiousness when he finds a ripe piece of carrion on the bank. He will dive onto a rotting carp with a gusto that is a wonder to watch.

The raccoon, a true omnivore, will take fruits and vegetables when available. The 'coon fondness for corn, melons, and other produce is legendary. The raccoon might balance his vegetarian diet by eating eggs, and even those that lay the eggs. Eating sprees can turn his stocky body into a lard barrel. That stored fat will see the raccoon through the cold weather of winter.

The raccoon is an intermittent hibernator, not a hibernator in the true sense of the word. The raccoon will become less active or inactive during cold weather when food is scarce and will maintain cozy groupings in the hollows of trees and other natural openings. If the weather warms slightly the 'coon might come out to forage. The raccoon is likely to stay active year-round in the temperate climates.

Raccoons breed in midwinter, usually February and March. In warm climates they may breed year-round. The three to six young may be born in the hollow of a tree or in a rock crevice in a rock jumble. The kits show about two months after breeding. Male raccoons, being polygamous, do a lot of traveling during the breeding season. The female is a good mother, sometimes tending the kits for almost a full year, until she is ready to breed again.

All raccoon are skilled swimmers. And all can climb a tree as well as any animal can. The tree climbing might involve a search for food (persimmons and such) or might be because the 'coon needs a sanctuary. Even so, an adult boar 'coon has few natural enemies. Some weigh fifty pounds and are full of fight. Most large predators would prefer a supper less cranky.

The raccoon pelt is a staple of the fur industry. Prices fluctuate, just as the price paid for all fur fluctuates. Raccoon pelts prime about November and remain prime through February in much of the raccoon range. Raccoon meat is dark and moist. Depression babies born in the hardwood hills of the Missouri Ozarks gummed the tasty 'coon meat before the first tooth appeared. I speak from experience.

Raccoon are not often found far away from water. Tracks can easily be found in the mud at water's edge. Rear raccoon tracks are about three to four inches long and somewhat resemble a human foot. The rear is narrow and the front wide. Toe marks are not always present.

'Coon droppings vary as diet varies. Look for crawfish shells or vegetable matter in the scat. Some areas of high raccoon population will show well defined trails leading from the feeding grounds to the bed grounds. As mentioned earlier in this chapter, a Raccoon Fight tape played through a battery powered caller is most effective. I like to scout my raccoon calling locations during daylight to get a better concept of the lay of the land. If I am not totally familiar with the area I may mark stand locations using plastic pennants.

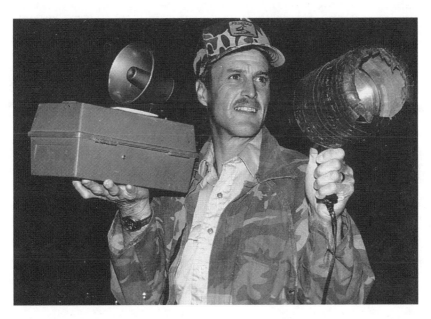

The right kind of light and a raccoon distress tape can be a deadly combination for 'coon.

Make the 'coon hunt during the dark; raccoon are almost totally nocturnal. Daylight, even crepuscular calls, will have low response. Park your vehicle away from the calling stand and walk in the final two or three hundred yards. Will the raccoon be alarmed because of the vehicle? Maybe yes maybe no. Other critters that might respond most certainly will be alarmed. I set the battery powered caller close to my sit-down and turn to low volume. If nothing shows in the first two or three minutes I turn the caller into a blaster, moving the volume knob extra loud.

Keep the beam of the finding light moving. A fast-moving raccoon might gallop too close when you swing slowly. Make an effort to flash the light high when there are trees close by. The raccoon I have met will sometimes climb a nearby tree to enjoy a better look. When eyes are located, on the ground or in the tree, reduce the call volume and prepare for the shot.

What kind of gun does a good job on raccoon? The Mag-10, mentioned earlier, can be dandy when loaded with copper plated BB's. A three-inch twelve, loaded the same way, does dandy also. Riflemen will want to consider the 22 WRFM (shooting hollow points) or the 22 Hornet. Both do a deadly job on close range raccoon. The 222, loaded to somewhat slow velocity, can be effective. Larger calibers, obviously, will do as well but might kill the critter deader than need be.

Callers who live near lakes, rivers, marshes, and backwaters might consider using a boat to patrol the banks, calling about each third of a mile. I prefer to stay about fifty feet out. Work the scanning light so as much of the bank as possible becomes illuminated. Much of the time the critter appears as a flash of eyes in the brushy shoreline. Shooting at such requires your reflexes to be quick. 'Coon calling, when it comes right down to basics, is not that tough. Work the night shift, just as they do. Set up close to raccoon habitat. Choose a setup that makes it easy for the raccoon to get to you and easy for you to get to the raccoon. Play or blow a sound that is interesting to the raccoon. After that it is a matter of practice.

Chapter 30

Calling Red Fox

It was nine in the morning when I made the setup. Constant clouds covered the sun, causing a dismal aspect to come to the Iliamna Barren Grounds. More dismal than ordinary. Those same clouds provoked a gentle rain and a miserable wind. The same miserable wind that had blown without relief for the past week. I snugged my big, wet body to the west (I think it was west, it can be difficult to know on the barren grounds) of an insignificant willow thicket and made a last minute check of the muzzle loader. The cap was on the recessed and inline nipple. The plastic cup covered to afford a degree of moisture protection. Plastic wrap covered the bore and covered the front of the telescope sight. Minutes before I had poked in the powder and the lead. "If the grizzly comes," I muttered to myself as I ungloved to reach for the TallyHo, "I hope this miserable wet bastard goes bang."

Ten minutes into the screaming, a flowing flash of red came at the lope from the south (I think it was south), from the Iliamni Lake side. Not a grizz, not even close. The customer was one of those big and beautiful Alaska reds, coming at the gallop. I let that dog fox come close, licked the call slobbers from my lips, and raised the Knight rifle. A semi-second later the trigger released and the bolt flew forward. The cap did not go bang and the powder did not go BANG. Only a depressing click as wet bolt smashed wet cap. I cocked and did it again. Another click. Several clicks later Gary "Slammer" Hull came at the charge from the far side of the willows, bringing the back-up gun, an A-Bolt Browning in 25-06. What did the red think of all of this? Curious. The fox considered it all to be damn odd. The critter sat 40 yards out to do a scratch. The 117 grain Sierra took him amidships during mid-scratch. I had called and killed my first Alaska red, killed him a lot deader than necessary. I collected the big pieces and we trudged off, looking for another.

The red fox ranges Alaska, parts of Canada, and nearly all of the continental United States. The coastal regions of some southeastern states have no reds. Nor does some of the West and much of the Southwest. A redless gap can be found in the Great Plains. As compensation, sort of, reds can be found in good numbers in much of the U.S. and that range is increasing even as we communicate.

The red fox found in much of the United States is likely a mutant. Our native red *Vulpes fulva* (tawny fox) was not widely distributed in much of the East during pioneer times. Our English progenitors, lonesome for the foxhunts held among the rolling hills of home, sicced the beagles and the bassets onto the somewhat plentiful gray fox. Not much fun at all. The gray had a habit of holing up and a worse habit of climbing a tree to look down smugly at the hounds. The limeys sent home for a transplant. A few months later a load of reds arrived. *Vulpes vulpes.* The good kind.

The refugees looked around, got friendly with the local reds, and more or less thrived. The red found in much of the East and Midwest is a product of that friendship, probably. Just as all black bears are not black, all red foxes are not red. The few reds found in the northeast corner of Arizona, as an example, have fur that is blonde, somewhat the color of a blonde cocker spaniel. That sandy fox (tawny?) is less red than the red accent found on some of the grays.

Some red fox further confuse as they mutate. Some red fox are silver and some are black. One color variation has the typical reddish color but has a dark cross over the shoulders and down the back. All of the assorted colors can be found in a single litter but seldom are.

The typical red can range up to fifteen pounds when fully mature. The average weight is less, maybe as low as ten or eleven pounds. The coat is true fur, not hair as is the case with the gray fox, and is full and fine, rich reddish underfur protected by long guard hair. The body is a couple of feet long. The tail adds another foot of length, is bushy and is almost always white tipped. Throat, neck, and chest are also white and the feet are black accented. The red aspect, in totality, is grand.

This Alaska red came at the gallop and stayed for the comedy.

Red fox fur lets them survive miserably cold winters.

The price paid for red fox pelts, as is the case with all other raw fur, cycles, responds to the twin masters of fashion and supply. Red fox fur has excellent insulation qualities. A red can bed when the temperature is so low it has to warm up to get damn cold. The red will find a hole when he can, maybe dig into the snow when he cannot, curl into a ball with that handsome tail around his nose, and stay somewhat warm. Maybe not toasty but sure in hell warm enough to stay alive. The red will stay holed during the blizzard and during the baddest part of a storm, coming out to hunt when weather improves.

The red is an opportunistic feeder. He eats when he can and what he can. Favored foods are mice and voles and any other rodent he can catch and kill. A hungry red can hear a mouse wearing Reeboks at fifty yards. That red will pause to pose with a foot aloft until he has zeroed to the target, maybe deciding direction of travel. That done, the red will leap and pounce, usually pinning the creeper in a mat of grass or leaves. Fox in agricultural areas (a favored habitat) regularly feed on rats, rabbits, birds (ground nesters like the bobwhite quail, the ringneck pheasant, waterfowl, and the wild turkey are particular targets), and even eggs and poultry. As is the case with other foxes, actually with all members of the wild dog family, the red owns a stomach that can find nourishment in fruits and vegetables as well as meat. A true omnivore.

Carrion can taste good to a red. I have seen hide and bones from young antelope and deer decorating the front porch of a red fox den. Nope, it is not likely the red made the kill, even though such has been documented. The scraps, much of the time, have been collected from kills effected by bigger dogs.

The vixen red come into heat once each year (monestrous) and that estrus occurs during late January, maybe a little before or after. The males commonly fight for the right to shake the sugar tree and that fight can be exciting. The males stand nose-to-nose with feet interlocked, striving mightily to show dominance. They leap and cavort with full tails flowing. When dominance has been established, the loser skulks away and the winner leaves with the girl.

It is likely red fox pair somewhat permanently. The male and the female share denning duties. When the kids are old enough to make it on their own, the adults may go their separate ways to lead their own lives until the mating urge returns. Some biologists feel the same two fox will get together the following year, if both are still around.

A red fox den might be established in an enlarged badger or woodchuck hole. If none such is available, the red will dig one, maybe selecting a site in the roots of a tree or under a substantial rock. Multiple tunnels commonly lead to the den, providing escape routes and ventilation. The mainly used tunnel is likely to face the east in colder climates so that the rising sun will warm somewhat.

Most reds have alternate dens, moving the kids to a new site when the parents perceive a threat. Working as a team the male and female can vacate suddenly, carrying the protesting pups in their mouth.

The red fox litter can be substantial. Dens containing ten pups have been documented. The average is lower, probably a half dozen or so. Pups are furred but blind at birth. Red fox milk is rich, much more rich than milk from a cow. Pups nurse frequently. The rich milk is supplemented by an equally rich regurgitated meat. The

When food is easily available, red fox pups might establish territories close by; others may travel hundreds of miles.

vixen is likely to bring bits of fur and feathers so that the pups might be amused as they learn a bit of the real world. Later, when the pups are ready, a live mouse or vole will be brought. Red fox pups learn the art of killing early on. The pups hunt with the adults when about two months old, starting on grasshoppers and such and then graduating to big game, mice, voles and other fox delicacies. When the pups are about five months old, when the frost hits, they are invited to get the hell gone, and they do. If the area around the den has a good food supply the young fox might not go far from home. If times are hard the young might travel a substantial distance looking for a piece of ground that offers survival advantage.

A biological study done at the University of Wisconsin documented an interesting dispersal. A young red fox, captured and tagged near Madison, was shot by a hunter near Montgomery County, Indiana, nine months later. The distance traveled? A straight line measure of 250 miles. A litter mate, tagged at the same time, was recaptured a year later, a few hundred yards from the original capture site. Go figure.

During dispersal can be a dandy time to scream at the red. There are more red fox to be called than at any other time of the year. The young of the year are out and about, a hungry gang of teenagers desperate to survive. Generally low hunting and poor survival skills cause them to eagerly cooperate. Look for dispersal in October, or thereabouts.

Fox are territorial. No surprise there. Most critters are so. The size of the red fox territory will be determined by prey density and food availability. A red might make a living on a few hundred acres if plenty of groceries are available. Areas less endowed might cause the fox to claim and protect a territory of five square miles. A Minnesota study showed an average territory of two square miles. That same study showed that collared animals did not often visit the neighbors.

Red fox, like all dogs, mark territory with urine and scat and will vocalize to warn off other fox. A fox that visits will be attacked. What causes the red fox to be such a grump? They have to be. They are not just fighting for their territory, they are fighting for their life. Red fox droppings are often seen along fence borders, farm roads, and paths. The scat is dog-like and is between coyote scat and gray fox scat in size. All such eat about the same kind of groceries, however, and absolute identification can be difficult. Scat found without a supporting track can remain a mystery.

The red fox track is somewhat distinctive. It is dog-like in configuration, is smaller than a coyote track, and larger than the track left by a gray fox. Front feet are larger than the rear. Prints made by a walking fox will appear in a nearly straight line. Prints left on firm ground will likely show as a partial, maybe only toes and a part of the pad.

Some fox dens will be found near elevated land features. A North Dakota biologist found red fox dens on mounds and hillocks scattered in overgrazed ground, maybe in hayed or otherwise idle land. That same study established that the reds there did not hibernate.

Reds are mainly nocturnal. I say so even though reds are at times seen hunting during daylight, most often during dead winter when food from night hunts is not enough. Winter fox will sometimes curl

Red fox might live close to human habitation. This red lived in a culvert near the Grand Coulee Project Office in Washington state. (U.S. Bureau of Reclamation Photo by N. Boekel)

atop a high point (a hill, a hummock, a hay bale, a rockpile, all such) to sun and survey. Hunters who know this will drive farm roads and glass those high points. A located fox is stalked to within rifle range, or screamed to rifle range.

Reds can be a tough call, particularly during daylight. Daytime activity can cause the fox to just say no to the best articulated scream. Night calling is most effective in most of the red fox range.

It is critical to scout night calling areas during daylight to get a feel for the land and to learn of hazards that might be a concomitant to shooting. Plan your setup so that you know the direction of likely approach. If the wind is more or less constant, consider that also. Use skunk musk as a masker. More information on night calls can be found in the chapter on night calling. A day visit will allow the opportunity to shake and howdy with the landowner. Midnight, as previously noted, is a poor time to go door knocking.

Day or night you are likely to have the best luck when calling to reds during the hungry months of January and February. The red has used up his fat reserve by then. The fox has to hunt or hunger. That hunger can cause him to respond to a screaming, even though he may stay suspicious.

Calling the weather, as mentioned in that chapter, can cause the red to cooperate. The red will be out and hunting as a storm front arrives and will be hungry and hunting when the storm leaves. The day before the storm and the day after can be dandy if such is not plagued by strong wind. I have also had luck calling on cloudy days. Such unsettled weather can cause the red to be nervous—maybe *restless* is a better word—and they will interrupt their routine to travel and hunt during daylight. Foggy days are also good. The fog helps to hide the hunter. The fox feels hidden also and shows an unusual confidence. The fog can cause the screaming to be subdued. Reduce the amount of distance between stands to compensate. Calling foggy nights can be frustrating. The fog disperses the beam of the light causing it to be difficult to see eyes.

The red fox I have met have not come to the call showing the eagerness seen in a gray or in a naive coyote. A red is wary by nature and his suspicion will increase each time he is fooled by a screaming. His keen nose can cause him to become alarmed, maybe before you sight him. Some red fox will circle to get downwind, to take a taste of the wind. Watch wind direction. Scream to the upwind when you can. When you cannot, scream to a crosswind. Use skunk musk as a masker.

The red fox is mainly a mouser. Calls that imitate the distress cry of a mouse or a bird, any non-threatening little critter, can be particularly effective. I like the sound made by the close-in callers for the first calls. I sometimes lip squeak to start the stand, hoping to suck in customers that might be close. If you use a battery powered caller, consider using a tape containing the distress scream of a baby cottontail or one of the bird distress tapes. I have had good luck using the flicker (sometimes labeled as the Yellowhammer Woodpecker) distress on reds. Play either at medium volume. I scream to reds for between ten and fifteen minutes, just as I do to other dogs. Do I say no red fox will come after that time? I do not say so at all. I say, instead, it is unlikely you will see a lot of action after that amount of time. It is better, the way I see it, to pack up the junk and travel to a fresh setup where the odds of response will increase.

Reds become call shy after a bad experience or two. They must do so if they are to survive. Even an educated fox can be called. Try a different sound on these Ph.D. fox. If most in your area blow a TallyHo, go to a Crit'R•Call, or vice versa. Switching to a battery powered caller can make sense. The variety of sounds available can be mind-boggling. Please remember one fact. The paranoid red is a real wimp. Play a gray fox distress or a coyote pup distress, even a coyote howl, and you are not likely to fetch in a red. The metal reeded calls sound similar—at least to my ear—no matter the mouth. The scream from a plastic reeded call can change as the mouth changes and as the position of the same mouth moves a bit to titillate the plastic. The red fox range is widespread and there are a lot of reds within. The screamer who keeps on hunting, those that understand the red nature and tailor the technique to respond, are in for a lot of calling excitement.

Chapter 31

The Uncalled and the Unexpected

I consider the predator call to be misnamed. Sure, a call that imitates the distress scream of a prey animal will cause predators such as coyote, bobcat, fox, lion, bear, and too many others to mention, to come close. That same distress scream can cause other animals, a bunch of them not the least bit predatory, to come equally close. I have had songbirds come to nearly perch on my hat brim as they made the effort to seek out the source of bird distress sounds. Jackrabbits have come like grapes, in bunches, to investigate sounds that simulated the distress scream of a jackrabbit. I have had deer, elk, antelope, javelina, cattle, and horses come close to investigate a screaming. On one stand I called in a hippie. You want the truth? About anything with ears might respond to a properly sounded distress scream.

Why do non-predators come to a screaming when logic suggests they should run the other way? Don't know. Those who have responded have not shared their thinking. I speculate that most prey animals come to defend. The critters might lope in believing a son, daughter, or other relative might be in jeopardy. They respond, perhaps, hoping to effect a rescue. I offer a couple of examples to support this speculation.

Larry and I set up within the greasewood bordering a mesquite-lined wash to do a screaming for coyote. A coyote came, trotted close, and received a .54 caliber maxiball between the eyes. We kept on calling as we almost always do after the shot. Minutes later a crashing of brush announced the arrival of a heavy-bodied animal. A doe deer bounded into view, and boy, was she mad. Her ears were laid flat to her neck to show hostility. The body language that showed hostility doubled when she came upon the carcass of the coyote. Every hair stood at attention. She snorted and reared, bringing her front feet down to within inches of the coyote's head. That doe was a hundred pounds of ugly, each ounce of that ugly hating that poor dead coyote. Larry had to laugh and when he did I did. The doe retreated at an indignant trot. As she left a second deer, a half grown immature, trotted down the wash to join momma.

Distress screams not only call predators close but can attract other animals as well.

Another call caused a sounder of javelina to spook and disperse. Some, including several very young javelina, made a hard run away from the setup, obviously hoping to get as far away from the screaming as possible. Four of the gang did not run away. They came straight to the screams at a charge, making no attempt to be neighborly. The salt-and-pepper hair of their backs was at attention, causing them to look twice as big as their 35-pound size. And that was not enough. Tusks clacked dangerously and all of that was decorated with the most ferocious grunting. The foursome, obviously, hoped to intimidate the screamer, and they did. I sat tight and sat quiet until the outraged peccaries tired of being tough and trotted off to rejoin the sounder.

The hunter who understands the full potential of the screamer can use that knowledge to good advantage. Bird photographers and those who simply like to see birds at close range can play a screech owl distress tape to cause about every kind of songbird to come close. That same sound, played during the dark, can cause great horned owls to swoop to brush the cap brim with a wing tip, and at times, to light upon the limb of a nearby snag. Such visits offer excitement and offer the opportunity to capture somewhat shy wildlife on film.

The fawn distress scream can be a dandy way to call deer to the camera or to the gun. My experience has convinced me doe are the most common respondent. I say that even though I have used the fawn bleat to call buck deer. Screaming to deer can be an effective hunting technique when hunting during the rut. The screaming that brought the Child Molester Buck to the muzzleloader illustrates the point.

Larry and I had worked the alluvial ridges on the north side of the Harcuvar Range for two days. On each of those days I had used the fawn distress scream to bring a buck close. The first day the buck was a small-horned four-point that came to about 250 yards, then hung up to begin a nervous stomping and snorting. The distance was beyond comfortable range for the black powder gun. Also, I was not that interested. I walked one way and the buck walked the opposite.

The second day the buck was big, mighty big, probably more than 250 pounds on the hoof and carrying a grand four-point rack (Western count) that was dandy, maybe an honest 34" spread. I screamed the big buck, and his harem of does, to within fifty yards of Larry O. Trouble was, no clear shot was offered. A palo verde, a mesquite, or one of the does was always between. No shot. Larry and I returned to the area the next day, hoping for a second chance. I was set up on the lip of a desert bowl when I settled in to make a screaming. I blew as I almost always blow for deer. I placed the TallyHo to the corner of my mouth and huffed out air to sound a series of somewhat long moans, doing my best to imitate a fawn in distress.

The four-point came a few minutes into the call, bringing along a pair of young does, jail bait. All three ran close, to about thirty yards, providing an excellent opportunity. The Child Molester weighed a bit over 200 pounds when field dressed. Using the distress scream to bring javelina close to the camera, the bow or the gun increases success. Those who know javelina best know the main range of the pig-like critter is within Arizona, parts of New Mexico, Texas, and Old Mexico. Javelina run in herds (called

A screaming during the deer rut can cause big racks to follow the does to the gun.

A screaming brought these adult boars, then caused them to fight to establish dominance.

sounders) and each adult member of that herd is committed to the integrity of the herd. That commitment causes a response when a danger is perceived. A threat causes adult members of the sounder to scatter. Immature javelina, those too little to keep up, freeze, hoping to become obscure or invisible. The adults will almost always halt the escape when they hear a distress scream that might be from one of the young. Some, I call them the enforcers, return to make the rescue.

Can it be dangerous to scream at javelina? I think not, although some might not agree. A calling companion who shared a close experience of the javelina kind most surely would disagree. It happened this way.

I took Fred to the high desert for a coyote screaming, the first time for him. A tusk-clacking sounder of javelina showed at one stand and Fred showed a total lack of control when he shouted a warning, leaped to his feet, and took off down canyon at a brisk pace. Trouble was, down canyon was the way the pigs decided to go. Convinced the slavering horde was after him, Fred plowed through mesquite, cat claw, and at least one Teddy Bear Cholla. He would have been better to surrender to the pigs. I had one hell of a time running him down.

The ringtail cat, actually the cacomistile, is a nocturnal predator somewhat common to certain parts of the southwestern U.S., Mexico, and Central America. The ringtail cat is not a cat at all, but one of the three members of a family that includes raccoon and coatimundi. The ringtail is a sleek and slender animal about two feet long, half of that being tail. The body fur is short and gray-brown grading to a cream on the belly. The tail is decorated with alternating bands of black and white. A big bull ringtail will weigh less than three pounds. Ringtail are night hunters and day sleepers. Do not expect to call many during the day. Do a screaming during the dark, in ringtail habitat, however, and the action can be

The ringtail cat is nocturnal but can be called during dusk and dawn.

The screech owl distress tape will bring songbirds like this cactus wren camera close.

dandy. I have my best luck calling within an area where scat or tracks show ringtail presence using a non-threatening bird distress sound. As is the case with most night hunters, the ringtail has oversize eyes that illuminate like a pair of miniature moons when hit by the light. I have not found the little furbearers to be light shy, having used the flash on a camera to take more than one exposure before the cat-like critter leaves.

Birds of every sort will come to a proper screaming. Songbirds and owls have been mentioned. Hawks, eagles, ravens, and crows come about as well. I can't count the number of redtails I have called close during a screaming directed at other critters. I called seven Harris hawks during one stand one winter, at a time when these communal hunters were passing. Golden and bald eagles have responded. It can be difficult to make a screaming and not attract a raven or a crow in certain areas. All lend interest to the screaming. All can provide photo opportunities to those who are so inclined.

About every kind of game animal from bull buffalo to bighorn sheep has come to a screaming. I used the distress scream on one hunt to harvest a decent buck antelope. I had glassed the fifteen-inch buck on the fringe of a juniper push. A deliberate stalk caused me to be within about a half mile of his position when I blundered into a group of does. Knowing I would spook the does and they would spook the buck as they fled, I holed up. Knowing the antelope were in the rut, knowing the herd of does almost surely had a buck close by, I whipped out the predator call and started a screaming. The buck, nervous because he thought one of his sweeties was in anguish, came at a hop I call the rutting strut, a hopping that cause the four feet to bunch and to hit the ground together. Each time the feet hit, the buck sounded an explosive grunt. Even though he was not a buck to write home to mother about, I took the shot. The horns were fifteen-and-a-half inches and massive with decent paddles. I crouched to begin the dirty work. Halfway through a grunt caused me to look. A second buck antelope, likely the one I had stalked originally, watched from a hundred yards out.

Domestic and feral dogs will sometimes come to the screaming. Free-running dogs show regularly in country where an abundant population is present. The vast span of the Navajo Indian Reservation, lands that occupy about a fourth of the state of Arizona and then slops over into parts of New Mexico, Colorado, and Utah, is one such. Feral and free-running dogs are a problem there, so much so that tribal authorities have placed free-running dogs at risk, causing them to be a legal target to any screamer who buys the moderately-priced small game hunting license.

A screamer never knows what to expect when he or she sets out to squeeze the rabbit. Nothing may come. The next screaming might cause a curious deer to come close. A call a quarter of a mile away might bring in a mountain lion or a bear. The suspense created, the not knowing what might show, creates an excitement that keeps us screaming.

Chapter 32

Skinning

Fur care begins with the shooting, continues during the retrieve, the transportation, the skinning, the repairs, the washing, stretching, and manicuring. "WHOA," you say. "Seems to me there is a lot more to precise fur handling than is obvious." You are exactly right, I answer. Read on to learn techniques that can cause the pelts you handle to look good on the wall and at the taxidermist, pelts that will bring out the generous nature of the most squinty-eyed fur-buyer.

Enlightened fur handling starts before the shot. I say so even though I know critters coming to the call must be "harvested" (God, how I hate that word) and know that such harvesting can be imprecise and somewhat destructive. Even so, the screamer has options when it comes time to do the wet work. One option, favored by some, involves the use of the moose gun, the elk gun, or the bear gun. And they light into the customer with the enthusiasm usually reserved for the charging and close-range grizzly. SHOOT THAT SUCKER, and if he wriggles, shoot him again.

Honesty causes me to say such technique will almost always cause death, often a very messy death. The corpse, sad to say, is killed deader than need be. The collecting of the big pieces from the various zip codes can be time-consuming and depressing. You want my advice? Read the chapter dealing with caliber selection, read, and heed.

Shooting the precise caliber needed to cause the critter to become only moderately dead can be dandy when shot placement is precise. An imprecise hit with a precisely correct caliber, sad to say, can also cause the wet work to turn nasty. Later in this chapter I will describe a wonderful technique that can cause a holey hide to become nearly pristine. That technique is called sewing.

Screamers who hope to "harvest" the pelt (and that includes about all of us) will benefit if they address pre-skinning concerns. Critters shot with a high velocity centerfire, much of the time, will show an insignificant entry wound and no exit. No blood. "HOO BOY," some will say, "I did good on that 'un!!!" Such is not always the case. The entry wound, following the nature of warm flesh, is puckered. That pucker will almost surely unpucker as body temperature decreases. What happens then? Blood, brother, and lots of it. I carry paper towels in the pocket or the day pack and use such and a stick to poke in a plug.

The trip to the vehicle should show respect for the critter corpse. Resist the temptation to drag. The draggings I have seen (and participated in) have never caused an improvement to the critter hide. Some draggings have caused damage; broken hair, the collection of grass and sticks, and soiling by dirt or mud. Those who do not skin in the field should protect the carcass during transport. Protect from what? Dust, rain, snow, sun, grease, oil, and all such. Protect the carcass also from pee and poop that is likely to ooze from the pooter as the sphincters relax. All such soilings are easily prevented but not easily corrected.

The timing of the skinning can be important. I have skinned hot critters, lukewarm critters, cold critters, and a few times, (shudder) frozen solid critters. Those experiences have provoked a strong opinion. The longer a skinning is delayed, the tougher the job. You want that put another way? Hot skinning a coyote might take ten minutes. That same coyote will demand two or three times as long when cold.

Skinning technique can vary as the experience and personality of the skinners vary. Even so, certain constants endure, particularly so when the skinning involves one of the most commonly called land predators—coyote, fox, and bobcat. I find it most convenient to hang the animal during skinning. I say so even though I know skinners, some mighty good ones, who do not. Legendary caller Murry Burnham of Marble Falls, Texas, can skin a grounded coyote fast

Dragging degrades the fur. Enlightened hunters find better ways to transport.

and easy. Others, Larry Gates being one, start the skinning on the ground and transfer to the hang after the hind legs are exposed. Me? I hang from the get-go.

Those of us who are hangers need some sort of suspension device to cause the carcass to be at a convenient height. Something sturdy, a device that will resist the muscular manipulations common to my style of skinning. The best suspender I have found is a

Murry Burnham is a ground skinner, whereas the author prefers to hang-skin.

choke chain, available at the pet supply sections in discount department stores. I use one end of the choker to suspend a hind foot and attach the opposite end to a stout limb.

Skinning begins with knife selection. I skin using a sharp knife. The sharper the better. Knowing that most of the skinning will be done using the first half-inch of the blade, I choose a knife that is light weight. Comfortable. A knife that does not unnecessarily tire the hand and wrist during the skinning of multiples.

There are two techniques used during the skinning of most fur-bearers, open and cased. Most critters, those destined for the fur trade, will be case-skinned. Open skinning is reserved for those animal pelts to be used as rug mounts. Some fatsos—badger, beaver and that sort—will be open-skinned also. Case skinning, simply described, is a skinning that causes the pelt to be separated from the carcass at the rear legs and at the tail. The pelt is then pulled and cut away from the carcass, a bit like grabbing the top of a tube sock and pulling it from off the leg and the foot. Simple? Maybe. Read on to learn tips that cause the technique to be less traumatic.

I use the pointed blade of the knife to make a cut on the inside of each hind leg, extending from the crotch to the foot. Look for the color line that will always be visible, the place where the belly fur meets the back fur. Slip the point of the knife inside the fur, making the cutting from the inside out. Make the cut along that line. Cut a ring around each hind foot to release the fur, then use the fingers (and the knife when necessary) to strip the fur away from the hind legs down to the base of the tail. Use finger strength and maybe a bit of knife work to part the tail fur from the tailbone. You will be able to expose about two or three inches of the tailbone. Use a tail stripper (available from advertisers in *Trapper & Predator Caller* magazine), a pair of sticks, and a couple of big nails to facilitate the further stripping of the tail. Place the selected device to top and bottom of the exposed tailbone, at the place where the fur starts, and use strength and strong language to strip the tail completely free.

Gerry Blair skins while critters are freshly dead.

Place your fingers on the leather and use strength to pull the hide away from the flesh until you reach the front shoulders. Some hides strip easily and some strip reluctantly. The hides of hot critters strip most easily. If resistance is encountered, use the knife, returning to the pull as soon as practical. One caution—use finesse instead of brute strength when you encounter the wound caused by the bullet. Too much enthusiasm can cause a further tearing.

Freeing the pelt from the front shoulders can be tricky. I use a length of steel rod, maybe a big screwdriver or a no-longer-needed sharpening steel from the kitchen knife set, to intrude between the front of the shoulder, at its joining with the chest. Pressure applied to the rod can cause some of the front leg hide to strip away. Hand and finger pressure can further strip the legs. How much leg fur is enough? I strip down to the elbow, make a cut around the elbow, and pull the leg through. Muscle power can cause the skin to strip down to the start of the neck after the front legs are released. The hide at the neck becomes tight and it is almost always necessary to use the knife. Do so with caution. The big arteries, the carotids, are close to the surface. Cutting into one will cause bleeding, usually a lot of bleeding.

240

The fox, it should be mentioned, is very small-necked. The hide will almost always hang up at the head. It will be necessary to cut and pull until the neck hide enlarges enough to pull over the head. Pull and cut the hide to the ear butts, using your fingers to locate such, and cut to release the ear butts from the meat of the skull. Continue to cut to the eyes and use the knife to skin out each eye. The membrane stays with the skin. Skin on down to the lips and beyond, leaving the dark membrane with the skin. Finally, at the nose, cut the hide so that the nose stays attached. Case skinning has been completed. If done in the field turn the hide leather side in, hair side out. Use the knife to make a cut from tail butt to tail tip, exposing the leather. Doing so lets the tail leather be exposed to the air so it will dry properly. Those who leave the tail uncut risk inside decay, causing the hair of the tail to slip. Start at the nose and roll the pelt to a compact bundle, then store in a ZipLoc gallon-size freezer bag. Why freezer bag? If I do not intend to handle the fur immediately I can place it as is in the freezer to be handled some other time.

Skinning open, although seldom done on fur to be sold, fur intended to be tanned to serve as a wall hanger, or fur headed for a new life as a taxidermy mount, is done about the same as case (or tube) skinning. Hang the unskinned carcass and use the knife to make a cut at the color line on the inside of the rear legs, extending the cut from crotch to ankle, just as you would do with case skinning. Strip the tail away from the tailbone, just as you would do when case skinning. Now take the point of the knife and make a cut that extends from the crotch cut to the chin. Make another cut that extends from the inside ankle of each front foot to the center cut on the chest. Pull with the fingers, using the knife when needed, to remove the skin. Finally, make the tail cut described during the case skinning instruction.

Open-skinned pelts can be placed within the ZipLocs to be refrigerated or frozen. Fold the pelt, leather to leather, so that the pelt is halved long ways. Now make the roll. Some buyers will be willing to buy fur from unskinned carcasses. Others will buy skinned fur that is not handled (buying green). In each case the price paid will be less than the price paid for fully-handled fur. The next chapter will cover the techniques of fur cleaning, fur repair, stretching, drying, and grooming.

Chapter 33

Fur Handling

Fur handling is a series of simple steps that cause the green pelt to turn into a stretched and dried pelt of uncommon beauty. The term "stretching" is somewhat of a misnomer. Pelts are not stretched in the true sense of the word. They are, instead, tautened on a wood or wire stretcher so that the air dries the leather, permitting storage until the fur is sent to the tannery. Much of the time, intermediate steps are necessary before the pelt is ready for the stretcher.

Some pelts will be soiled. Blood, mud, or fecal material may have contaminated the fur. A part of the time those contaminants can be mostly brushed away when the pelt has dried. Other times the soiling will be so severe it is necessary to wash the pelt prior to handling. Some fur handlers, the purists, wash every pelt to make it look as good as can be. Why would an unsoiled pelt need washing? Coyote, fox, and bobcat do not often bathe. Try never. The pelts from wild critters almost always have natural oils to cause the fur to be somewhat waterproof. That natural oil will cooperate with dust and dirt to cause a dingy aspect to the fur. Washing takes out the grease and takes out the dust. A properly washed pelt presents a bright aspect, looking as good as can be.

Pelt washing takes a bit of time but is not difficult. Use a pail or sink full of lukewarm water flavored with a bit of liquid detergent. Turn the unhandled pelt hair side out and slosh that pelt around in the water until most of the contaminants transfer from pelt to water. Empty the pail, refill with more water, and repeat. Continue until the water stays clean.

Hold the wet pelt by the nose and use the other hand to strip water as you move the hand down, following the lay of the hair, to the tail. Repeat until excess water has been removed. Place the still wet pelt hair side out on a wood or wire stretcher frame and place it in a somewhat warm room. When the hair has dried it is time to attend to other aspects.

Some pelts, as mentioned earlier, have holes in need of repair. Those that have been shot with a shotgun loaded with copper-plated BB's, or anything smaller, are not likely to need repair. Even though there may be a lot of holes, all small, such is not likely to alarm the fur buyer. Larger holes, those made by high velocity centerfires, almost always need a stitch or two. Maybe more. Do the stitching with a needle having a somewhat large throat.

I have used waxed fishing line and have used monofilament line. Waxed dental floss also works. Turn the pelt leather side out and use the knife to trim away bits of fat, leather and bloodshot meat. Pinch the tear together and use the needle and thread to single stitch, pushing through the leather only, avoiding the hair. Tie off each stitch using a square knot. Repeat, stitching every quarter inch or so, until the wound is closed.

Most hides need fleshing before being dried. The fleshing does take off bits of flesh left by the skinning but mostly takes off plates of muscle and fat. A fleshing knife and fleshing board, both available from advertisers in *Trapper & Predator Caller,* make the job easy. Place the pelt leather side out on the fleshing beam and then use the fleshing knife, held at an angle, to scrape the leather. Do not over-flesh. Doing so can harm the hair roots and cause hair loss.

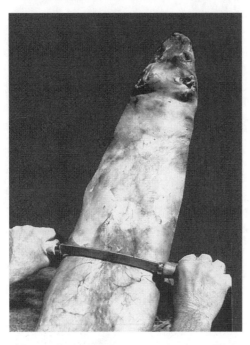

The fleshing beam and fleshing knife cooperate to remove fat and muscle.

Some pelts will contain burrs, pitch, and hair mats. Remove all such before starting the fleshing. If left, the fleshing knife will hang up there to cause a tear, provoking unnecessary repair. Hides that have been sewn can be fleshed, but must be fleshed carefully so that the knife does not cause a rippage. Some areas, the ear butts for example, will not accommodate the fleshing knife. Use a knife to cut meat, muscle, and fat away. Is it a good idea to salt the ear butts and the leather of the tail? Absolutely not. Salting causes water to gather rather than leave. Something in the salt messes up the tanning operation. Do a good job of fleshing and no salt is needed.

Stretching can be done using wood or wire. Even though I am convinced fur stretched on wood has a better look, I am equally convinced the buyer does not have a preference. I use wire most often because it is faster to do so. Position the pelt on the wood stretcher and pull taut, using brads or small nails to attach the pelt to the stretcher at the hips, or using the clamps provided on the wire stretcher. Place the stretched fur in a moderately warm room to dry. How long does it take the leather of a pelt to crust? Don't know. Crusting will depend on temperature and humidity. Crusting might take an hour or two or might take a day or two. I suggest you experiment to learn crusting time where you live.

When the leather has crusted, maybe being eighty or ninety percent dry, remove it from the stretcher and turn the pelt so that the hair is out. This turning is most easily accomplished by turning the nose back into the mouth and pushing the head as far into the opening as reasonable. Push a pole, maybe the handle from a broom, into the opening to catch the nose. Stand the pole on a solid surface. Turn the hips so that the hair side is out and pull until the fur is completely turned.

What do you do if you mess up and let the leather get too dry to turn? Use a wet rag or wet paper toweling to slightly moisten the leather. Watch the drying closely (it will not take long) and make the turn when the time is right. Return the pelt to the stretcher, hair side out, and store upright, in a cool dry place, until the leather is completely dried. The dried fur can now be removed from the stretcher for storage. Before doing so, use a wire brush (I use a poodle brush) to comb and fluff the fur. Some fur handlers use air pressure from a compressor to do the job. Do not ignore the hair or fur on the tail.

Parts of the carcass can be salvaged, as a personal trophy or as a cash crop. If you call and handle a lot of predators, think about collecting the urine and the glands. The most desirable glands, the anal glands, are those located to the right and the left of the pooter. Others are located between the muscles of the hips and below the ears. Each is kidney bean shaped and is of a nasty gray color. Urine and glands can be sold to trappers or sometimes sold to a trapper supplier.

Skulls are also salable, the price determined by rarity. Some callers clean the skull and retain such as a trophy

Pelts remain on stretcher until leather is about eighty percent dry . . . removed . . . turned, and returned to the stretcher hair side out.

245

of the hunt. Some (I am one) have an extensive skull collection. Some are natural while others have painted-on decoration. How can a skull be cleaned? There are those about who provide a skull cleaning service. Skulls Unlimited, P.O. Box 6741, Moore, Oklahoma 73149 is one. Owner Jay Villamemarette has been a trapper and caller. He cleans using dermestid beetle (carrion beetles) colonies, no boiling to weaken the bone. Cleaned skulls are handsome.

Those who wish to clean their own skulls (actually, the skull of called and killed predators) can do so. Cut the skull away from the vertebra. Use the knife to cut out the tongue and as much of the

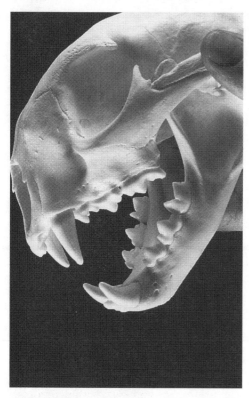

meat and muscle easily available. Place the skull in enough water to cover, adding a cup full of laundry soap and boil for about a half hour. Shut off the heat and leave the skull in the water until it cools. Use a section of clothes hangar wire to get into the brain cavity (through the vertebra hole) and mush up the cooked brains. Use air pressure or water pressure to remove the brains. Use a stiff bristle brush to clean away residual meat.

Predators can host an amazing variety of vermin. I shot a female coyote on one hunt that carried enough fleas to pull a wagon. Some fur handlers have advised leaving the pelt out overnight to allow the fleas the opportunity to abandon. This has not worked for me. The fleas I have come in contact with prefer warm fur to cold ground. I have

Cleaned skulls (small cougar pictured) are attractive and salable.

hung hides out in sub-zero temperature for days and found fleas when I made an inspection. I have placed pelts within plastic bags and placed those plastic bags in the freezer. Some fleas, almost always, survive. What to do? Carry a 30-gallon trash bag on the hunt. Place the carcass of the customer within, spray a few squirts of a strong flea killer within, and tie shut. An hour or so of such can cause the most healthy flea to call in sick, maybe turn belly up, or to become too sick to worry about jumping on a screamer.

A couple of other precautions can help. Cut the tops from a holey pair of tube socks and carry those in a ZipLoc liberally dosed with flea powder. Pull the tubes over the wrists at the start of the skinning. Use a spray insecticide, specific to the flea, to spray the feet and legs of a hung critter before starting the skinning. Finally, wear gloves to discourage fleas and to inhibit the transfer of critter blood to a cut on the human hand. Not heavy gloves. Wear the thin rubbers used by surgeons, almost always available at the pharmacy. Practice safe skinning.

Why worry about something as small as a flea? Because they are blood sucking little boogers that deserve to be hated, mostly. And too, the wrong kind of flea can transmit the dreaded bubonic plague. Such can be treated if diagnosed early. The fleas that have given me trouble made the transfer as I posed for photos. Having a coyote, a fox, or a bobcat on the shoulder can cause an eye-catching photo. Trouble is, a bunch of fleas can transfer from the cooling carcass to my mostly warm one.

Fur handling is a skill that appears to be complicated but is actually not. Each step is simple and the simple series can cause a raw pelt to turn into a thing of beauty, for the wall or for the trade. Either way, the right kind of fur handler will take pride in his or her handiwork. That finished fur makes a statement about the standards of the handler.

Spraying hips with a flea killer can help. It is better to place the carcass within a trash bag, spray, then tie shut.

Chapter 34

Marketing

Some fur hunters do not sell the fur they collect. Some have the pelts tanned to serve as hunt trophies. Others send the fur to a furrier to have coats and jackets, maybe even hats and mittens, made for personal use. Others do sell. They sell the fur each time the buyer comes to town, or save the fur and sell it as a collection at season's end. This payday can be used to offset hunting expenses or can be used to buy the new fur gun or the battery-powered caller.

The amount of the check will be determined by market conditions, the number of fur in the collection, and the skill of the fur handler. The condition of the individual pelts can have a major influence on the price paid. The fur buyer looks at a number of circumstances as he grades the fur to determine a fair price. What circumstances? The size of the pelt is one. Pelts from large and extra large animals bring a better price than do pelts from average or under-size animals. The lushness of the fur, both underfur and guard hair, can affect price. Pelts taken during the coldest part of the year almost always bring a better price than do pelts taken early in the season.

The buyer also checks to see if the pelt is prime. That word describes fur that is taken during the winter months when cold weather causes the fur to thicken and causes the leather to thin and become creamy. Prime refers to the condition of the leather. Unprime fur causes the leather to show a gray color, called blue in the trade. The grader also looks at fur or hair color. Most furbearers show color variation. That variation can be greatest when habitat conditions change but can be present in a common habitat. Bobcat from the West can be dandy, showing a desirable blue color to the back and a snow white belly covered with stark spots. The fur from bobcat taken near the California coast, or from parts of the South and the East, will show a muddy body color with minimal fur on the belly. The price paid for each can vary substantially.

At certain times of the year the hide may be prime, but the hair or fur degrades to cause the price to drop. Some animals rub the hip area in the spring to rid themselves of the thick winter coat. This rubbing is most noticeable on coyote and fox. As summer causes warming temperature, the guard hair on some furbearers begins to curl, creating a condition called singeing, a second condition that can cause price to plummet.

The market condition is a circumstance that is beyond the seller's control. The fur market can be influenced by fashion, the amount of hold-over fur (pelts in storage from the previous season), and by the amount of a particular fur that is available to the market. Some sellers hesitate to sell early in the season, figuring the market price is indefinite. Such hold the fur to season's end, hoping for the best price then. Selling early can be a gamble. So can selling late. If I knew all there was to know about the fur market I would likely be rich, or at least richer, and wouldn't have to write for a living.

A second circumstance within the seller's control is the amount of care devoted to fur handling. Well-handled fur will always bring a better price.

The fur taker has three general options when it comes time to sell. Option number one involves the country buyer, a person in the community who buys and sells fur for a living, or as a concomitant to another business; perhaps a trapping supply house or a sporting goods store. Maybe both. Other country buyers travel regular routes during the fur season, stopping at announced locations to grade and make an offer on fur collections. A country buyer must offer a fair price if he or she is to stay in business. His or her reputation as one who offers a fair price or as one who takes advantage can influence business longevity.

The country buyer, sometimes a trapper or a screamer himself, knows local conditions and knows local fur. He has time, usually, to offer good advice on ways to improve fur handling skills. Some will buy fur on the carcass or "green" fur, fur that is skinned but not handled.

One further advantage comes to the screamer who sells locally. He or she can have the fur graded and has the opportunity to discuss grading technique with the buyer. The offer can be considered and

The country buyer is often the best market for small collections.

accepted or rejected. Selling to a fur house is a second option. The seller packages the collection and sends it off to the fur house. It is wise to call or write the fur house ahead of time, to learn conditions of acceptance and shipping regulations. Most of the fur houses grade the collection, call or mail an offer, then hold the collection for a certain time (maybe ten days) to give the seller the opportunity to accept or reject. Rejection of the offer causes the fur to be shipped back to the seller, at the seller's expense.

The last fur selling option is the fur auction, selling the fur collection through a consignment house. Auctions are organized by groups and individuals who receive and market the fur in a warehouse sort of setting. Some state trapping associations sponsor auctions. Fur can be delivered personally or can be shipped. Employees arrange the fur into logical lots and sometimes groom the fur a bit to disguise transportation evidence. The auction sponsors charge a percentage of the bid price as a commission.

Multiple buyers walk the floor to inspect and grade the lots. If inclined to bid, the buyer marks his or her bid on a sheet. The advantage of competition causes the offer to be generally fair. Sellers are offered protection through the minimum bid mechanism. Each lot of fur (a lot of fur is fur from the same species or same subspecies and same seller, sometimes of similar grading) has a space where the seller can mark the minimum price they will accept. If no offer meets or exceeds that minimum the fur is not sold. The seller pays a flat fee to the auction house and gets the fur back.

My experience causes me to believe the local buyer (when fair) is the best buyer for the small collection. That country buyer usually markets the fur he has purchased through one of the auction houses, increasing paid price by about twenty percent to make his

Fur auctions encourage competitive bidding.

profit. That same experience causes me to think mid-season (January) is the time to sell. There is not often a lot of new fur on the market during early season sales; much of the material offered is stale stuff, hold-over fur. Buyers do not dig deep for such. Season prices have stabilized by mid-season. Fresh fur hits the market. Much of that fur comes from the prime fur time of winter. End of season sales can be good or can be bad. I have seen years when prices peak at the last sale of the season. Some buyers have delayed buying, hoping for a better price, and now must scurry to find enough fur to satisfy their contract commitments. Screamers who feel the price offered is unfair have the option of holding the fur through the summer to place it on the market during the next season. In climates that enjoy mild summer temperatures the fur can be hung in a cool and well ventilated area. Hot summers can be hard on fur. It is better to freeze the handled or green fur to retain a degree of freshness.

Complicated market conditions can cause prices that are puzzling. Those market conditions will sometimes conspire to take much of the profit out of fur selling. No market condition, fortunately, can take the fun out of the screaming.

Appendices

ACCURACY AIDS

DIEBOLD BIPODS
P.O. Box 10
Gerlach, NV 89412

HARRIS BIPODS
Barlow, KY 42024

PIPER SHOOTING REST
Box 297
Lexington, OR 97839

UNDERWOOD SHOOTING
STICKS
Route 9, Box 564
Mocksville, NC 27028

CATALOG COMPANIES

BASS PRO SHOPS
1935 S. Campbell Ave
Springfield, MO 65895

CABELA'S
812 13th Avenue
Sidney, NE 69160

DUNNS
Grand Junction, TN 38039

GANDER MOUNTAIN
Box 248, Hwy W
Wilmot, WI 53192

WING SUPPLY
P.O. Box 367
Greenville, KY 42345

HUNTING LIGHTS

BURNHAM BROTHERS
P.O. Box 1148
Menard, TX 76859

BURNHAM GAME CALLS
P.O. Box 1018
Marble Falls, TX 78654

KOHLER WHEAT LIGHT
123 Felton Street
Marlborough, MASS 01752

LIGHTFORCE
4021 Aurora Avenue North
Seattle, WA 98103

NITE LITE
P.O. Box 8210
Little Rock, AR 72221

OPTRONICS
350 N. Wheeler Street
Fort Gibson, OK 74434

OTHER GOOD STUFF

Michael's of Oregon
P.O. Box 13010
Portland, OR 97213

TEX ISBELL's COVERSCENT
Johnny Stewart Wildlife Calls
P.O. Box 7594
Waco, TX 76714

SKULLS UNLIMITED
P.O. Box 6741
Moore, OK 73153

VAN DYKE'S TAXIDERMY
SUPPLIES
Woonsocket, SD 57385

PREDATOR CALL MAKERS & MARKETERS

BILL AUSTIN'S CALLS
Box 284
Kaycee, WY 82639

BUCKLEY'S GAME CALLS
97A4 Leary Road
Honey Brook, PA 19344

BURNHAM BROTHERS
P.O. Box 1148
Menard, TX 76859

BURNHAM GAME CALLS
P.O. Box 1018
Marble Falls, TX 78654

CIRCE
Lohman Game Calls
P.O. Box 220
Neosho, MO 64850

CRIT'R•CALL
P.O. Box 999
LaPorte, CO 80535

DAN THOMPSON CALLS
P.O. Box 624
Rawlins, WY 82301

FAULKS
616 18th St.
Lake Charles, LA 70601

HAYDEL'S GAME CALLS
5018 Hazel Jones Road
Bossier City, LA 71111

HUNTER SPECIALTIES
5285 Rockwell Dr. N.E.
Cedar Rapids, IA 52402

PRIMOS WILD GAME CALLS
4436 N. State Street, A-7
P.O. Box 12785
Jackson, MS 39206

QUAKER BOY INC
6426 W. Quaker Street
Orchard Park, NY 14127

JOHNNY STEWART WILDLIFE
CALLS
P.O. Box 7594
Waco, TX 76714-7594

KNIGHT & HALE GAME CALLS
U.S. HWY 68E
Cadiz, KY 42211

LOHMAN MANUFACTURING
P.O. Box 220
Neosho, MO 64850

OLT CALLS
Box 550
Pekin, ILL 61554

SCOTCH HUNTING
PRODUCTS
6619 Oak Orchard Road
Elba, NY 14058

WOODS WISE PRODUCTS
P.O. Box 681552
Franklin, TN 37068

TALLYHO
Beastmasters
3941 N. Paradise Road
Flagstaff, AZ 86004

RECOMMENDED VIEWING

HUNTING COYOTE EAST &
WEST
Krause Publications
700 E. State Street
Iola, WI 54990-0001

HUNTING THE HUNTERS
Rocky Mountain Wildlife Products
P.O. Box 999
LaPorte, CO 80535

MASTERS' SECRETS TO PRED-
ATOR CALLING
Beastmasters
3941 N. Paradise Road
Flagstaff, AZ 86004

RECOMMENDED READING

CALLING EAST & WEST by
Gerry Blair. Beastmasters, 3941
N. Paradise Road, Flagstaff, AZ
86004.

GUN LIST. Krause Publications,
700 East State Street, Iola, WI
54990.

TRAPPER & PREDATOR
CALLER, Krause Publications,
700 East State Street, Iola, WI
54990.

VARMINT HUNTER, Box 759,
Pierre, SD 57501.

Index